EXTINCT BIRDS

EXTINCT BIRDS

AN ATTEMPT TO UNITE IN ONE VOLUME A SHORT ACCOUNT OF THOSE BIRDS WHICH HAVE BECOME EXTINCT IN HISTORICAL TIMES THAT IS, WITH IN THE LAST SIX *OR* SEVEN HUNDRED YEARS TO WHICH ARE ADDED A FEW WHICH STILL EXIST, BUT ARE ON THE VERGE OF EXTINCTION

The Hon. WALTER ROTHSCHILD, PH. D., F. Z. S.

GYAN

Published by

Gyan Publishing House
5, Ansari Road
Daryaganj, New Delhi-110002
Phone: 011-47034999, 9811692060
E-mail: books@gyanbooks.com

Distribution Network
gyanbooks.com
India, USA, Canada, UK, Australia, France

ISBN: 978-81-212-9094-4(PB)
First Published, 1907

2nd Impression 2023

Printed at: Gyan Press, Delhi.

EXTINCT BIRDS

Author: The Hon. WALTER ROTHSCHILD

EXTINCT BIRDS.

An attempt to unite in one volume a short account of those Birds which have become extinct in historical times—that is, within the last six or seven hundred years. To which are added a few which still exist, but are on the verge of extinction.

BY

The Hon. WALTER ROTHSCHILD,
Ph. D., F.Z.S.

With 45 Coloured Plates, embracing 63 subjects, and other illustrations.

LONDON.
HUTCHINSON & CO., PATERNOSTER ROW, E.C.
1907

This copy is No. 25 of the limited edition of 300 copies for the British Empire, of which 280 are for sale, the names of Subscribers being registered at our office.

Signed Walter Rothschild

November 12th *1907.*

Paternoster Row,
London.

PREFACE.

WHEN I decided to read a paper before the Ornithological Congress of 1905 on Extinct and Vanishing Birds, I found it necessary to illustrate my paper by a number of drawings. These drawings roused special interest among those who listened to my lecture, and I was asked by many if I could not see my way to publish the lecture and drawings, in book form, as these plates were far too numerous for the proceedings of the Congress. After some hesitation I determined to do this, greatly owing to the persuasion of the late Dr. Paul Leverkühn. The preparation of a book required considerably more research than the lecture, and therefore my readers will find, in the following pages, a totally different account to that in the lecture, as well as corrections and numerous additions. The lecture itself has been published in the "Proceedings of the IVth International Ornithological Congress."

I wish to thank very heartily all those of my ornithological friends, who have kindly helped me with the loan of specimens or otherwise, and especially Dr. H. O. Forbes, Dr. Scharff, Professor Dr. K. Lampert, Dr. O. Finsch, Professor Dr. A. Koenig, Dr. Kerbert, Mr. Fleming, Dr. von Lorenz, and others.

WALTER ROTHSCHILD.

INTRODUCTION.

THE study of the forms of life no longer existing on the earth, from the scanty remains preserved to us, has provoked a very great interest almost from the commencement of historical times. The very small portion of this vast field I am treating of in the following pages has a special attraction, as it deals to a great extent with forms familiar in a living state to our immediate forefathers and even to some of ourselves. Although I have here arranged the species systematically, they fall into two distinct categories, namely those known externally as well as internally, and those of which we know bones and egg-shells only. Under the former category might be included those merely known from descriptions or figures in ancient books, as well as those of which specimens exist. In the present work several plates have been reconstructed from such descriptions in order to give some idea of their probable appearance. There is considerable difference of opinion as to the approximate date of the disappearance of many of the species known from bones dug from deposits which have been variously determined as pleistocene and post-pleistocene. It seems to me that this problem can never be entirely solved, but the significant fact remains, that while many bones of these species in one locality have been collected in the kitchen-middens of the former inhabitants, in other localities the same bones occur in what seem to be much older formations.

In view of this and kindred facts, I have mentioned many species which some ornithologists will probably consider outside the range of the present treatise, viz., birds which have become extinct in the last seven- or eight-hundred years. Taking my first category, viz., those species whose exterior is more or less known, our knowledge is very variable in scope; about some we have a very full and even redundant literature, such as the Great Auk, the Labrador Duck, and Notornis, while of others, such as most of the extinct Parrots from the West Indies, the "Giant" of Mauritius, the "Blue Bird" of Bourbon, and so forth, we have the very scantiest knowledge. Even in the times of Leguat and Labat there must have been many species, now extinct, of which no mention has ever been made, for these old writers only mentioned such species which impressed themselves on their memories either from their size, peculiar shape, beauty of plumage, or excellence and usefulness for food—in fact the culinary property of the various birds seems to have been their principal interest. One of the most interesting phenomena connected with recently extinct birds is the resemblance of the fauna of the Mascarene Islands and that of the Chatham Islands in the possession of a number of large flightless Rails, though the significance of this fact has been much exaggerated.

On the whole, this book is confined to species actually known to be extinct, but a few are included of which a small number is still known to exist, because firstly there seems no doubt that they will vanish soon, and secondly, as in the case of *Notornis*, it was necessary to clear up certain misconceptions and contradictory statements. In the case of a few species believed to be quite extinct, it is possible that some individuals may still exist in little known parts of their range, while on the other hand it is more than likely that several of the species referred to in my lecture (Proc. Orn. Congress pp. 191-207, 1907) as threatened with destruction, have already ceased to live. This may also be the case with some birds not alluded to at all.

In several instances I have treated of extinct flightless species under genera including existing species capable of flight. This may appear to be inconsistent, seeing that I maintain *Notornis* separate from *Porphyrio*, but, while not considering flightlessness in itself a generic character, the great development of the wing-coverts and the modification of the toes appear of sufficient generic value in this case. I know that several of the most eminent ornithologists of the day, among them Dr. Sharpe, differ from me, and are convinced that the loss of the power of flight is so profound a modification, that it is imperative that we should treat it as sufficient for generic distinction.

While agreeing that many genera are founded on much less striking modifications, I cannot concur in this opinion, for, unless the loss of the power of flight is also accompanied by other changes, in some cases it is difficult to find at first sight even specific differences other than the aborted wings.

The cause of recent extinction among birds is in most cases due directly or indirectly to man, but we also have instances of birds becoming extinct for no apparent reason whatever.

Man has destroyed, and is continually destroying species directly, either for food or for sport, but also in many other ways he contributes to their destruction. Some species have been exterminated by the introduction of animals of prey, such as rats, cats, mongoose, etc., and we know that also the acclimatisation of other birds, such as the mynah, etc., has proved to be harmful to the native birds. Again we find that the introduction of domestic creatures or others kept as pets has brought diseases which may prove fatal to the indigenous fauna. Another means by which man causes immense destruction, is by destroying the natural habitat of various species. By cutting down or burning the forests, prairies, or scrub, and by bringing the land under cultivation, man indirectly kills off a species through starvation, from extermination of certain insects or plants on which it depends for food. Many species, such as the Moas, were evidently greatly reduced in numbers by cataclysms of Nature, such as volcanic outbreaks, earthquakes, floods, bush fires, etc., and then died out from what appears only explicable by the natural exhaustion of their vitality. The chief cause of the extermination of the Moas was undoubtedly their slaughter by the Maoris for food, but in several inaccessible parts of the interior large numbers of Moa remains have been found which undoubtedly had died for no apparent reason.

This cause also seems to be the only explanation of the dying out of such birds as *Aechmorhynchus*, *Chaetoptila*, *Camptolaimus* and others.

The melancholy fact however remains that man and his satellites, cats, rats, dogs, and pigs are the worst and in fact the only important agents of destruction of the native avifaunas wherever they go.

I have not included in the body of this work the fossil species from the pleistocene of Europe, Asia, Australia and America, as I believe that these belonged to an avifauna of an epoch considerably anterior to those attributed to the pleistocene of New Zealand and the adjacent islands, as well as that of the Mascarenes and Madagascar. I, however, give here the list of the species described from the above mentioned regions which I have been able to find in our literature, to serve as a guide to those who may think I ought to have included them in the work itself.

Strix melitensis Lydekker .... Malta.
Vultur melitensis Lydekker .... Malta.
Pelecanus proavus De Vis .... Queensland.
Phalacrocorax sp. Lydekker .... New Zealand.
Aythya robusta De Vis .... Queensland.
Anas elapsa De Vis .... Queensland.
Anas benedeni Sharpe .... Belgium.
Alopochen pugil Winge .... Brazil.

Dendrocygna validipennis (De Vis)	....	Queensland.
Branta hypsibata Cope	....	Oregon.
Branta propinqua Schufeldt	....	Oregon.
Anser scaldii Van Beneden	....	Belgium.
Anser sp. Lydekker	....	England.
Anser coudoni Schufeldt	....	Oregon.
Cygnus sp. Lydekker	....	Malta.
Cygnus falconeri Parker	....	Malta.
Palaeopelargus nobilis De Vis	....	Queensland.
Prociconia lydekkeri Ameghino	....	Brazil.
Platibis subtenuis De Vis	....	Queensland.
Grus proavus Marsh	....	New Jersey.
Grus melitensis Lydekker	....	Malta.
Grus turfa Portis	....	Italy.
Grus primigenia Milne Edwards	....	France.
Fulica prior De Vis	....	Queensland.
Fulica pisana Portis	....	Italy.
Porphyrio mackintoshi De Vis	....	Queensland.
Gallinula strenuipes De Vis	....	Queensland.
Gallinula peralata De Vis	....	Queensland.
Microtribonyx effluxus De Vis	....	Queensland.
Progura gallinacea De Vis	....	Queensland.
Columba melitensis Lydekker	....	Malta.
Lithophaps ulnaris De Vis	....	Queensland.
Gallus sp. Lydekker	....	New Zealand.
Gallus sp. Lydekker	....	Central Germany.
Phasianus sp. Lydekker	....	Germany.
Perdix sp. Issel	....	Italy.
Tetrao sp. Issel	....	Italy.
Metapteryx bifrons De Vis	....	Queensland.
Dromaius queenslandiae (De Vis)....	....	Queensland.
Dromaius gracilipes (De Vis)	....	Queensland.
Dromaius patricius (De Vis)	....	East Australia.
Genyornis newtoni Sterling & Zeitz	....	South Australia.

Casuarius lydekkeri nom. nov.

"The distal extremity of the tibio-tarsus is narrow, without a semilunar pit on the lateral surface of the ectocondyle, and with a very deep extensor groove" (Lydekker, Cat. Fossil B. Brit. Mus., p. 353).

Type, a caste of the distal portion of the right tibio-tarsus, in the British Museum. The original is preserved in the Museum at Sydney and was obtained from the pleistocene cavern-deposits in the Wellington Valley in New South Wales.

A bird usually stated to be extinct is *Monarcha dimidiata*, from Rara-Tonga, but in March, 1901, two specimens, male and female, were procured by the Earl of Ranfurly. Doubtless this is a species which will one day vanish entirely, but at present it hardly comes within the scope of this work.

The birds known to be more or less on the verge of extinction which I have not thought advisable to give in the main part of this book might, for convenience of reference and to avoid possible controversy as to my having omitted any species, be given here, but it must be understood that of these species I only know the fact that their numbers have been greatly reduced and mostly almost to vanishing point. I have already mentioned before that some of them may already have disappeared, but in many cases recent investigations are wanting, and all, therefore, that can be said of them is that they are threatened and may soon become extinct, if they still exist.

Myadestes sibilans	St. Vincent.
Myadestes genibarbis	Martinique.
Cinclocerthia gutturalis	Martinique.
Rhamphocinclus brachyurus	Martinique.
Ixocincla olivacea	Mauritius.
Phedina borbonica	Mascarene Islands.
Trochocercus borbonicus	Mascarene Islands.
Oxynotus typicus	Mauritius.
Foudia newtoni	Bourbon.
Drymoeca rodericana	Rodriguez.
Cyanorhamphus cooki	Norfolk Island.
Cyanorhamphus erythrotis	Antipodes Island.
Cyanorhamphus unicolor	Antipodes Island.
Turnagra tanagra	North Island, New Zealand.
Sceloglaux albifacies....	Middle Island, New Zealand.
Miro albifrons	North Island, New Zealand.
Miro australis	Middle Island, New Zealand.
Clitonyx albicilla	North Island, New Zealand.
Pogonornis cincta	North Island, New Zealand.
Hypotaenidia mülleri	Auckland Island.
Mergus australis	Auckland Island.

Nesonetta aucklandica	Auckland Island.
Ocydromus ? sylvestris	Lord Howe's Island.
Puffinus newelli	Hawaiian Islands.
Telespiza flaviceps	Hawaii.
Nesochen sandvicensis	Hawaii.
Pareudiastes pacificus	Samoa.
Nesomimus trifasciatus	Charles ? and Gardener Island, Galápagos Islands.
Phalacrocorax harrisi	Galápagos Islands.
Meleagris americana	United States.
Conurus carolinensis	Southern United States.
Pseudgryphus californianus	California.
Amazona guildingi	St. Vincent.
Campephilus principalis	Southern United States.
Pyrrhula pyrrhula murina	Azores.
Stringops habroptilus	New Zealand.
Anthornis melanocephala	Chatham Islands.
Gallinago pusilla	Chatham Islands.
Thinornis novaezealandiae	Chatham Islands.
Amazona augusta	Dominica.
Amazona bouqueti	St. Lucia.
Amazona versicolor	Dominica.
Hemignathus lanaiensis	Lanai, Sandwich Islands.

Many of my readers will, I fear, find fault with me for having bestowed names on a number of forms, known only from fragments of bones, single bones, or two or three bones. Especially will they, I fear, blame me for doing this when these forms have been described by other authors who have refrained from giving names. My reasons for doing so are very simple: in such cases as Dr. Parker's species which are fully described, but quoted under the formula *Pachyornis species A* or *Anomalopteryx species B*, the danger lies in different authors using the same formula for quite other species. In the case of others, where an author fears to name a form, but gives the distinctive characters and quotes only *Casuarius species* or *Emeus sp.*, unless the author and page are quoted, confusion must arise, and so in both cases I have thought it easier for reference and also more concise to name all these forms which have been described or differentiated without a binomial or trinomial appellation. I have, however, refrained from doing so in the foregoing list of Pleistocene species in the following eight cases as I was not able to decide anything about them with the material or literature at my disposal, viz.:—

Phalacrocorax sp. Lydekker	New Zealand.
Anser sp. Lydekker	England.
Cygnus sp. Lydekker	Malta.
Gallus sp. Lydekker	New Zealand.
Gallus sp. Lydekker	Central Germany.
Phasianus sp. Lydekker	Germany.
Perdix sp. Issel	Italy.
Tetrao sp. Issel	Italy.

LITERATURE

REFERRING TO

EXTINCT BIRDS.

No attempt has been made to quote all books in which extinct birds have been mentioned; not only would that mean a tedious, long work, and a book in itself, but, the repetitions being so numerous, it would have been of very little use. On the other hand, I have tried to quote the most important literature referring to Extinct Birds, and I have specially been anxious to cite and verify the principal ancient literature. Well known general works on birds in which extinct species have, of course, also been mentioned, are, as a rule, not quoted; such as: The 27 volumes of the Catalogue of Birds; Brisson's Ornithology; Daubenton's, Buffon's and Montbeillard's works; Latham's Ornithological Writings; Linnaeus' Systema Naturae in all its editions; Vieillot's writings; popular natural histories and school books; Brehm's Thierleben in its various editions; Finsch's Papageien; Gray's and Sharpe's Hand-lists; Dubois' Synopsis Avium, lists of specimens in Museums, and many others, in which extinct birds are as a matter of course mentioned.

Three most complete detailed bibliographies must be named: The "Bibliography of the Didinae," forming Appendix B. of Strickland's "Dodo and its Kindred" (1848), the Bibliography of *Alca impennis* by Wilhelm Blasius in the new Edition of Naumann, vol. XII, pp. 169-176 (1903), and the Bibliography referring to the Moas by Hamilton, in the Trans. New Zealand Institute XXVI and XXVII (1894, 1895).

Most of the books and pamphlets quoted hereafter are in my library at the Zoological Museum at Tring, in the ornithological part of which Dr. Hartert and I have been specially interested for many years. Those books that are not in my library are marked with an asterisk, but several of these I have been able to consult in other libraries.

The chronological order appeared to be best suited to the particular subject treated of.

1580 or 90. COLLAERT, ADRIAN. Avium vivae icones, in aes incisae & editae ab Adriano Collardo.

(On one of the plates is figured the "Avis Indica." This figure seems to have been the original of the representations in Dubois' and Leguat's works.)

1601. JACOB CORNELISZ NECK. Het tweede Boek, Journael oft Dagh-register, inhoudende een warachtig verhael, etc., etc. Middelburch, Anno 1601.

(On picture No. 2, page 7, the Dodo is figured and described as follows: "Desen Voghel de is soo groot als een Swaen, gaven hem de naem Walchvoghel, want doen wy de leckere Duyfkens ende ande cleyn ghevoghelte ghenoech vinghen, doen taelden wy niet meer naer desen Voghel." This appears to be the first mention of the Dodo in literature.)

1605. CLUSIUS. Caroli Clusii Atrebatis . . . Exoticorum libri decem: Quibus Animalium, Plantarum, Aromatum historiae describuntur. Ex Officina Plantiniana Raphelengii, 1605.

(On p. 100 van Neck's Dodo is reproduced, on p. 103 the Great Auk, sub nomine "Mergus Americanus.")

1606. DE BRY. Achter Theil der Orientalischen Indien, begreiffend erstlich ein Histor. Beschr. d. Schiffahrt, so der Adm. Jacob von Neck ausz Hollandt, etc., etc. Frankf. 1606.

(Figure and mention of the Dodo.)

1619. JACOB CORNELISZ NECK. Historiale Beschryvinghe, Inhoudende een waerachtich verhael vande veyse ghedaen met acht Schepen van Amsterdam, etc., etc. Amsterdam, 1619.

(Evidently another edition of Neck's voyage of 1601. On page 5 and on Picture No. 2 (page 7), which is the same as in the other editions of Neck's voyage, the Dodo is described. There is also a French edition of 1601.)

1625. CASTLETON. Purchas his Pilgrimes. In five books.

(On p. 331, in chapter XV., first mention of the Réunion Dodo.)

1626. SIR THOMAS HERBERT. A relation of some years' Travaile.

(First mention of *Aphanapteryx bonasia.*)

1635. NIEREMBERG. Joannis Evsebii Nierembergii . . . . . Historia Naturae, maxime peregrinae, libris XVI distincta. In quibus rarissima Naturae arcana, etc., etc., etc. Antverpiae MDCXXXV.

(Clusius' account and figure of the Dodo reproduced on pp. 231, 232. On p. 237 the Great Auk ("Goifugel") mentioned).

*1638 and 1651. CAUCHE. Rélations véritables et curieuses de l'isle de Madagascar. (Two editions.)

(See *Aphanapteryx bonasia.*)

1640. PÈRE BOUTON. Relation de l'établ. des Français dep. 1635, en l'ile Martinique, l'vne des antilles de l'Amérique.

(Describes, among other birds, the Aras and Parrots of the island of Martinique.)

1646. BONTEKOE. Journ. of te gedenckw. beschr. van de Ost. Ind. Reyse. Haarlem 1646.

(On p. 6 mention of the Réunion Dodo.)

1655. WORM. Museum Wormianum.

(On pp. 300, 301, lib. III, description and figure of a Great Auk from the Faroe Islands.)

1658. HISTOIRE NATURELLE ET MORALE DES ILES ANTILLES DE L'AMÉRIQUE. Enrichie de pleusieurs belles figures des Raretez les plus considerables qui y sont d'écrites. Avec un vocabulaire caraïbe. Rotterdam 1658.

(The title-page has no author's name, but according to Père du Tertre the author is "Le Sieur de Rochefort, Ministre de Rotterdam." Contains important notes on former bird-life on the Antilles.)

1665. The same. Second Edition. Rotterdam 1665.

1658. BONTIUS. Gulielmi Pisonis Medici Amstelaedamensis de Indiae Utriusque re naturali et medica libri quatuordecim. Third Part: Jacobi Bontii, medici civitatis Bataviae Novae in Java Ordinarii, Historiae Natur. et Medici Indiae Orientalis libri sex.

(On p. 70 an excellent figure of the Dodo. Caput XVII. Appendix: De Dronte, aliis Dod-aers.)

1667. DU TERTRE. Histoire générale des Antilles habitées par les François. Tome II, contenant l'Histoire Naturelle. Paris 1667.

(On p. 246. Traite V. Des animaux de l'air. § I, Les Arras. § II, Des Perroquets. § III, Des Perriques.)

1668. HISTORISCHE BESCHREIBUNG DER ANTILLEN INSELN IN AMERICA GELEGEN. In sich begreiffend deroselben Gelegenheit, darinnen befindl. natürl. Sachen, sampt deren Einwohner Sitten und Gebraüchen. Von dem Herrn de Rochefort, zum zweiten mahl in Französischer sprach an den Tag gegeben, nunmehr aber in die Teutsche übersetzet. Frankfurt 1668.

(Translation of the second edition of Rochefort's book.)

*1668. CARRÉ, Voyage des Indes Orientales.

(Page 12 the "Solitaire." Cf. *Didus solitarius*.)

1668. J. MARSHALL. Memorandums concerning India.

(In the article on Mauritius occurs a mention of Geese.)

1674. PÈRE DUBOIS. Les Voyages faits par le Sieur D.B. aux Isles Dauphine ou Madagascar, and Bourbon, ou Mascarenne, ès années 1669-70-71-72.

(Of this extremely rare work I possess a beautiful copy, together with the map of Sanson belonging to it.)

(On p. 168 we find "Description de quelques Oyseaux de l'Isle de Bourbon," with figures of the "Géant" and "Solitaire.")

1696. THEVENOT, M. MELCHISEDEC. Rélations de divers voyages curieux qui nont point este' publié'es. Nouvelle Edition. Vol. I, II, 1696.

(A very interesting collection of ancient voyages, translated into French. In Vol. II is a translation of Bontekoe's travels to the "East Indies," with figures of the Dodo and other interesting notes.)

1707. LEGUAT, FRANÇOIS. Voyages et Avantures de François Leguat, et de ses Compagnos, en deux Isles desertes des Indes Orientales. Londres 1707.

1708. LEGUAT, FRANCIS. A New Voyage to the East Indies by Francis Leguat and his companions. Containing their adventures in two desert islands. London 1708.

(Valuable notes on the birds of Rodriguez and Mauritius.)

1707. SLOANE, HANS. A Voyage to the islands Madera, Barbados, Nieves, S. Christofers and Jamaica, with the Natural History of the Herbs and Trees, four-footed Beasts, Fishes, Insects, Birds, Reptiles, etc. Vol. I, 1707; vol. II, 1725.

(Gives most valuable notes on the birds, including the Goatsucker, *Aestrelata* and Parrots.)

1722. LABAT, JEAN BAPTISTE. Nouveau Voyage aux Iles de l'Amérique contenant l'histoire naturelle de ces pays. Paris 1722. 6 vols.

In Vol. II, chapter VIII, the different species of Parrots are described, and it is stated that each island had three kinds, viz., an "Aras," a "Perroquet" and a "Perrique," evidently meaning a Macaw, an Amazona and a Conurus.)

1742. Nouvelle Edition. 8 vols.

1752. MOEHRING. Avium Genera.

(In this ominous work, which, through an article by Poche in Zool. Anz. 1904, has recently caused so much quite unnecessary disturbance among nomenclatorists — cf. Hartert, Zool. Anz. 1904, p. 154, and Proc. IV. Int. Orn. Congress, pp. 276—283. The Dodo is mentioned under the name "Raphus.")

1763. L'ABBÉ DE LA CAILLE. Journal Historique du Voyage fait au Cap de Bonne—espérance.

(Some birds from Mauritius mentioned, but no descriptions.)

1773. VOYAGE A L'ISLE DE FRANCE, à l'isle de Bourbon, au Cap de Bonne Espérance, etc. Avec des observations nouvelles sur la nature and sur les hommes. Par un officier du roi. Neuchatel 1773.

1775. A voyage to the island of Mauritius, etc. By a French Officer. (Translation of the above).

(Lettre IX, page 67, treats of the "Animals natural to the isle of France.")

1782. SONNERAT. Voyage aus iles orientales et à la Chine. Two volumes, 1782.

(In Volume II, on plate 101, opposite page 176, the extinct *Alectroenas nitidissima* is figured, under the name of "Pigeon hollandais.")

*1783 (?) CALLAM. Voyage Botany Bay.

(According to Gray *Notornis alba* is mentioned under the name of "White Gallinule.")

1786. SPARRMANN. Museum Carlsonianum I.

(On pl. 23 *Pomarea nigra* Sparrm.)

1789. G. DIXON. Voyage round the World.

(On p. 357 is note and figure of the extinct *Moho apicalis*, under the name of the "Yellow-tufted Bee-eater.")

1789. BROWNE, PATRICK. The Civil and Natural History of Jamaica.

1789. THE VOYAGE OF GOVERNOR PHILLIP to Botany Bay, etc. London 1789.

(Among other interesting birds *Notornis stanleyi* is figured on the plate opposite p. 273.)

1790. J. WHITE. Journal of a Voyage to New South Wales with sixty-five Plates of Nondescript Animals, Birds, Lizards, Serpents, etc. London MDCCXC.

(I have a copy with black and white, and another with coloured plates. *Notornis alba.*)

1804. HERMANN. Observationes Zoolog.

(On page 125 the extinct Bourbon *Palaeornis* is described as *Psittacus semirostris.*)

1807. M. F. PÉRON. Voyage de découvertes aux terres australes, exécuté par ordre de Sa Majesté l'Empereur et Roi, etc., etc. 2 vols. 1807 and 1816 and Atlas.

(On p. 467 is described the Little Emu from Kangaroo Island, which I have named *Dromaius peronii*, in honour of its discoverer, François Péron. A memoir of this extraordinary and admirable man's short and brilliant life will be found in Vol. VI of the "Naturalist's Library," Edinburgh, 1843.)

1810. ANDRÉ PIERRE LEDRU. Voyage aux iles de Tényériffe, la Trinité, Saint-Thomas, Sainte-Croix et Porto-Ricco, exécuté par ordre du Gouvern. français, etc., etc. Two volumes, 1810.

(In Vol. II, page 39, are mentioned various birds as occurring on the Danish West-Indian Islands, which are not found there at present. "Un todier, nommé vulgairement perroquet de terre" and seven species of Humming-Birds!)

*1826. Bloxam. Voyage of the Blonde.

(See *Phaeornis oahensis, Loxops coccinea rufa.* Also interesting notes on other Sandwich-Islands Birds.)

1827. PALLAS. Zoogr. Rosso—Asiat. II p. 305: *Phalacrocorax perspicillatus*, the now extinct Cormorant from Bering Island.

1830. QUOY ET GAIMARD. Voy. Astrolabe, Zool. I p. 242 pl. 24.
(*Coturnix novaezealandiae* described.)

1830. KITTLITZ. Mémoires Acad. Sc. Pétersburg I.
(Kittlitz describes *Turdus terrestris* and *Fringilla papa*.)

*1838. POLACK. New Zealand.
(First mention of Moas.)

*1838. DON DE NAVARETTE. Rel. Quat. voy. Christ.

1838. LICHTENSTEIN. Abhandl. K. Akademie d. Wissenschaften p. 448, plate V.
(*Hemignathus ellisianus* — sub nomine *obscurus* — and *Hemignathus lucidus* described.)

1843. DIEFFENBACH'S Travels in New Zealand, 1843. Appendix, Birds, by J. E. Gray. On page 197 *Rallus dieffenbachii* described.

1843. OWEN. P.Z.S. 1843, p. 1., letter read from Rev. W. C. Cotton, mentioning remains of gigantic birds in New Zealand, p. 8 the name *Dinornis novaezealandiae* given to the first Moa-bones exhibited.

1846. In the "VOYAGE OF EREBUS AND TERROR," Birds, Gray describes and figures *Nesolimnas dieffenbachii*.

1847. GOSSE. Birds of Jamaica.
(Cf. *Ara erythrocephala*, *Siphonorhis americanus* and other Jamaican birds.)

1848. EDM. DE SÉLYS-LONGCHAMPS. Résumé concern. les Oiseaux brévipennes mentionnés dans l'ouvrage de M. Strickland sur le Dodo.
In Rev. Zool. 1848, pp. 292-295.

1848. STRICKLAND AND MELVILLE. The Dodo and its kindred; or the history, affinities, and Osteology of the Dodo, Solitaire, and other extinct birds of the islands Mauritius, Rodriguez and Bourbon. London 1848.
(141 pages and 15 plates.)

*1848. PEALE. U.S. Expl. Exp. Birds.
(On p. 147, pl. XL, is described and figured the extinct *Chaetoptila augustipluma*, under the name of *Entomiza augustipluma*. This work is not available, as only 3 or 4 copies exist of it, but see:
CASSIN. U.S. Expl. Exp. Mamm. and Orn. p. p. 148 pl. XI (1858).

1851. IS. GEOFFROY-SAINT-HILAIRE. Notice sur des ossements et des oeufs trouvés a Madagascar dans les alluvions modernes, et provenant d'un oiseau gigantesque.
In Annales des Scienc. Naturelles, 13 série, Zoologie, tome 40.
(This volume is dated "1850," but the above article is said to have been read before the Academy on January 27, 1851, therefore the date of publication must be rather 1851 than 1850.)

1854. H. SCHLEGEL. Ook een woordje over den Dodo en zijne verwanten.
In: Verslagen en Mededeelingen der Koninglijke Akademie der Wetenschappen, Afdeel. Naturkunde, Deel II, p. 254.

1857. JAPETUS STEENSTRUP. Bidrag til Geirfuglens Naturhistorie, etc.
In: Naturh. Forening. Vidensk. Meddel. for 1855, Nos. 3-7.
(The first history and bibliography of the Great Auk.)

1858. H. SCHLEGEL. Over eenige uitgestorvene reusachtige Vogels van de Mascarenhas-eilanden. (Een tegenhanger tot zijne geschiedenis der Dodo's.)
In: Verslagen en Mededeelingen der Koninglijke Akademie van Wetenschappen, Afdeel. Naturkunde, Deel VII, pp. 116-128.
(*Leguatia gigantea*, *Porphyrio (Notornis ?) caerulescens*.)

1860. A. v. PELZELN. Zur Ornithologie der Insel Norfolk.

In: Sitzungsberichte der Mathemat. Naturwiss. Cl. Akademie Wien Bd. XLI, No. 15, pp. 319-332. (Mit 1 Tafel.)

(Lengthy account of *Nestor norfolcensis*, from Bauer's Manuscript, *Notornis alba*, etc.)

1681. ALFRED NEWTON. Abstract of Mr. Wolley's Researches in Iceland respecting the Gare-fowl.

In Ibis, 1861, pp. 374-399.

1862. W. J. BRODERIP. Notice of an Original Painting, including a figure of the Dodo.

In Trans. Zool. Soc. London IV, p. 197.

1862. WILLIAM PREYER. Ueber *Plautus impennis*.

In Journ. f. Orn. 1862, pp. 110-124, 337-356.

1865. ALFRED NEWTON. The Gare-fowl and its Historians.

In Natural Hist. Review XII (1865), pp. 467-488); id. in Encylcl. Britannica Ed. IX, Vol. III; id. Dict. Birds, p. 220-221.

1866. OWEN. *Psittacus mauritianus* named, in Ibis p. 168; also mentioned in Trans. Zool. Soc. VI, p. 53, 1866.

(See *Lophopsittacus*.)

1866-1873. ALPH. MILNE-EDWARDS. Recherches sur la Faune Ornithologique Eteinte des iles Mascareignes et de Madagascar. Paris 1866-1873.

(With 37 plates. This volume consists of reprints of the author's articles on the suhject in French periodicals, though not a word of this is mentioned. To the plates originally issued with the articles, several new ones are added.)

1867. ALFRED NEWTON. On a Picture supposed to represent the Didine Bird of the Island of Bourbon (Réunion).

In Trans. Zool. Soc. London VI, pp. 373-376. Plate 62.

1867. GEORGE DAWSON ROWLEY. On the Egg of *Aepyornis*, the Colossal Bird of Madagascar.

In Proc. Zool. Soc. London 1867, pp. 892-895.

1868. FRAUENFELD, GEORGE RITTER VON. Neu aufgefundene Abbildung des *Dronte* und eines zweiten kurzflügligen Vogels, wahrscheinlich des poule rouge au bec de bécasse der Maskarenen, in der Privatbibliothek S.M. des verstorbenen Kaisers Franz. Wien 1868. Mit 4 Tafeln.

1868. SCHLEGEL & POLLEN. Mammifères et Oiseaux, in: Pollen et von Dam, Recherches sur la faune de Madagascar et de ses dépendances. Leyde 1868.

1868. OWEN, on Moas in Trans. Zool. Soc. London, VI.

(*Dinornis maximus* established.)

***1868.** H. C. MILLIES. Over eene nieuw ontdekte afbeelding van den Dodo.

In: Verhandlingen der Koningl. Akad. d. Wetenschappen, Deel XI, Amsterdam 1868.

1869. OWEN. On the osteology of the Dodo.

In: Trans. Zool. Soc. London VI, 1869, p. 70.

1869. ELLIOT. New and heretofore unfig. sp. N. American Birds.

(In Vol. II, part 14, No. 3, the now extinct *Carbo perspicillatus* from Bering Island figured.)

1872. F. W. Hutton. On the Microscopical structure of the Egg-shell of the Moa.

In Trans. & Proceed. New Zealand Inst. IV, pp. 166-167, with illustrations.

1872. F. W. Hutton. Notes on some Birds from the Chatham Islands, collected by H. H. Travers, Esq.

In Ibis 1872, pp. 243-250.

(*Miro traversi* and *Sphenoeacus rufescens* (*Bowdleria rufescens* of this book) only found on Mangare. First description of "*Rallus modestus*" (*Cabalus modestus*), "*Rallus dieffenbachi*" already extinct.)

1872. J. Hector. On Recent Moa Remains in New Zealand.

In Trans. and Proc. N. Zealand Inst. IV, p. 110.

1872. Julius Haast. Notes on Harpagornis Moorei.

In Trans. and Proc. N. Zealand Inst. IV, p. 192.

1873. A. v. Pelzeln. On the Birds in the Imperial Collection at Vienna obtained from the Leverian Museum.

In Ibis 1873, pp. 14-54, 103-124.

(Most important notes on some of Latham's types. Cf. *Drepanis pacifica*, *Platycercus ulietanus*, *Notornis alba*.)

1873. Christmann und Oberländer. Ozeanien.

(On pages 138-144 a popular account and wood cuts—from Brehm's Thierleben—of Moas and other Gigantic Birds.)

1873. Buller. The Birds of New Zealand.

1874. A. Milne-Edwards. Recherches sur la faune ancienne des iles Mascareignes.

In Ann. Sciences naturelles sér. V, Tome XIX, article 3 (*Erythromachus*, *Strix murivora*, *Columba rodericana*, etc.)

1875. Rowley. *Porphyrio Stanleyi.*

In Ornith. Miscell. I, pp. 37-48, plate.

1875. Hutton. Description of the Moa Swamp at Hamilton.

In Trans. & Proc. N. Zealand Inst. VII, p. 123, pl. V.

1875. Hutton & Coughtrey. Description of some Moa Remains from the Knobby Ranges.

In Trans. & Proc. N. Zealand Inst. VII, p. 266, pl. XIX.

1875. Alfred Newton. P.Z.S. 1875, p. 350: the name *Lophopsittacus* established.

1875. Hutton. On the Dimensions of Dinornis bones.

In Trans. & Proc. N. Zealand Inst. VII, p. 274.

1875. Julius von Haast. Researches and Excavations on, in and near the Moa-bone Point Cave, Sumner Road, in the year 1872.

In Trans. and Proceed. New Zealand Institute VII, pp. 54-85, pls. I, II.

*1875. Van Beneden. Journ. Zool. IV, p. 267.

(Description of *Anas finschi*.)

1876. A. & E. Newton. On the Psittaci of the Mascarene Islands.

In Ibis 1876, pp. 281-288, plate VI.

1876. Tommaso Salvadori. Nota intorno al *Fregilupus varius*.

In: Atti della Reale Accademia delle Scienze di Torino, Vol. XI, pp. 482-488.

1877. G. D. Rowley. On the Extinct Birds of the Mascarene Islands.

In Orn. Miscell. II, pp. 124-133, plates LII, LIII.

1878. G. D. Rowley. Remarks on the Extinct Gigantic Birds of Madagascar and New Zealand.

In Ornith. Miscell. III, pp. 237-247, pls. CXII-CXV.

1879. Dole. List of Birds of the Hawaiian Islands. Corrected from the Hawaiian Almanack.
Reprint: Ibis 1881, p. 241.

(Pennula millsi, Ciridops anna.)

1879. Owen, Richard. Memoirs on the Extinct Wingless Birds of New Zealand; with an Appendix on those of England, Australia, Newfoundland, Mauritius and Rodriguez.

(Memoirs on the *Dinornithidae*, their bones, eggs, integument and plumage, *Notornis, Aptornis, Cnemiornis, Alca impennis, Didus* and *Pezophaps*. With many wood-cuts and plates.)

(See also Owen's articles in Trans. Zool. Soc. London III, IV, VI, X, XI.)

1879. Günther and E. Newton, on *Aphanapteryx leguati* in Philosophical Transactions. Vol. 168, pp. 431-432, pl. XLIII.

1879. W. A. Forbes. On the systemat. position and scientific name of "Le Perroquet mascarin" of Brisson.

In Ibis 1879, p. 303.

1884. Wilhelm Blasius. Zur Geschichte von *Alca impennis*.

In Journ. f. Orn. 1884, pp. 58-176.

(The most accurate and complete list—till 1884—of specimens of *Alca impennis*.)

1885. A. B. Meyer. *Notornis hochstetteri*.

In: Zeitschr. ges Orn. II, p. 45, pl. I.

1885. Symington Grieve. The Great Auk or Garefowl. Its History, Archaeology, and Remains. London 1885.

1897. Id.: Supplementary note on the Great Auk; in Trans. Edinburgh Field Nat. Soc. 1897, pp. 238-273.

1886. December. Julius von Haast. On *Megalapteryx hectori*, a new Gigantic Species of Apterygian Bird.

In Trans. Zool. Soc. London XII, p. 161, pl. XXX.

1887. Henry Seebohm. The Geographical Distribution of the family *Charidriidae*.

(Plates of *Prosobonia leucoptera* and *Aechmorhynchus cancellata*.)

1888. Buller. A History of the Birds of New Zealand.

In two volumes. Second Edition. (See 1873.)

1889. Sir Edward Newton. Presidential address.

In Trans. Norfolk and Norwich Natural. Society IV, pp. 540-547.

1889. A. de Quatrefages. Nouvelle Preuve de l'Extinction récente des Moas.

In: Le Naturaliste 1889, p. 117.

1889. F. C. Noll. Die Veränderung in der Vogelwelt im Laufe der Zeit.

In: Bericht über die Senckenberg. Naturf. Gesellsch. in Frankf.-a.-M. 1887-1888, pp. 77-142.

1890. Stejneger and Lucas. Contributions to the History of Pallas' Cormorant. With plates II-IV.

In Proc. U.S. Nat. Mus. XII, pp. 83-94.

1890-99. Scott B. Wilson & Evans. Aves Hawaiienses: The Birds of the Sandwich Islands. With numerous plates.

1891. Richard Lydekker. Catalogue of the Fossil Birds in the British Museum. London 1891.

(Pages I-XXVII, 1-368. With 75 figures in the text.)

1891. FREDERIC A. LUCAS. Animals recently extinct or threatened with extermination, as represented in the collection of the U.S. National Museum.

In Report of the Smithson Inst. (U.S. Nat. Mus.) 1889 (1891 !), pp. 609-649, pls. XCV-CV.

(An account of some of the larger animals which have become extinct within historic times, or are threatened with extinction, with reasons suggested for their disappearance.)

1891. HARTERT. Katalog der Vogelsammlung im Museum der Senchenberg. Naturf. Ges. Frankfurt-a-M.

(*Alca impennis*, *Turdus terrestris*, *Chaunoproctus ferreorostris*, *Hemiphaga spadicea* mentioned.)

1891. WILL. DUTCHER. The Labrador Duck. A revised list of the extant specimens in North America, with some historical notes.

In Auk 1891, pp. 301-316, pl. 2.

1894. WILL. DUTCHER. The Labrador Duck. With additional data respecting extant specimens.

In Auk 1894, pp. 4-12.

1892. FORBES, H. O. Preliminary Notice of Additions to the Extinct Avifauna of New Zealand (Abstract).

In Trans. and Proceed. New Zealand Inst. Vol. XXIV, pp. 185-189.

(The editors say that the paper is published in abstract, as it had been impossible to prepare the drawings for its illustrations in time.—It is a most pitiful and unscientific proceeding to publish such preliminary abstracts containing insufficiently founded names and complete "nomina nuda" without publishing a fuller account; such, as far as I know, has never appeared.)

1892. H. O. FORBES. *Aphanapteryx* and other remains in the Chatham Islands.

In Nature, Vol. XLVI, p. 252.

(Short notes on avian remains which, unfortunately, were never properly studied afterwards.)

1892. HUTTON. The Moas of New Zealand.

In Trans. and Proceed. New Zealand Institute Vol. XXIV, pp. 93-172, pls. XV-XVII.

1892. HAMILTON. Notes on Moa Gizzard-stones, t.c. p. 172.

1892. HAMILTON. On the genus *Aptornis*, t.c. pp. 175-184.

1892. HARTLAUB. Vier seltene Rallen.

In: Abhandl. d. Naturwiss. Vereins zu. Bremen XII.

1893. H. O. FORBES. A List of the Birds inhabiting the Chatham Islands.

In Ibis 1893, pp. 521-546.

(Notes on the living and extinct forms. The genus *Palaeolimnas* established. Egg of *Cabalus modestus* figured, etc.)

1893. W. W. SMITH. Notes on certain species of New Zealand Birds.

In Ibis 1893, pp. 509-520.

(Methods of colonization and their disastrous results to the birds described.)

1893. MILNE-EDWARDS & OUSTALET. Notice sur quelques espèces d'oiseaux actuellement éteintes qui se trouvent représentées dans les collections du muséum d'histoire naturelle. In: Centenaire de la fondation du muséum d'histoire naturelle. Volume commémoratif publié par les professeurs du Muséum. Pp. 189-252, pls. I-V.

(Only 6 species: *Mascarinus mascarinus*, *Alectroenas nitidissima*, *Alca impennis*, *Fregilupus varius*, *Camptolaemus labradorius*, *Dromaius "ater*," but these beautifully figured and masterly described and discussed.)

1893. SIR E. NEWTON AND GADOW. On additional Bones of the Dodo and other Extinct Birds of Mauritius obtained by Mr. Théodore Sauzier.

In Trans. Zool. Soc. London XIII, pp. 281-302. Pls. XXXIII-XXXVII.

(*Strix sauzieri*, *Astur alphonsi*, *Butorides mauritianus*, *Plotus nanus*, *Sarcidiornis mauritianus*, *Anas theodori*, etc.)

1893. A. de Quatrefages. The Moas and Moa-hunters.

In Trans. and Proceed. New Zealand Inst. XXV, pp. 17-49.

(Translation of the French article which appeared in the Nos. for June and July of the "Journal des Savants" by Laura Buller.)

1893. Parker. On the classification and mutual relations of the *Dinornithidae*. By T. J. Parker.

In Trans. and Proc. New Zealand Inst. XXV, pp. 1-6, pls. I-III.

1893. F. W. Hutton. New Species of Moas.

In Trans. and Proc. New Zealand Inst. Vol. XXV, pp. 6-13.

(Dinornis strenuus, Anomalopteryx fortis, Euryapteryx compacta, Pachyornis inhabilis, P. valgus.)

1893. F. W. Hutton. On *Anomalopteryx antiqua*. T.c. p. 14, pl. IV.

*1893. R. Burckhardt, in Palāontolog. Abhandl. VI, Heft 2, pp. 127-145, Taf. 1-4.

(Aepyornis.)

1893. H. O. Forbes. The Moas of New Zealand.

In Natural Science II, pp. 374-380.

1893. A. Hamilton. On the Fissures and Caves at the Castle Rocks, Southland; with a description of the remains of the Existing and Extinct Birds found in them.

(In Trans. and Proceed. New Zealand Inst. XXV, pp. 88-106; with figures.)

1893. A. Newton. "Extermination." In A Dictionary of Birds.

(See also in Encyclopaedia Britannica.)

1893-1900. Walter Rothschild. The Avifauna of Laysan and the Neighbouring Islands: with a complete history to date of the Birds of the Hawaiian Possessions. London 1893-1900. With numerous plates.

(Account and coloured plates of the extinct birds of Oahu and Hawaii.)

1894. Milne-Edwards et Grandidier. Observations sur les *Aepyornis* de Madagascar.

In: Comptes Rendus hebd. des Séances de l'Acad. d. Sciences, Paris, Vol. CXVIII, Part I, pp. 122-127.

1894. J. Parker. Notes on Three Moa-Skulls.

In Trans. and Proc. N. Zealand Inst. XXVI, p. 223.

1894. Hamilton. On Avian Remains in Southland.

In Trans. and Proc. N. Zealand Inst. XXVI, p. 226.

1894. Hamilton. Materials for a Bibliography of the *Dinornithidae*.

In Trans. and Proc. N. Zealand Inst. XXVI, pp. 229-257.

(A careful list to which I refer my readers.)

1895. C. W. Andrews. On some remains of Aepyornis in the Hon. Walter Rothschild's Museum at Tring.

In: Novitates Zoologicae II, pp. 23-25.

1895. Hamilton. Further contributions towards a Bibliography of the Moas.

In Trans. and Proc. N. Zealand Inst. XXVII, p. 228-232.

1895. Jeffery Parker. On the Cranial Osteology, Classification, and Phylogeny of the Dinornithidae.

In Trans. Zool. Soc. London Vol. XIII, pp. 373-431, pls. LVI-LXII.

1895. HAMILTON. On the Feathers of a small Moa.

In Trans. and Proc. N. Zealand Inst. XXVII, pp. 232-238.

*1895. C. W. ANDREWS. On Aepyornis bones, etc., in Geological Magazine 1895.

1896. HUTTON. On a deposit of Moa-bones at Kapua.

In Trans. and Proc. N. Zealand Inst. XXVIII, p. 627. Id. On the Moa-bones from Enfield, t.c.p. 645.

1896. C. W. ANDREWS. On the Extinct Birds of the Chatham Islands

In Novit Zoolog. III, p. 73-84 and 260-271.

(Diaphorapteryx hawkinsi, Palaeolimnas chathamensis, Nesolimnas dieffenbachii.)

1896. G. HARTLAUB. En Beitrag zur Geschichte der ausgestorbenen Vögel der Neuzeit, sowie derjenigen, deren Fortbestehen bedroht erscheint.

In : Abhandl. d. Naturwiss. Vereins gn. Bremen XIV Band, 1 Heft.

(Also : Second edition of the same, printed as manuscript, with a few alterations and additions.)

(The most useful, comprehensive pamphlet on recently extinct birds.)

1897. ANDREWS. On some fossil remains of Carinate Birds from Central Madagascar.

In Ibis 1897, pp. 343-359, pls. VIII and IX.

1897. H. O. FORBES. On an apparently new, and supposed to be now extinct, species of Bird from the Mascarene Islands, provisionally referred to the genus *Necropsar*. With plate.

In Bull. Liverpool Museums, I, p. 34, pl. Sturn. I *(Necropsar leguati)*.

1897. FORBES AND ROBINSON. Note on Two Species of Pigeon, t.c. p. 35.

(Hemiphaga spadicea.)

(On pl. I of the same vol. is figured *Nestor norfolcensis*. See p. 5.)

1900. W. WOLTERSTORFF. Ausgestorbene Riesenvögel. Vortrag, gehalten im Naturwissenschaftlichen Verein zu Magdeburg. Mit zwei Abbildungen. Stuttgart. Verlag von E. Nägele.

1900. A. MERTENS. Die Moas im Naturwissenschaftl. Museum zu Magdeburg. Mit 2 Abbildungen.

In : Jahresbericht Naturwiss. Vereins zu Magdeburg für 1898-1900. (Pp. 1-24 in separate copy.)

1901. W. A. BRYAN. Key to the Birds of the Hawaiian group.

1902. WALTER ROTHSCHILD AND ERNST HARTERT. Further notes on the fauna of the Galápagos Islands.

In Nov. Zool. 1902, pp. 381-418; cf. also Nov. Zool. 1899, pp. 154, 163.

(*Geospiza magnirostris* and *dentirostris*.)

1902. H. W. HENSHAW. Birds of the Hawaian Islands, being a complete list of the Birds of the Hawaiian Possessions, with notes on their habits. Honolulu 1902.

1903. GRAHAM RENSHAW. The Black Emu.

In : Zoologist 1903, pp. 81-88.

1903. WILHELM BLASIUS. Der Riesenalk, *Alca impennis* L. In the New Edition of Naumann called "Naumann, Naturgeschichte der Vögel Mitteleuropas" (sic), vol. XII, pp. 169-208, pls. 17, 17A-17D, 1903.

(Among others the most complete bibliography and very detailed descriptions.)

1903. FLEMING, J. H. On the Passenger Pigeon.

In Auk 1903, p. 66.

1903. M. GUILLAUME GRANDIDIER. Contribution à l'etude de l'Epiornis de Madagascar.

In : Comptes Rendus des Séances de l'Acad. Sc., Paris 1903 (pp. 1-3 in separate copy.)

1903. G. GRANDIDIER. Note au sujet du squelette de l'*Aepyornis ingens*.

In Bull. Mus. Paris 1903, pp. 318-323, with figures.

1903. PAUL CARIÉ. Observations sur quelques oiseaux de l'ile Maurice.

In Ornis XII, p. 121-128.

(We are informed that neither *Palaeornis echo*—sub nomine *eques*—nor *Nesoenas mayeri* are extinct.)

1905. A. H. CLARK. Extirpated West Indian Birds.

In Auk 1905, pp. 259-266.

1905. A. H. CLARK. The Lesser Antillean Macaws.

In Auk 1905, pp. 266-273.

1905. A. H. CLARK. The West Indian Parrots.

In Auk 1905, pp. 337-344.

1905. A. H. CLARK. The Greater Antillean Macaws.

In Auk 1905, pp. 345-348.

1905-1906. SIR WALTER BULLER. Supplement to the "Birds of New Zealand." Two volumes.

(Though containing very interesting notes on extinct and threatened birds, these two volumes are rather disappointing. They contain very little that is new, and are mainly composed of quotations from other people's writings or letters. Buller's former great book on the Birds of New Zealand was a most important and creditable work, though not without shortcomings. Our knowledge of New Zealand Birds might have been brought up to date in his supplement, but we cannot say that this has been done properly, and errors are frequent.)

1906. BALDWIN SPENCER. The King Island Emu.

In The Victorian Naturalist XXIII (1906), pp. 139, 140.

(*Dromaius minor* described.)

1907. WALTER ROTHSCHILD. On Extinct and Vanishing Birds. A short Essay on the Birds which have presumably become extinct within the last 500 years, and also of those birds which are on the verge of extinction, including a few which, though not yet so far gone, are threatened with extinction in the near future.

In Proceed. of the IV Intern. Ornith. Congress, London 1905, pp. 191-217.

LIST OF PLATES.

PALAEOCORAX FORBES.

THIS genus is founded on cranial characters: Basipterygoid processes of parasphenoid present but rudimentary. The vomer broad, flat, and three-pointed in front. Maxillaries anchylosed to the premaxillaries, the latter anchylosed to the expanded ossified base of the nasal septum. The ossified mesethmoid stretches backward and is lodged in the concavity of the upper surface of the vomer, so that it presents a form intermediate between the complete aegithognathous forms, such as *Corvus*, and the compound aegithognathous forms, such as *Gymnorhina*, in which desmognathism was superadded by "anchylosis of the inner edge of the maxillaries with a highly ossified alinasal wall and nasal septum" (Parker).

PALAEOCORAX MORIORUM (FORBES).

Corvus moriorum Forbes, Nature XLVI p. 252 (1892).
Palaeocorax moriorum Forbes, Bull. B.O.C. I p. XXI (1892).

DR. FORBES says this bird is of about half the size again of a *Corvus cornix*. The principal characters are cranial, and the same as those of the genus.

Habitat: Chatham Islands, and possibly the Middle Island, New Zealand.

Many skulls and bones in the Tring Museum.

PALAEOCORAX ANTIPODUM FORBES.

Palaeocorax antipodum Forbes, Ibis 1893, p. 544.

THIS is said to be distinguished from *P. moriorum* by its considerably smaller size. Habitat: North Island, New Zealand.

FREGILUPUS LESSON.

HUGE crest, bill long and curved. One species, extinct.

FREGILUPUS VARIA (BODD.)

(PLATE I.)

"*Huppes ou Callendres*," Voyages du Sieur D.B. (Dubois) aux Iles Dauphine on Madagascar, and Bourbon ou Mascarenne, etc., p. 172 (1674—Bourbon).

Huppe du Cap de Bonne Espérance Daubenton, Pl. Enl. 697.

Huppe noire et blanche du Cap de Bonne Espérance Montbeillard, Hist. Nat. Ois. VI, p. 463 (1779).

Madagascar Hoopoe Latham, Gen. Syn. B. II pt. I, p. 690 (1783).

Upupa varia Boddaert, Tabl. Pl. Enl. p. 43 (1783—ex Daubenton).

Upupa capensis Gmelin, Syst. Nat. I, p. 466 (1788—ex Montbeillard).

La Huppe grise Audebert et Vieillot, Ois. Dor., "Promerops" p. 15 pl. 111 (1802).

Le Mérops huppé Levaillant, Hist. Nat. Promérops, etc., p. 43, pl. 18 (1806).

Upupa madagascariensis Shaw, Gen. Zool. VIII, pt. I, p. 140 (1812).

Coracia cristata Vieillot, Nouv. Dict. d'Hist. Nat. VIII, p. 3 (1817).

Pastor upupa Wagler, Syst. Avium, Pastor, sp. 13 (1827).

Fregilupus borbonicus Vinson, Bull. Soc. d'Acclimat 1868, p. 627.

Fregilupus varius Hartlaub, Vög. Madagasc. p. 203 (1877); Sharpe, Cat. B. Brit. Mus. XIII p. 194 (1890); Milne-Edwards & Oustalet, Centenaire Mus. Hist. Nat., p. 205, pl. II (1893).

AS long ago as 1674 a note about the "Huppe" exists, by "Le Sieur D.B.," *i.e.*, Dubois. He says, when describing the birds of Réunion (translated): "Hoopoes or 'Callendres,' having a white tuft on the head, the rest of the plumage white and grey, the bill and the feet like a bird of prey; they are a little larger than the young pigeons; this is another good game (*i.e.*, to eat) when it is fat."

This description has generally been accepted as referring to the *Fregilupus*, though that of the bill and feet is then due to an error of the author, for *Fregilupus* has the bill and feet of a member of the *Sturnidae* or family of Starlings.

Good descriptions and representations of the "Huppe" have been given in many places (see literature), but whether they were taken from males or females is generally not known. The sexes seem to be alike in colour, but the female is smaller, and has a shorter and straighter bill than the male. At least, this is the conclusion of Dr. Hartert, who saw the four examples in the museum at Troyes. As far as he could see through the glass all four seemed to be adult birds, but two were larger with longer and more curved bills, two smaller and with shorter and straighter beaks, so that they are evidently two pairs.

This bird seems to have become extirpated about the middle of the last century. The late Monsieur Pollen wrote in 1868 (translated): "This species has become so rare that one did not hear them mentioned for a dozen years. It has been destroyed in all the littoral districts, and even in the mountains near the coast. Trustworthy persons, however, have assured us that they must still exist in the forests of the interior, near St. Joseph. The old creoles told me that, in their youth, these birds were still common, and that they were so stupid that one could kill them with sticks. They call this bird the "Hoopoe." It is, therefore, not wrong what a distinguished inhabitant of Réunion, Mr. A. Legras, wrote about this bird with the following words: "The Hoopoe has become so rare that we have hardly seen a dozen in our wanderings to discover birds; we were even grieved to search for it in vain in our museum."

We are certain that *Fregilupus* existed still on Réunion in 1835, as Monsieur Desjardins, living on Mauritius, wrote in a manuscript formerly belonging to the late Professor Milne-Edwards: "My friend, Marcelin Sauzier, has sent me four alive from Bourbon in May, 1835. They eat everything. Two have escaped some months afterwards, and it might well happen that they will stock our forests."

It seems, indeed, that specimens were killed in 1837 on Mauritius, where they did not originally exist. Verreaux shot an example in Réunion in 1832.

The names "La Huppe du Cap" and "*Upupa madagascariensis*" arose out of the mistaken notions that this bird lived in South Africa or Madagascar, but we know now that its real home was Réunion or Bourbon.

WE ARE AWARE OF THE FOLLOWING SPECIMENS PRESERVED IN COLLECTIONS.

2 stuffed ones, one in good, one in bad condition, and two in spirits, in the Paris Museum.
4 stuffed in Troyes.
1 stuffed, from the Riocour collection, in the British Museum.
1 in the Florence Museum.
1 in Turin.
1 in Pisa.
1, rather poor and old, in Leyden.
1 in Stockholm.
1 in the Museum at Port Louis, on the island of Mauritius.
1 in the collection of the late Baron de Selys Longchamps.
1 in Genoa.

NECROPSAR GÜNTHER & NEWTON.

THE authors state that this genus was very closely allied to *Fregilupus*, and, besides some minor differences, give as the principal difference the shorter and less curved bill.

NECROPSAR RODERICANUS GÜNTH. & NEWT.

(PLATE 2, FIG. 2.)

Necropsar rodericanus Günther & Newton, Phil. Trans. vol. 168, p. 427, pl. XLII, figs. A-G (1879).

THE original description given by the anonymous author of the "Relation de l'Ile Rodrigue" is as follows:—"These birds are a little larger than a blackbird, and have white plumage, part of the wings and the tail black, the beak and the legs yellow, and make a wonderful warbling." Our author also says they inhabited the Islet au Mât, and fed on seabirds' eggs and dead turtle.

The bird evidently became extinct on Rodriguez before 1730, and lingered a little longer on the outlying islets. Only known from bones, mostly collected by the Rev. H. H. Slater, and the above description.

Habitat: Rodriguez and neighbouring islets.

There is one tibia in the Tring Museum.

The figure is coloured according to the description, while the shape of the bird is evident from its bones and relation.

NECROPSAR LEGUATI FORBES.

(PLATE 2, FIG. 3.)

Necropsar leguati Forbes, Bull. Liverp. Mus. I, p. 34, pl. *Sturnidae* I (1897-1898).

DR. FORBES' description is as follows :—" General colour white everywhere, except on the outer webs of distal half of the primaries and secondaries and the outer webs of the newly moulted and both webs of the unmoulted rectrices, which are marked with lighter or darker ferruginous."

Dr. Forbes then gives an exhaustive description of the structure, to which I refer my readers, and the following measurements :—

Culmen	32 mm.
Wing	109 ,,
Tail	98 ,,
Tarsus	31·5 ,,

I should have been inclined to consider this bird an albinistic specimen of the bird described in "Relation de l'Ile Rodrigue," but for the fact that the tibia of *Necropsar rodericanus* is 52-59 mm. in length, while this is only 46 mm. in length, while the metatarsus measures 31·5 mm. as opposed to 36-41 mm. in *N. rodericanus*. I cannot accept the theory that this is the Islet au Mât bird, and therefore different from *N. rodericanus*, as the islet is too close to Rodriguez to have had a different starling. I therefore believe this bird to have been an albinistic specimen of the Mauritius species of *Necropsar*, for there can be little doubt that it is albinistic, as the ferruginous colour is much stronger on one wing than on the other ; and I conclude that the colour in the wings and tail in normal specimens was black like the Rodriguez bird, and that *N. leguati* was a close ally of *N. rodericanus*, from which it differed principally in its much smaller size.

Habitat doubtful.—The type specimen bears Lord Derby's Museum number, 1792, and a label of Verreaux giving Madagascar as the habitat, which is certainly erroneous.

FOUDIA BRUANTE (P.L.S. MÜLL.)

(PLATE 2, FIG. 1.)

Bruant de l'isle de Bourbon Daubenton, Pl. Enl. 321.

Le Mordoré, Montbeillard, Hist. Nat. Ois., Quarto Edition IV., p. 366 (1778—Bourbon).

Fringilla bruante P.L.S. Müll., Natursyst., Suppl. p. 164, No. 51 (1776—ex Daubenton Pl. enl).

Emberiza fuscofulva Boddaert, Table Pl. Enl. p. 20 (1783—based on Pl. Enl. 321 and Montbeillard's "Morderé").

Emberiza borbonica Gmelin, Syst. Nat. I p. 886 (1788—ex Daubenton and Montbeillard).

Foudia bruante Newton, Trans. Norf. and Norw. Nat. Soc. IV., pp. 543 and 548 (1889).

Nesacanthis fusco-fulvus Sharpe, Cat. B. Brit. Mus. XIII p. 484 (1890).

WE know absolutely nothing about this bird, except Daubenton's figure and the description by Montbeillard. In the plate the whole body, including the back, is uniform red, about the same red as in other species of *Foudia*, while the wings and tail are dark brown with yellowish-brown borders. In the description the body plumage is described as rufous ("morderé") and the wings, wing-coverts and tail as more or less bright rufous ("d'un mordoré plus ou moins clair"). The size is said to be about that of a Bunting, but the tail shorter and the wings longer.

According to Dr. Sharpe (Cat. B. XIII, p. 484) "it has generally been considered identical with *Foudia madagascariensis*," but the latter has the back marked with longitudinal black spots, while both the figure and description of *F. bruante* represent a uniform red upperside; moreover the locality of the latter is expressly stated, and as we know other forms of *Foudia* from the Seychelles, Mauritius, Comoros, Aldabra and Madagascar, we have no reason to doubt the statement. We are not aware of any specimen existing of this doubtless extinct bird, though it would be worth while to search the Paris Museum for this treasure.

Habitat: Réunion or Bourbon.

CHAUNOPROCTUS Bp.

Chaunoproctus Bonaparte, Consp. Av. I p. 526 (1850).

THE genus *Chaunoproctus* contains only one species, which is characterized by its enormous bill, the depth of the mandible being greater than the distance between the nasal apertures. The cutting-edge of the maxilla is nearly straight, and there is no tooth in the posterior half of the maxilla. The total length is about seven to eight inches. The adult male has red in the plumage, the female is brown, above and below.

Dr. Hartert (Vögel pal. Fauna I, p. 115) is of opinion that this bird is connected with *Carpodacus* and allies, and not with the Greenfinches and Hawfinches, among which it is placed in the Catalogue of Birds in the British Museum.

CHAUNOPROCTUS FERREOROSTRIS (VIG.)

(PLATE 3, FIG. 4.)

Coccothraustes ferreorostris (*sic*) Vigors, Zool. Journ. IV p. 354 (1828); id. in Beechey's Voy. Blossom, p. 22, pl. 8 (1839).

Fringilla papa Kittlitz, Mém. Acad. Imp. Sc. Petersbourg I p. 239, pl. 15 (1830); id. Kupfertaf. Vög. p. 24, pl. 32, 2 (1832).

Chaunoproctus papa Bonaparte, Consp. I p. 526 (1850); Bp. and Schlegel, Monogr. Loxiens p. 32 pls. 37, 38 (1850).

Chaunoproctus ferreirostris Sharpe, Cat. B. Brit. Mus. XII p. 31 (1888).

VIGORS' original description, translated from the Latin, is as follows: Dark brown; head, breast and upper part of abdomen scarlet. Bill very strong, feet plumbeous. Length of body $8\frac{1}{2}$, bill $\frac{7}{8}$, at gape $1\frac{3}{16}$, height $\frac{7}{8}$; wings from the carpus to the third quill $4\frac{1}{2}$; tail 3, tarsus $\frac{7}{8}$ inches."

In the "Catalogue of Birds," XII, p. 31, both sexes are carefully described.

It appears that only one pair, now in the British Museum, was obtained during Captain Beechey's voyage. Curiously enough, Vigors suggested that the brilliantly coloured adult male might be the young, the female the adult bird, "as is the case in the Pine-Grosbeak" (*Sic !*).

Kittlitz, who visited the largest of the Bonin Islands in May, 1828, obtained a number of specimens, of which some are in St. Petersburg, two in Frankfurt-a.-M., one or two in Leyden, and, I believe, in Paris.

These seem to be all the specimens known in European museums. Mr. Seebohm's collector, the late Holst, failed to obtain it, and Mr. Alan Owston's men, who several times went to the Bonin group to obtain it, and who were promised good prices for specimens, did not get one. I am therefore convinced that for some unknown reason this bird became extinct, though there is still the possibility that the recent collectors did not collect on the main island of the group, which alone was visited by Kittlitz.

Kittlitz tells us that he found it in the woods along the coast, but not numerous. That it keeps concealed, is very phlegmatic, and is so little shy that one is obliged to go back for some distance, before shooting, if one wishes to preserve the specimen. Kittlitz saw it but seldom on high trees, mostly on the ground. Its frequently heard note is a very fine piping sound. In the crop and stomach small fruit and buds of one kind of tree were found.

Habitat: The largest of the Bonin Islands, south of Japan.

GEOSPIZA MAGNIROSTRIS GOULD.

(PLATE 3, FIG. 1.)

Geospiza magnirostris Gould, Proc. Zool. Soc. London 1837, p. 5 (Galapagos Islands); Rothschild & Hartert, Nov. Zool. 1899 p. 154, 1902 p. 388; Sharpe, Cat. B. Brit. Mus. XII, pp. 6, 7 (Fig.); Ridgway, B. North and Middle America I, p. 495 (1901).

AS explained in Nov. Zool. 1899, p. 154, it is uncertain where Darwin obtained the type specimens of Gould's *G. magnirostris*, as "Unfortunately, most of the specimens of the finch-tribe were mingled together," as Darwin tells us in his "Journal of Researches" (New Edition 1890, p. 420), and he had only "strong reasons to suspect that some of the species of the sub-group *Geospiza* are confined to separate islands." We are, however, convinced that the types of *G. magnirostris* can only have come from Charles Island, where it is, probably, the representative of *G. strenua strenua*. It seems, however, that *G. magnirostris* exists no longer, for all subsequent collectors have failed to obtain specimens, unless an immature specimen in the U. S. Nat. Mus., from Charles Island (No. 115,905), is a young *magnirostris* (cf. Nov. Zool. 1902, p. 388).

The dimensions of the three black specimens in the British Museum are as follows: Culmen 26·5, 27, 27; height of bill at base 23·5-24; wing 91, 91, 95; tarsus 25 mm. These measurements—a culmen of over 26·5 and a wing of 91 mm. combined—do not occur among our large series of *strenua*, and therefore it is hardly possible that *G. magnirostris* is composed of huge examples of *strenua* only.

As Charles Island has been inhabited for many years it is not at all unlikely that a bird became extinct on that place. On plate 3 is figured *G. magnirostris* and a head of *G. strenua* for comparison.

GEOSPIZA DENTIROSTRIS GOULD.

Geospiza dentirostris Gould, Proc. Zool. Soc. London 1837, p. 6; Rothschild & Hartert, Nov. Zool. 1899 p. 163, 1902 p. 396.

THIS curious form differs from *G. fortis fortis* (Charles Island !) in its bill, which is bowed in towards the end of the upper mandible, and slightly "toothed" on its cutting edge. The one specimen in the British Museum certainly came from Charles Island, and we may, therefore, conclude that the other also came from there, and there is certainly no reason to think that it came from Chatham Island. As the skins in the British Museum slightly differ from each other, there is some reason to suspect that they are both aberrations of *G. fortis fortis*. Otherwise it must have become extinct, as, in spite of special attention being paid to it, none of the recent collectors met with *G. dentirostris*.

POMAREA NIGRA (SPARRM.)

Muscicapa nigra Sparrmann, Mus. Carlson. I, pl. 23 and text (1786—Society Islands).
Pomarea nigra Sharpe, Cat. B. Brit. Mus. IV, p. 434 (1879—Full synonymy, description, etc., "Society Islands, Marquesas group").

IN the list of birds now fully extinct, in the Proceedings of the Fourth Intern. Orn. Congress, I enumerated *Pomarea nigra*, on the strength of E. L. Layard's statement, P.Z.S. 1876, p. 501, who says: "This bird has undoubtedly become extinct. Large sums have been offered by Messrs. Godeffroy's collectors for the acquisition of a single specimen, but in vain! The *very* old natives say they remember the bird and call it "Moho."

I, however, overlooked the fact that this note of Layard's referred to the Friendly Islands only, and that this bird has afterwards been obtained in numbers on the Marquesas group. It would, nevertheless, be very interesting to compare specimens from the various islands, viz.: the Society group, Marquesas and Tongatabu, to see if they are perfectly similar.

MIRO TRAVERSI BULLER.

(PLATE 5, FIG. 1.)

Miro traversi Buller, B. New Zealand, Ed. I p. 123 (1873—Chatham Islands).
Petroeca traversi Hutton, Ibis 1872, p. 245.
Myiomoira traversi Finsch, Journ.-f.-Orn. 1874, p. 189.
Miro traversi Sharpe, Cat. B. Brit. Mus. IV p. 236 (1879).
Miro traversi (partim) Buller, Suppl. B. N. Zealand II p. 125 ? pl. XII (October, 1906).

THE late Sir Walter Buller described, in 1873, *Miro traversi* as follows: "Adult male. The whole of the plumage black, the base of the feathers dark plumbeous; wing-feathers and their coverts tinged with brown, the former greyish on their inner surface; tail-feathers black, very slightly tinged with brown. Irides dark brown; bill black; tarsi and toes blackish brown, the soles of the feet dull yellow. Total length 6 inches; wing, from flexure, 3·4; tail 2·6; bill 0·5, tarsus 1·1; middle toe and claw 0·1, hind toe and claw 0·8 inch."

"Female. Slightly smaller than the male, and without the brown tinge on the wings and tail."

It may be added that *Miro traversi* is not pure black, but of a somewhat brownish slaty black.

Miro traversi is only known from the Chatham Islands, where it was formerly very common, but, according to a letter from the late W. Hawkins, the cats, which have been introduced to destroy rats and rabbits, have exterminated it. It seems to have disapppeared from Warekauri, the main island of the Chatham group, long ago, for H. O. Forbes (Ibis 1893, p. 524) and Henry Palmer found it, in 1890 and 1892, only on the outlying islets of Mangare and Little Mangare.

The bird from the Snares is quite different, being deep glossy black and having a shorter and narrower first primary. I named it *M. dannefaerdi*. It is to be feared that a similar fate will one day befall it as has, apparently, already befallen its congener from the Chatham Islands.

Sir Walter Buller (Suppl. B.N.Z. II, p. 125) has confounded *M. traversi* and *dannefaerdi*, and the figure he gave on his plate looks so black, that I do not doubt it represents rather the latter than the former. Of course *M. dannefaerdi* alone occurs on the Snares, and Buller's *traversi* from the Snares were all *dannefaerdi*. Dr. Finsch's statement (Ibis 1888, p. 308) that Reischek's specimen from the Snares "agreed in every respect with specimens from the Chatham Islands" is entirely wrong, for, even if one prefers unscientifically to lump allied forms, one cannot say that a *Miro* from the Chathams agrees in every respect with one from the Snares. Buller's doubts about the distinctness of the latter might easily have been removed, if he had taken the trouble to compare them, for it does not require any genius to see the differences. I admit that with my present views on geographical forms I would regard the two *Miro* as sub-species, and call them *M. traversi traversi* and *M. traversi dannefaerdi*, but most ornithologists would still consider them to be "good species."

I may add that Buller, l.c., p. 125, has not quoted my description correctly, for in his rendering are several disturbing misprints, and in the fourth line from the bottom occurs a "not" which ought not to be there, and which makes the sentence incomprehensible. Also the name itself is spelt incorrectly.

I have a series from Mangare and Little Mangare, taken by Henry Palmer in 1890. The egg seems to be unknown.

Habitat: Chatham Islands.

TURDUS TERRESTRIS KITTL.

Turdus terrestris Kittlitz, Mém. Acad. Sc. Pétersburg I p. 245, pl. 17 (1830—Boninsima).

Geocichla terrestris Bonaparte, Consp. Av. I, p. 268 (1850); Seebohm, Cat. B. Brit. Mus. V, p. 183 (1881); Hartert, Kat. Vogels. Senckenb, p. 6 (1891); Sharpe, Monograph Turdidae, I p. 107, pl. 33 (1902).

Cichlopasser terrestris Bonaparte, C.R. XXXVIII, p. 6 (1854).

THE following is Dr. Sharpe's description from a specimen in the Leyden Museum: "General colour of the upper parts olive-brown, shading into chestnut-brown on the rump, upper tail-coverts, and tail; the inside web of each feather much darker, approaching black on the back; lores dark brown; eye-stripe very obscure; lesser wing-coverts brown, darkest on the inside web; median coverts dark brown, with large olive-brown tips; greater coverts nearly black, broadly tipped, and narrowly margined towards the base with olive-brown; primary coverts black, with a broad olive-brown patch on the outer webs; tertials dark brown on the inner web, and olive-brown on the outer web; secondaries brown, margined with olive-brown on the outer webs: primaries brown, with the basal half of the outer webs, and a spot where the emargination begins, olive-brown; tail-feathers chestnut-brown; ear-coverts brown; underparts olive-brown, shading into white on the chin, throat, and centre of belly; under tail-coverts dark brown, with irregular diamond-shaped white tips; axillaries brown; under wing-coverts brown. Geocichline markings on inner webs of quills dirty white. Wing 3·8 inches, tail 2·6, culmen 0·85, tarsus 1·07, bastard primary 0·8."

The only person who ever collected this short-tailed Ground-Thrush was Kittlitz, who obtained four specimens, one of which is in St. Petersburg, one in Frankfurt, one in Vienna, and one in Leyden. Neither Holst, nor Alan Owston's Japanese collectors obtained specimens, though their special attention was called to it. Therefore, unless these recent collectors left unvisited the most important island of the group, we must suppose that it became extinct.

Habitat: Bonin Islands, south-east of Japan.

PHAEORNIS OAHENSIS WILSON & EVANS.

Phaeornis oahensis Wilson & Evans, Aves Hawaiienses, Introd. p. XIII (1899—Based on *Turdus sandwichensis var.* Bloxam, Voy. "Blonde" App. p. 250 (1826-Oahu) and "*Turdus woahensis*" Bloxam M.S.)

NOTHING is known about this evidently extinct bird, which formerly existed on the island of Oahu, except Bloxam's short description, which is as follows :—" Length 7½ inches ; upper parts olive-brown, extremities of the feathers much lighter colour ; tail and wings brown ; bill bristled at the base."

The corresponding description of *Phaeornis obscura* in Bloxam's M.S. notes is :—Length 8 inches ; belly light ash ; back, tail and wings an ash-brown ; bill slender, ¾-in. long, bristled at the base. A beautiful songster."

It is thus evident that Bloxam considered both forms to be distinct, and Messrs. Wilson and Evans were perfectly justified in naming the extinct Oahu form.

We are not aware of any specimens being preserved in any Museum, though Bloxam obtained a skin. Messrs. Wilson and Evans (l.c.) write :— "All the specimens obtained by Mr. Andrew Bloxam, properly prepared and labelled, were placed at the disposal of the Lords of the Admiralty, as shewn by a copy of the letter he wrote to their Secretary, and probably all were sent, as some certainly were, to the British Museum ; but no other trace of this unique specimen of a vanished species, which may be properly called *Phaeornis oahensis*, is now forthcoming."

BOWDLERIA RUFESCENS (BULLER).

(PLATE 5, FIG. 3.)

Sphenoeacus rufescens Buller, Ibis 1869, p. 38.
Megalurus rufescens Gray Hand-l. B. I, p. 206. No. 2913. (1869.)

BULLER'S original description is as follows: "Upper parts, sides, and tail dark rufous brown, brightest on the crown and hind-neck; the feathers of the shoulders and sides centred with black. Quills dusky black, margined with rufous brown. Streak over the eye, throat, breast and abdomen pale fawn colour; sides of the head and ear-coverts marked with black. Bill light brown with the ridge black, feet dark brown." Buller's type probably had been preserved in spirit, as the colouration of fresh specimens is very different to his description. The general colour above and on the flanks chestnut rufous, most feathers with darker or black centres; chin, throat, breast and abdomen pure white; crissum and under tail-coverts whity buff or buffy brown. Wing 2·6 inches, tail 3·9 inches, culmen 0·65 inch."

Habitat: Chatham Islands.

Cats, rats and weasels have exterminated this fine species, which is now quite extinct. Messrs. Travers and Dannefaerd have supplied the specimens in most colonial museums, while Henry Palmer collected the 14 at Tring. A few in Liverpool and two in the British Museum are all known to me in Europe, in addition to those at Tring.

TRAVERSIA ROTHSCH.

See description below. Only one species known.

TRAVERSIA LYALLI ROTHSCH.

(Plate 5, Fig. 3.)

Traversia lyalli Rothschild, Bull. B.O.C. IV p. X (December 29th, 1894); Nov. Zool. 1895, p. 81.

Xenicus insularis Buller, Ibis 1895, p. 236, pl. .

Traversia insularis Buller, Suppl. B.N.Z. II p. 109, pl. X (1906).

IN 1894 I described this remarkable little bird as follows: "*Traversia*, gen. nov. *Xenicidarum*. Differs in several important points both from *Xenicus* and *Acanthidositta*. Bill much larger and stouter, very little shorter, if at all, than the tarsus; the latter about as long as middle toe without claw, or the hind toe and claw, while in *Xenicus* and *Acanthidositta* it is about twice as long as the hind toe. The principal difference, however, is the weakness of the wing, which suggests flightlessness, as does also the very soft and loose character of the entire plumage, and the very Ralline aspect of the bird. There are only ten tail-feathers, and the scutellation of the tarsus is like that of *Xenicus*. These two points determine its position in the *Xenicidae* at once (cf. Sclater, Cat. B. XIV, p. 450).

"The type is: *Traversia lyalli*, sp. nov.

"Male. Above dark brownish olive-yellow, each feather with a brownish-black border. A narrow distinct yellow superciliary line. Wings and tail umber-brown, the inner webs darker; wing-coverts like back. Chin, throat, and breast chrome-yellow, each feather slightly edged with greyish brown. Flanks, abdomen, and vent pale brown, centre of feathers paler.

"Female. Upper surface umber-brown, each feather bordered with very dark brown; wings and tail similar. Under surface buffy grey, the feathers edged with pale brown. Total length about 4 inches, culmen 0·6, wing 1·8 to 1·9, tail 0·8, but much concealed, tarens 0·75, middle toe 0·65, hind toe without claw 0·5.

Habitat: Stephens Island, New Zealand. Discovered by Mr. Dr. Lyall, lighthouse-keeper, and sent to me by Mr. Henry H. Travers."

I received nine specimens of this new bird, and was not aware that any others had been taken at that time. As I was unable to attend the December meeting, 1894, of the British Ornithologists Club, I asked Dr. Hartert to exhibit the birds in my name. When he had done so and had read the description, the Chairman, Dr. P. L. Sclater, said that the bird had also been received for illustration and description in the Ibis, from Sir Walter Buller, and he asked Dr. Hartert if I would not withdraw my description. Dr. Hartert said that this was unfortunate, but he had no authority to withdraw my description, and he and Dr. Sharpe thought that the proceedings of the meeting should be printed without consideration of any manuscripts which might refer to the same bird. No doubt this was hard luck on Sir Walter Buller, but it would have been equally hard luck for me if he had forestalled me with the new bird. He had only one specimen, I had nine, of both sexes, and I had paid a high price for them, as types of a new bird. My type is in Tring, and, as everybody knows, available for study by any competent ornithologist, while Buller's type was not in any museum, and it was uncertain to whom he would sell it afterwards. I suppose it is now in the Carnegie Museum, Pittsburgh, to which Buller's "third collection," 625 specimens, was sold for a thousand pounds, as Buller himself tells us in his Supplement II, p. 167, under the heading of *Glaucopis wilsoni!* On the same page Sir Walter Buller also tells us that his "second collection" was sold to me, but he makes a mistake about the price, as I certainly did not pay a thousand pounds for it.

I mentioned these unimportant details, because Buller rather bitterly and severely complained about my describing the Stephens' Island Wren, on p. 111 of his supplement. I may only add that of course my name, being published in December, 1894, has the priority over his, which was not published before April, 1895.

The history of *Traversia lyalli* is perhaps the most extraordinary of any bird known. All the specimens I am aware of, viz., the eight now in my collection, the type of "*Xenicus insularis*" in Buller's former collection, one in the late Canon Tristram's collection, one in the British Museum (ex Tring), and two or more offered some years ago by Mr. Travers, were brought in by the lighthouse-keeper's cat. Evidently this feline discoverer has at the same time been the exterminator of *Traversia lyalli*, and many may have been digested by that unique cat, as in letters received from Mr. Travers I have been told that no more specimens could be obtained, and Buller (l.c.) says: "Very diligent search has been made on Stephen Island for further specimens of the Island Wren, but without success, and there is too much reason to fear that this species has almost immediately after its discovery become extinct."

Habitat: Stephen Island, a small, partly wooded islet, about a square mile in extent, in Cook Strait. It is almost impossible that this bird has only existed on Stephen Island. It must have been overlooked on d'Urville Island or the "mainland," where it probably became extinct—through rats and cats, and similar pests—long ago.

MOHO APICALIS GOULD.

(PLATE 4A, 1.)

"*Yellow-tufted Bee-eater*" (non Latham!), Dixon, Voyage round the World, p. 357, plate (1789).
Moho apicalis Gould, Proc. Zool. Soc. London 1860, p. 381 (? Hawaii).
Acrulocercus apicalis Wilson & Evans, Av. Hawaii, pt. V text and plate (1894).
Moho apicalis Rothschild, Avif. Laysan, etc., p. 223 and plate (1900).

THIS rarest species of the Mohos formerly inhabited the island of Oahu, where specimens were obtained in 1837, near Enero, by Herr Deppe.

The localities of the specimens figured by Dixon and that of the type of Gould are uncertain, but they must have been obtained on Oahu. Since 1837 we have no further traces of *Moho apicalis*.

The only specimens known are those in Berlin, collected by Deppe, two in the British Museum, and one in my Museum at Tring. The latter, which I obtained in exchange from the British Museum, is the one brought home from the Sandwich Islands by Capt. Lord Byron. There is no specimen of *Moho apicalis* in the Vienna Museum.

Habitat: Oahu.

CHAETOPTILA SCL.

Chaetoptila Sclater, Ibis 1871 p. 358.

DR. SCLATER justly proposed a new generic term for the "*Entomyza*" or "*Moho*" *angustipluma* of former authors. This bird belongs doubtless to the family of *Meliphagidae* or Honey-eaters, and the genus is sufficiently distinct from all others. There are no fleshy wattles anywhere. The tail is long and strongly graduated; all the rectrices are obliquely pointed at their tips. The plumage of the body is very soft, that of the head, throat and chest almost fluffy; the feathers of the chin, throat and forehead end in hair-like bristles.

We know only one species.

CHAETOPTILA ANGUSTIPLUMA (PEALE).

(PLATE 4A, FIG. 2.)

Entomiza angustipluma Peale, U.S. Expl. Exp., Birds p. 147 pl. XL fig. 2 (1848—Hawaii).

Mohoa angustipluma Cassin, Proc. Acad. Philad. 1855 p. 440.

Moho angustipluma Cassin, U.S. Expl. Exp., Mamm. & Orn. p. 148 pl. XI fig 1 (1858—Hawaii).

Wilson & Evans, Aves. Hawai. pt. II and plate (1891—Hawaii).

Rothschild, Avif. Laysan, etc., p. 215 and plate (1900).

THIS remarkable bird, belonging to the family *Meliphagidae*, used to inhabit the island of Hawaii in the Sandwich Archipelago. It has been said by Mr. Dole to inhabit Molokai, but this is evidently an error. At present nobody on the island of Hawaii has any recollection of its presence, and its former native name is unknown—the name "Kiowea" erroneously quoted by Mr. Dole being that of *Numenius tahitiensis*. The bird is extinct, though we do not know the reason why it disappeared.

THE ONLY SPECIMENS WE KNOW OF ARE THE FOLLOWING:—

1. The type in the Museum at Washington, U.S.A.
2. One in the Bernice Pauahi Bishop Museum in Honolulu.
3. One in the Museum of the University at Cambridge, obtained in exchange from Honolulu by Mr. Scott Wilson.
4. One in my Museum at Tring, obtained in exchange from the Honolulu Museum.

The type was obtained by Peale, the three others by the late Mr. Mills on the island of Hawaii.

STRIGICEPS LEUCOPOGON LESS.

Strigiceps leucopogon Lesson, Echo du Monde Savant 1840 (?); Rev. Zool. 1840, p. 266; Suppl. aux œuvres compl. de Buffon, Descr. de Mammif. & Ois, récemm. découverts, p. 277 (1847—Nouvelle Hollande); Hartlaub, Beitrag Gesch ausgest Vögel, in Abhandl. Naturw. Ver. Bremen, 2te Ausgabe, als M.S. gedr., p. 40 (1896).

Nobody has hitherto identified the curious bird described by Lesson, l.c., under the above name. From the generic characters he gives it is evident that it was a bird with a long, curved bill, lanceolate feathers on the head and throat, and long, strongly graduated tail, doubtless belonging to the *Meliphagidae*. The description of the colouration is as follows:—

"Back, wings and tail bright greenish-olive; quills brown inside; shafts of the rectrices canary-yellow from below, glossy brown-red from above; top of head and neck chestnut, each feather being narrow and streaked with white, then with fawn-colour on the top; the feathers of the throat are elongated and fringed out on their edges, very narrow and lanceolate, grey at base, white at the tips; cheeks, sides of neck and chest ferruginous, some white streaks on the feathers of the chest and in the middle of the throat; flanks and belly clear rufous, passing into canary-yellow on the under tail-coverts. Tail from below greenish-yellow; tarsi horn-colour, bill above brownish, below yellowish with brown tip. Length about eight french inches and a half (0.23 centimètres)." (*Translated.*)

This bird was said to have come from Australia. I have made enquiries, but the type seems to have disappeared. There is something in the description reminding us of *Chaetoptila angustipluma*. Unless the description is faulty, this bird came probably not from Australia, but from one of the Pacific Islands. It has not been observed since, and is possibly extinct.

DREPANIS TEMM.

Drepanis Temminck, Man. d'Orn. Ed. II, I p. LXXXVI (1820—"Espèces: *Certhia pacifica* —*obscura*—*vestiaria* et probablement *falcata*, que je n'ai pas vu." Type by elimination: *Drepanis pacifica*.

THE name *Drepanis* is now restricted to the practically extinct "Mamo" of the natives of the Sandwich Islands. *Drepanis pacifica* has a very striking black and yellow colouration; the somewhat loose-webbed under tail-coverts cover about three-quarters of the tail. The bill is long, curved, non-serrated, the upper mandible a few millimetres longer than the lower jaw. Nostrils large, covered by an operculum. First primary rudimentary, hidden by its covert. There is a silky, soft and fluffy axillary patch of feathers. The tail is slightly rounded. The metatarsus is covered with large, partly fused scutes.

Only one species known.

DREPANIS PACIFICA (GM.)

Great Hook-billed Creeper Latham, Gen. Synops. I p. 703 (1782).
Certhia pacifica Gmelin, Syst. Nat. I p. 470 (1788—ex Latham).

BOTH Mr. Scott Wilson and myself have at length discussed this beautiful bird in our books on the Hawaiian Avifauna. Of the actual status of this bird in former times we know nothing. Latham described it first (Gmelin named this species after Latham's description) from a pair in the Leverian collection, which is now preserved in the Vienna Museum. About half a century ago several specimens were collected by the late W. Mills near Hilo, on the island of Hawaii, the only island where it existed. Nothing certain was heard of the "Mamo" until, in 1892, my collector Henry Palmer obtained a fine male, which was caught before his eyes by a native birdcatcher. In July, 1898, Mr. H. W. Henshaw saw "at least a pair, possibly a whole family," in the woods of Kaumana, and in 1899 a native heard the, to him, well-known call near the same place. This brings the existence of the Mamo down to the year 1898 or 1899. In view of the futile efforts of Messrs. Henry Palmer,

Perkins, Henshaw and others to observe this rare bird again, we may well suppose that this species is either extinct, or will very soon vanish if any are left.

In former times the Mamo was probably more or less common. Its golden yellow feathers were of great value, and, though the majority of the famous war-cloaks are composed of the feathers of *Moho nobilis*, a few such cloaks are known to consist of Mamo feathers. It is supposed that it took generations to complete such a cape.

I only know of specimens of this bird in Vienna, Leyden, Paris, Honolulu, Cambridge and Tring.

The two examples in the Vienna Museum were obtained by Fichtel at the sale of the Leverian collection. One is perfect, the other has the upper portion of the bill wanting.

HEMIGNATHUS OBSCURUS ELLISIANUS

GRAY.

(PLATE 4, FIG. 1.)

Hemignathus obscurus Lichtenstein (non Gmelin!), Abh. Akad. Wiss. Berlin, 1838, p. 440 pl. 5 fig. 1 (Oahu).

Drepanis (*Hemignathus*) *ellisiana* Gray, Cat. B. Trop. Is. Pac. Oc. p. 9 (1859—based on Lichtenstein's *H. obscurus* from Oahu.

Hemignathus lichtensteini Scott Wilson, Ann. & Mag. N. H. ser. 6, vol. IV, p. 401 (1889—Oahu, based on the Berlin specimen).

Hemignathus ellisianus Rothschild, Avif. of Laysan, etc., p. 87 (1893) p. 310 (1900).

WE know only of one single specimen, the type of the names *ellisianus* and *lichtensteini*, figured and described by Lichtenstein, in 1838, under the name of *Hemignathus obscurus*. It is true that Lichtenstein says, that Herr Deppe procured several specimens, but there is only one in the Berlin Museum, and we have no knowledge where the others may be, if they are still in existence.

There can hardly be any doubt that *H. obscurus ellisianus* is extinct on Oahu, where it was discovered by Deppe. All recent collectors, from Wilson and Palmer to this day, have failed to find a trace of it. Although collecting in the dense forests and rugged mountains of Oahu is most difficult, we may suppose that at least one of these collectors would have come across it, if it still existed.

The following is the description made by Dr. Hartert of the type in Berlin:—

"Above greenish olive-brown, more greenish on the back and rump, and somewhat more greyish on the head and hind-neck; the dark bases of the feathers on the head showing through, lores deep brown. A distinct yellow superciliary stripe. Chin, throat, and middle of abdomen dull brownish white (apparently somewhat faded). Upper breast olive-greenish, sides of breast and flanks dull olive-greenish, more olive-brown on the flanks. Wings and tail deep brown, bordered with yellowish green. Under-wing coverts dull white. Bill brown, somewhat horn-brown, but not blackish, as in the other forms of *Hemignathus*.

It is not probable that the bill and feet are faded, as in specimens of *Heterorhynchus lucidus* collected and stuffed at the same time and kept side by side with *H. o. ellisianus*, the bill and feet are still blackish and not brown.

Wing 83·5, tail 53, culmen 56, bill from gape to tip in a straight line 47·5, lower mandible from mental apex to tip 40 mm."

HETERORHYNCHUS LUCIDUS (LICHT.)

(PLATE 4, FIG. 2.)

Hemignathus lucidus Lichtenstein, Abh. d. Kön. Akad. Wissensch. Berlin 1838 p. 451, pl. V figs. 2 ♂ 3 ♀ (1839—Oahu).

Heterorhynchus olivaceus Lafresnaye, Mag. de Zool. 1839 pl. X. and text (Oct. 1839).

THE Oahu form of *Heterorhynchus* is now extinct, and specimens are only, as far as we know, preserved in the Museums of Berlin (types of *H. lucidus*), Boston (type of *H. olivaceus*), Francfort, Paris, Leyden, London, Cambridge, Liverpool.

In 1838 Deppe saw this bird in great numbers flying round the flowers of the banana plantations. As the bird was apparently common, it is quite possible that specimens are preserved in several other collections, and it would be most welcome if the officials of continental Museums would give information in case they should find specimens of this interesting extinct bird.

Habitat : Oahu.

PSITTIROSTRA PSITTACEA DEPPEI

(PLATE 4, FIG. 3.) ROTHSCH.

Psittirostra olivacea Rothschild, Avifauna of Laysan p. 193 (1900—Oahu, ex Lichtenstein nomen nudum & M.S.)

Psittirostra psittacea deppei Rothschild, Bull. B.O.C. XV. p. 45 (1905—new name for the above, the name *olivacea* being preoccupied by Ranzani).

PSITTIROSTRA PSITTACEA PSITTACEA is still one of the commoner birds on most of the Hawaiian Islands, except Oahu, where it was formerly replaced by a closely allied form, *P. p. deppei*, distinguishable by slightly smaller dimensions, more whitish abdomen in the male, and somewhat more olivaceous upperside. Specimens have been collected on Oahu by Prof. Behn and Herr Deppe, and besides a pair in my collection, I only know of examples in the museums of Berlin and Vienna. There is no trace left of this species in Oahu, and in spite of great efforts Mr. Palmer and all other recent collectors did not come across it. This form has thus shared the fate of *Hemignathus ellisianus*, *Heterorhynchus lucidus*, *Moho apicalis* and *Phaeornis oahensis*, which have all disappeared from Oahu, while *Loxops rufa* may still exist in a few pairs, or has possibly followed suit already.

LOXOPS COCCINEA RUFA BLOXAM.

Fringilla rufa Bloxam, Voy. "Blonde" p. 250 (1826).
Loxops wolstenholmei Rothschild, Bull. Brit. Orn. Club I, p, LVI (1893-Oahu).
Loxops rufa Wilson, Aves Hawaiienses part VI, plate and text (1896) ; Rothschild, Avif. of Laysan, etc., p. 177 (1900).

THIS form of *Loxops* is only found on Oahu, where it is doubtless very rare now, if not already extinct. The last known specimen was shot on April 20th, 1893, in the mountains of the Wailua district, on Oahu, and is in my collection. This is the only specimen obtained by the efforts of recent collectors, and, if any should still exist, we may suppose that their fate is sealed.

L. c. rufa differs from *L. coccinea coccinea* of Hawaii by its smaller size and more brownish, somberer coloration.

We know of specimens in the British Museum, including the type of Bloxam's *Fringilla rufa*, in Liverpool, Philadelphia, Berlin, Berlepsch Castle, Vienna and Tring.

CIRIDOPS WILSON.

Ciridops Wilson, Nature 1892, p. 469.

THOUGH formerly supposed to belong to the *Fringillidae*, it is now generally acknowledged to belong to the family *Drepanidae*, a peculiar family of different forms restricted in its distribution to the Hawaiian Islands. The genus *Ciridops* seems to stand nearest to *Loxops*, from which, however, it is easily distinguished by the form of the bill, the pattern of colouration, stronger feet, and the structure of its plumage, which is somewhat stiff and scanty, while it is soft and rich in *Loxops*. The feathers of the crown and throat are pointed.

We only know one species belonging to this genus.

CIRIDOPS ANNA (DOLE).

(PLATE 4, FIG. 4.)

Fringilla anna Dole, Hawaiian Almanac 1879, p. 49 (Hawaii); reprint in Ibis 1880.

Ciridops anna Wilson & Evans, Aves Hawaienses, Part IV, text and plate; Rothschild, Avifauna of Laysan, p. 183.

THE "Ulaaihawane" of the natives of Hawaii is one of the rarest birds known, only three specimens being on record—one, the type, in the Bernice Pauahi Bishop Museum in Honolulu, and two in my collection. One of these was brought home by Mr. Scott Wilson, who obtained it from Mr. Bishop in Honolulu, the other was shot by a native for my former collector, Mr. Palmer. No other examples have been obtained. As there are still a good many hawane palms in elevated districts of Hawaii, there is, of course, a possibility that a few examples still exist there; but to all intents and purposes *Ciridops anna* may be looked upon as extinct.

SIPHONORHIS SCL.

Siphonorhis Sclater, P.Z.S. 1861, p. 77. Type: *Caprimulgus americanus* L.

"THE bill is extremely broad at base, the tip strong and heavily decurved; nostrils tubular and very prominent; rictal bristles strongly developed. Wing pointed, third primary longest; tail rounded, almost graduated. Tarsi long and naked. The sexes differ slightly in coloration." (Hartert.)

SIPHONORHIS AMERICANUS (L.)

(PLATE 5A.)

"*Small Wood-Owle*" Sloane, Voy. Jamaica II, p. 296, pl. 255, fig. 1 (1725).

Caprimulgus americanus Linnaeus, Syst. Nat., Ed. X, p. 193 (1758—Ex Sloane. "Habitat in America calidiore").

Chordeiles americanus Bonaparte, Consp. Av. I, p. 63 (1850).

Siphonorhis americanus Sclater, P.Z.S. 1861, p. 77; id. P.Z.S. 1866, p. 144; Cory, B. W. Indies, p. 139 (1889); Hartert, Cat. B. Brit. Mus. XVI, p. 592 (1892).

THE whole diagnosis of Linnaeus is "Caprimulgus narium tubulis eminentibus," but the prominent tubular nostrils are just the character which distinguishes *S. americanus* most strikingly from all the other goatsuckers, and I think that Sloane's figure and description are sufficient to indicate this bird. Sloane says as follows:—

"This was seven Inches from the end of the Bill to that of the Tail, and ten from the end of Wing to Wing expanded, it had a quarter of an Inch long crooked black bill, with two *Tubuli* about one eight Part of an Inch long for the Nostrills, along the upper Mandible were several bristly Hairs in a Line, like those of a Cat's Mustachoes of a black Colour, the *Aperture* of Chaps or Swallow was extraordinary large. The Feathers on the Head and under the Chaps were many, the Tail was four Inches long, the Head and Back were cover'd with Feathers of a mixt Colour of *Feuille Morte*, grey and black, the Wings and Tail were of the same Colour only Lighter under the Chaps, Breast and Belly was also of the same, the Legs and Feet were an Inch and half cover'd with brown Scales, the Toes four, three before, that in the middle three-quarters of an Inch long, and one behind.

"Its Stomach was not very muscular, it was fill'd with Scarabei, &c. The rest of the Bowells agreed in everything with those of the greater Sort, concerning which see the description above.

"They feed on *Scarabei* and other Insects of that Kind.

"They are found with the former."

Specimens of this Goatsucker are very rare in collections, and I am only aware of the existence of examples in American museums and of the pair obtained by Osburn in Jamaica about half a century ago, and now in the British Museum. Recent collectors have failed to procure it, and it is therefore to be feared that, like *Aestrelata caribbaea*, it has been exterminated by the introduced mongoose and other animals.

Habitat: Jamaica.

NESTOR PRODUCTUS (GOULD.)

(PLATE 6, head.)

Wilson's Parrakeet Latham, Gen. Hist. B. II, p. 170 (1822).
Plyctolophus productus Gould, P.Z.S. 1836, p. 19.
Nestor productus Gould, Syn. Austr. B. and adj. Isl. pt. I, pl. , fig. 1 (183—?).
Centrurus productus Bp., Naumannia 1856, Consp. Psitt. No. 265.

LATHAM'S original description is as follows: "Length thirteen inches. Bill very long and hooked, and upper mandible measuring almost two inches, the under three-quarters, colour dusky; plumage in general greenish ash, inclining to brown, and clouded here and there with orange as in the 'Crossbill,' but the edges of the feathers of the back dun colour; all the under parts of the body mixed yellow and dull orange; rump dull red; under wing coverts dull yellow; thighs brown; the quills reach almost to the end of the tail, which is somewhat, but not greatly, cuneiform; both quills and tail are brown, the former marked on the inner webs with five or six whitish bars; legs dusky, toes very long. Inhabits New South Wales. I met with a fine specimen of it in the collection of Thomas Wilson, Esqre."

It has long been a question whether *Nestor productus* of Gould and *Nestor norfolcensis* of Pelzeln were really distinct or only individual varieties of one species. I had for a long time considered them to be merely individual varieties, for I could not persuade myself that a small island like Philip Island, almost contiguous to Norfolk Island, could have a different species of *Nestor* to that found on the larger island. Since commencing to write this book, however, I have come to somewhat different conclusions. In the first place no special locality is given for *N. productus* by the earlier authors, in the same way as in the case of *Notornis alba*, which, like the *Nestor*, was said to come from N. S. Wales. This fact is easily explained, as N. S. Wales and Norfolk Island were both penal settlements in the early days, and there was intercourse by regular vessels plying between these colonies and Lord Howe's Island. Now we find in the case of several other birds that distinct local forms occur on Norfolk and Lord Howe's Islands, while as far as I know there is no other record of a distinct bird from Philip Island. I therefore believe that *Nestor productus* inhabited both Norfolk and Philip Islands, and that all specimens extant are from Philip Island, where it lingered some years longer than on the main island, while the specimens of Ferdinand Bauer and Governor Hunter, and possibly the supposed *N. norfolcensis* of

Canon Tristram's collection, now in Liverpool, had been brought from Lord Howe's Island in cages and were kept as pets in Norfolk Island; and then, as the value of exact data in those early days of our science was unknown, the references were made to the place whence the specimens were seen or brought. One thing however is certain, the bill in Ferdinand Bauer's sketch is evidently a monstrous growth produced by captivity, for Latham expressly describes the bill of Governor Hunter's bird as ending in a long thin point. The differences of *N. norfolcensis* are the dull crimson sides of face, chin, and throat; dull green head and hind neck, and the total absence of bars on the tail. The plate given herewith is a reproduction of the Liverpool bird, with the bill of Ferdinand Bauer's sketch added, as this is wanting in that bird, and in the corner a head of the specimen of *N. productus*, purchased for the Tring Museum, when the late Mr. Wallace's Museum at Distington, Cumberland, was dispersed.

I have carefully examined the three fine specimens of *Nestor productus* in the British Museum, and the conclusion I have come to is that the bird described by Gould as the adult of his *N. productus* was an abnormal specimen, and was in relation to normal *N. productus* what the aberrations called "*superbus*" and "*esslingi*" are to *N. meridionalis*. The bills of the British Museum specimens are very different. The one from the Bell collection has the long, thin bill, but it is at least half-an-inch to three-quarters shorter than those in the Tring and Florence specimens.

Habitat: Philip Island and probably Norfolk Island.

One in Tring, three in London, one in Florence, two in Vienna, one in Prague, two in Leyden, one in Amsterdam, are known to me.

The two specimens in the Vienna Museum were both bought in 1839. One from Ward, with a short bill, brown chest and throat, and a very wide yellow breast-band. The other from Baron von Hügel, which has a long bill and very red cheeks and chin.

NESTOR NORFOLCENSIS PELZELN.

(PLATE 6, full figure.)

Long-billed Parrakeet Latham, Gen. Hist. II, p. 171 (1822).

Nestor norfolcensis Pelzeln, Sitzb. k. Akad. Wiss. XLI, pp. 322-325, pl. — (1860—detailed description from the manuscript of the late botanist, Ferdinand Lucas Bauer, and figure of head with an evidently abnormally developed bill. The specimen was from Norfolk Island; it had disappeared before Pelzeln's time).

LATHAM'S original description is as follows: "Length above 12 inches. Bill very long and curved, thick halfway from the base, but tapering quite to a point at the tip, and under mandible truncated at the end, colour of both, dusky; head and neck dull green; sides under the eyes, chin and throat pale crimson; upper parts of the body, wings and tail dusky; breast yellowish; belly, thighs and vent more or less crimson; tail cuneiform; legs brown."

"One of these was in possession of Governor Hunter, who brought it from Norfolk Island; from the bill it seems related to the other, but the tail is cuneiform in a much greater degree, without any bars across it."

The only bird of this species extant is the one in Liverpool, from the Tristram collection.

Governor Hunter's specimen and Bauer's bird were both brought from Norfolk Island, but as they were cage-birds, and differed so markedly from *N. productus*, I, for reasons given under *N. productus*, believe this bird came from Lord Howe's Island.

Habitat: Lord Howe's Island (?).

LOPHOPSITTACUS NEWTON.

THE huge bill and peculiar shaped crest, together with the—apparently, *i.e.*, if the figure is correct—very short wings are characteristic of this genus. (P.Z.S. 1875, p. 350.)

LOPHOPSITTACUS MAURITIANUS (OWEN).

(PLATE 7.)

Broad-billed Parrot Owen, Trans. Zool. Soc. VI, p. 53 (1866).
Psittacus mauritianus Owen, Ibis, p. 168 (1866).
Psittacus (*Lophopsittacus*) *mauritianus* A. Newton, P.Z.S. (1875), pp. 349, 350.
Lophopsittacus mauritianus Newton, Enc. Brit. (ed. 9) III, p. 732, ff. 44, 46 (1875).

THIS extraordinary parrot was first described and made known to science by Professor Owen in 1866. He described it from 2 lower mandibles, much damaged, which were dug up from the Mare aux Songes. Except a few further osseous remains, mostly collected by Sir Edward Newton, nothing more of importance was found relating to this bird till Professor Schlegel discovered in the Library of Utrecht the manuscript journal kept during the voyage to Mauritius in A.D. 1601-1602 of Wolphart Harmanszoon, in which among other items of natural history there is a sketch of *Lophopsittacus* from life, and the statement that it was wholly of a grey-blue colour. From the fact that this bird is not mentioned by the voyagers who visited Mauritius in the 2nd and 3rd decades of the 18th century, it is probable that it was one of the first of the Mascarene birds to become extinct. This is easily understood when we consider that the bird was apparently unable to fly, and would like all big parrots prove excellent eating.

Only known from osseous remains and the above-quoted drawing and notes.

35 tarsi and tibiae, and 60 complete and incomplete lower mandibles and fragments of palatine bones in the Tring Museum.

Habitat : Mauritius.

ARA TRICOLOR BECHST.

(PLATE 10.)

Le petit Ara D'Aubenton, Pl. Enl. 641.
L'Ara tricolor Levaill., Perr. I p. 17, pl. 5 (1801)
Psittacus tricolor Bechst., Kurze Ueb. p. 64, pl. I (1811).
Sittace? lichtensteini Wagl., fide Bp., Naumannia 1856, Consp. Psitt.

BECHSTEIN'S description, taken from Levaillant, is (translated) as follows: "This *Aras*, which others have held to be only a variety of *Macao*, is according to Vaillant a distinct species. It is one third smaller than the red-fronted species, or 1 ft. 10 in. long, of which the tail takes 11 inches and the bill 18 lines. The latter is of a black colour and has the upper mandible less curved, and the sides of the lower mandible more swollen than is the case in the other *Ara* species. The cheeks are naked and white, with three lines of red feathers. Head, front and sides of the neck, breast, belly and thighs red ; back of the neck pale yellow ; back, shoulders and smaller wing coverts brownish red bordered with yellow or green ; flanks yellowish, primaries above dark azure blue, below coppery red. Crissum violet blue, undertail coverts pale blue with green and brown-red borders; under-wing coverts red, the larger yellow, and brownish green. Two centre tail feathers all red with blue tips, the outer ones blue on outer webs and tips, red on the rest of the feather."

Of this bird I know only of two in the British Museum, one in Paris, one in Leyden, one in Liverpool. The specimen in the Paris Museum bears the inscription "Macrocercus tricolor (Bechst.) M. E. Rosseau. Cuba. Ménagerie 1842." Probably, however, there are more specimens in other museums.

Apparently the last specimen was shot in 1864 at La Vega (Bangs, Americ. Nat. XXXIX, p. 200).

Like all the extinct West Indian Macaws, Amazons and Conures, it became extinct through its persecution by the inhabitants for food.

Habitat: Formerly Cuba and Isle of Pines.

ARA GOSSEI ROTHSCH.

(Plate 11.)

Yellow-headed Macaw Gosse, Birds of Jamaica, p. 260 (1847).
Ara gossei Rothsch., Bull. B.O.C., XVI, p. 14 (1905); Proc. IV, Orn. Congr., p. 201 (1907).
Ara tricolor (non Bechstein) Clark, Auk 1905, p. 348.

MR. GOSSE'S description is as follows:—" Basal half of upper mandible black; apical half, ash coloured; lower mandible, black, tip only ash coloured; forehead, crown, and back of neck, bright yellow; sides of face, around eyes, anterior and lateral parts of the neck, and back, a fine scarlet; wing coverts and breast deep sanguine red; winglet and primaries an elegant light blue. The legs and feet are said to have been black; the tail, red and yellow intermixed (Rob.)"

Mr. Gosse also remarks, "If this is not the *tricolor* of Le Vaillant, which is the only Macaw I am aware of marked with a yellow nape, it is probably new."

In spite of the evident differences in the description, the Jamaican *Ara* has always been united with the Cuban *A. tricolor*, even as lately as October, 1905, by Mr. Austin H. Clark (Auk, 1905, p. 348), though he queries it in a footnote. The specimen described by Dr. Robinson, here quoted by Gosse, was shot about 1765, by Mr. Odell, in the mountains of Hanover parish, about ten miles east of Lucea.

Habitat: Jamaica.

The specimen described no longer exists, and there are none in any collection known.

There was a third member of the *tricolor* group of Macaws found on the large island of Haiti, which Mr. Clark has also united under *A. tricolor*, but I believe it must have been different, just as the Jamaica bird.

ARA ERYTHROCEPHALA ROTHSCH.

(PLATE 12.)

Ara militaris Gosse, Birds of Jamaica, p. 261 (1847).

Ara erythrocephala Rothsch., Bull. B.O.C., XVI, p. 14 (1905); Proc. IV Orn. Congr., p. 201 (1907).

GOSSE says the description given to him in a letter, just received from Mr. Hill, was as follows:—"Head red; neck, shoulders, and underparts of a light and lively green; the greater wing coverts and quills, blue; and the tail scarlet and blue on the upper surface, with the under plumage, both of wings and tail, a mass of intense orange yellow."

"The specimen here described was procured in the mountains of Trelawny and St. Anne's by Mr. White, proprietor of the Oxford estate." No specimen now known.

Habitat: Jamaica.

Mr. Gosse also relates that the Rev. Mr. Coward, in 1842, saw two large Macaws flying near the foot of the mountains in the parish of St. James, near the centre of the island. These birds were said to have been blue and yellow; if so, probably they were my *Ara erythrura*, whose precise island home is unknown.

ARA MARTINICUS (ROTHSCH.)

(PLATE 14.)

Les Aras Père Bouton, Rel. de l'étab. d. Français dep. 1635, en l'ile Martinique pp. 71.72 (1640)

Anadorhynchus martinicus Rothsch. Bull. B.O.C. XVI, p. 14 (1905); Proc. IV Orn. Congr., p. 202 (1907.)

PÈRE BOUTON says, "Les Aras sont deux ou trois fois gros comme les Perroquets et ont un plumage bien différent en couleur. Ceux que j'ai vus avaient les plumes leleucs et orangées."

No specimen preserved.

Habitat: Martinique.

ARA GUADALOUPENSIS CLARK.

Les Arras Du Tertre, Hist. gen. des Antilles Vol. II p. 248 (1667).
Ara Rouge D'Aubenton, Pl. Enl. 12 (1779).
Ara guadaloupensis Clark, Auk, XXII, p. 272 (1905).

DU TERTRE gives the following description :—" The Arras is a sort of Parrot bigger than all the others. This is proved because those of Guadaloupe are larger than all the other Parrots, both those from the Islands as well as from the Mainland; while this Arras is larger than these by one third. It has the head, the neck, the belly and the back of the colour of fire; its wings are a mixture of yellow azure, and crimson feathers; while the tail is entirely red and a foot-and-a-half long."

Macaws of this colouration are mentioned by Du Tertre, De Rochefort, and others of the older authors as being found on Guadaloupe, Dominica and Martinique, and Mr. Clark has united them under one name. This I feel sure is wrong, and I believe each of the three islands had a distinct species of Red Macaw, so I confine this name to the Guadaloupe form.

Habitat: Guadaloupe.

No specimen existing.

ARA ERYTHRURA NOM. NOV.

(PLATE 15.)

De Rochefort, Histoire Nat. & Mor. des Iles Antilles, &c. (1658), p. 154, Art. IX (Des Arras).
Anadorhynchus coeruleus (non Gmelin) Rothsch., Bull. B.O.C., XVI, p. 15 (1905).

IN the Bull. B.O.C. XVI, p. 15 (1905), I unfortunately described this bird under the name of *Anadorhynchus coeruleus* (Gm.), having misread his description, and also said it came from Jamaica. Professor Salvadori, in the Ibis (1906) Series 8, Vol. VI, "Notes on Parrots," p 451, calls attention to my double error, but failed entirely to realise what bird I really meant. The original description is (translated) as follows :—

" Among them are some which have the head, the upper side of the neck, and the back of a satiny sky blue; the underside of the neck, the belly, and undersurface of the wings, yellow, and the tail entirely red."

No specimen existing.

Habitat: One of the West Indian Islands.

ANODORHYNCHUS PURPURASCENS ROTHSCH.

(Plate 13.)

Le gros Perroquet de la Guadaloupe Don de Navarette, Rel. Quat. voy. Christ. p. 425 pl. II (1838).

Anadorhynchus purpurascens Rothsch. Bull. B.O.C. XVI, p. 13 (1905); Proc. IV Orn. Congr., p. 202 (1907).

THE original description of this bird says it was entirely deep violet. Native name *Oné couli*. No specimen extant. I have placed this species in the genus *Anodorhynchus* on account of its uniform bluish colour.

Habitat: Guadaloupe.

AMAZONA VIOLACEUS (GM.)

(PLATE 17.)

Perroquet de la Guadeloupe Du Tertre, Hist. Nat. Antill. II, p. 250, fig. p. 246 (1667).
Perroquets Labat, Voy. aux iles de l'Amér., vol. II p. 214 (1742).
Psittacus violaceus Gmelin, Syst. Nat. I, p. 337 (1788).

LABAT'S translated original description is as follows :—" Those of Guadaloupe are a little smaller than the *Aras;* they have the head, the neck, and the belly slate colour with a few green and black feathers, the back is entirely green, and the wings are yellow and red."

Gmelin's description reads thus :—Ps. violaceus viridi et nigro admisto varius, dorso ex fusco viridi, remigibus majoribus nigris, reliquis ex luteo, viridi, et rubro variis, tectricum macula rosea. Rostrum et orbitae incarnata."

Du Tertre's description is as follows :—" He is about as big as a fowl, has the beak and eyes bordered with red. All the feathers of the head, neck and belly are of a violet colour, a little mixed with black and green, shot like the throat of a pigeon. All the upper part of the back is green, strongly washed with brown. Outer primaries black, rest yellow, green and red."

No specimens in collections.

Habitat : Guadaloupe.

AMAZONA MARTINICANA CLARK.

(PLATE 18.)

"*Perroquets*" Labat's Voy. aux iles de l'Amér. II p. 214 (1742).
Amazona martinicana Clark, Auk. XXII, p. 343 (1905).

LABAT'S description reads thus :—" Those of Dominica have some red feathers on the wings, under the throat, and in the tail; all the rest is green (Amazona bouqueti, W.R.). Those of Martinique have the same plumage as the last mentioned, but the top of the head is slate colour with a small amount of red."

No specimen now known.

Habitat : Martinique.

CONUREUS LABATI ROTHSCH.

(PLATE 16.)

Perriques Labat, Voy. aux iles de l'Amér. II p. 218 (1742).

Conurus labati Rothsch. Bull. B.O.C. XVI, p. 13 (1905); Proc. IV Orn. Congr., p. 202 (1907).

LABAT'S translated description of this bird is as follows :—" Those of Guadaloupe are about the size of a blackbird, entirely green, except a few small red feathers, which they have on their head. Their bill is white. They are very gentle, loving, and learn to speak easily."

No specimens known.

Habitat : Island of Guadaloupe.

NECROPSITTACUS MILNE-EDW.

Necropsittacus Milne-Edwards, Ann. Sc. Nat. (5) XIX, Art. 3, p. 18 (1874).

MILNE-EDWARDS considered *Necropsittacus* closely allied to the genus *Palaeornis*, and at the same time to show affinities with the *Loriidae*. At the same time the two mandibles were sufficient, in his opinion, to show that this bird belonged to a little generic group standing near *Palaeornis*.

NECROPSITTACUS RODRICANUS (MILNE-EDW.)

Psittacus Rodricanus A. Milne-Edw., Ann. Sc. Nat. (5) VIII, pp. 151-155, pl. 7, ff. 1, 2 (1867).
Necropsittacus rodericanus A. Newt., P.Z.S. p. 41 (1875).

THIS parrot was described from a portion of the upper mandible by Professor Milne-Edwards, and then was more fully described by Dr. Günther and Sir Edward Newton, who examined a nearly complete skull and other bones.

A manuscript discovered in the Archives of the Ministry of Marine in Paris proves that this bird only became extinct at a not very distant date, it having been seen alive by the writer of the manuscript about the year 1731. In this manuscript the bird was said to have a body considerably larger than a pigeon, with a *very* long tail and a *very* large head and bill. Unfortunately the writer does not mention the colour, but adds that the smaller green and blue parrot (*Palaeornis exsul*) was much handsomer; so we can safely assume that our bird was of sombre colouration. It was undoubtedly closely allied to the genus *Palaeornis*. The two following, though much brighter coloured and but scantily described, apparently belong to the same genus.

Habitat: Rodriguez.

NECROPSITTACUS (?) BORBONICUS

NOM. NOV.

(PLATE 8.)

THIS parrot is described by the Sieur D.B. (Dubois) in the following terms :—" Body the size of a large pigeon, green ; head, tail and upper part of wings the colour of fire." As he compares it with the other parrots which are true *Palaeornis*, it is evident that this bird must have been a *Necropsittacus*.

This description is the sole evidence we have of the existence of this bird.

Habitat : Bourbon or Réunion.

NECROPSITTACUS (?) FRANCICUS

ROTHSCH.

Necropsittacus francicus Rothsch., Proceedings Int. Ornith. Congress 1905, p. 197 (1907).

ORIGINAL description :—" Head and tail fiery red, rest of body and wings green." We only know this bird from the descriptions in the various "Voyages" to Mauritius in the 17th and early 18th centuries.

Habitat : Mauritius.

MASCARINUS LESSON.

Mascarinus Lesson, Traité d'Orn. p. 188 (1831—A mixture of forms. By elimination the name *Mascarinus* has been restricted to the Mascarine Parrot).

THE generic affinities of this bird have been discussed by various authors. Wagler, Gray, Pelzeln, Hartlaub (1877) and Messrs. A. and E. Newton united it with the Vaza Parrots in the genus *Coracopsis*, Finsch included it, together with the Vazas and the Grey Parrot (*Psittacus erithacus*), in the genus *Psittacus*. Recent authors—Oustalet 1893, W. A. Forbes 1879, and Salvadori (Cat. B. XX, p. 421, 1891)—have admitted a separate genus, *Mascarinus*. This is evidently the proper course, and I agree with W. A. Forbes, Oustalet and Salvadori that its nearest affinities appear to be the genus *Tanygnathus* rather than *Coracopsis*, and that the place of *Mascarinus* is among the *Palaeornithinae* of Salvadori.

The large red bill, with distinctly ridged gonys, concealed nostrils and moderately long, strongly rounded tail, are peculiar characters. The colouration is unique. Only one species is known.

MASCARINUS MASCARINUS (L.)
MASCARINE PARROT.

(Plate 9.)

"*Perroquets un peu plus gros que pigeons, ayant le plumage de couleur de petit gris, un chaperon noir sur la teste, le becq fort gros, & couleur de feu*" Le Sieur D.B, (Dubois), Voyages aux Iles Dauphine ou Madagascar, and Bourbon ou Mascarenne. p. 172 (1674—" Bourbon ou Mascarenne").

Psittacus Mascarinus Brisson, Orn. IV., p. 315 (1760); Hahn, Orn. Atlas, Papageien p. 54, pl. 39 (1835).

Psittacus mascarin. Linnaeus, Mantissa Plantarum, regni animalis appendix p. 524 (1771 —" Habitat in Mascarina." Ex Brisson).

Perroquet Mascarin Levaillant, Perroquets II, p. 171, pl. 189 (1805—" Madagascar," errore).

Mascarinus madagascariensis Lesson, Traité d'Orn, p. 189 (1831—" Madagascar," ex Levaillant).

Coracopsis mascarina Wagler, Mon. Psittac. p. 679 (1832); Pelzeln, Verh. Zool. Bot. Ges. Wien 1863, p. 934.

Mascarinus obscurus (non *Psittacus obscurus* L.) Bonaparte, Rev. & Mag. de Zool. 1854 p. 154 (Linnaeus, *Psittacus obscurus*—Syst. Nat. Ed. X, p. 97, 1758, ex Hasselquist M.S.—though identified by himself with the Marcarine Parrot in 1766—Syst. Nat. Ed. XII, I, p. 140—cannot be the same as *P. mascarinus;* the description disagrees entirely, and the bird was described from a specimen probably seen alive by Hasselquist, with uncertain locality. What Linnaeus' *P. obscurus* was, is difficult to say; if it was not for the long tail, one might consider it a variety of the Grey Parrot).

Psittacus madagascarensis Finsch, Papageien II pp. 306, 955 (1868—Finsch was not acquainted with the history of this Parrot, as he still considered Madagascar to be its home, and wondered why it had not been found there by recent collectors).

Psittacus madagascariensis Pelzeln, Ibis 1873, p. 32.

Mascarinus duboisi W. A. Forbes, Ibis 1879, pp. 304, 305 (figures), 306; Milne-Edwards & Oustalet, Centenaire Mus. d'Hist. Nat. pp. 191-205, pl. I (1893—excellent lengthy account).

Mascarinus mascarinus Salvadori, Cat. B. Brit. Mus. XX, p. 421 (1891—Réunion).

IT has been mentioned above that " Le Sieur D. B." (Dubois) described this Parrot clearly in 1674, and that it lived on Réunion, and not on Madagascar. Linnaeus in 1771 (see above) was the first to bestow a scientific name on it, though Brisson had already again described it in 1760. Linnaeus' diagnosis is, as usual, rather poor, and not quite correct*, but his reference to Brisson leaves no doubt as to what he meant.

This parrot is one of the rarest of extinct birds, only two stuffed specimens being known. One normally coloured specimen is preserved in the Museum of Natural History in Paris, and it is evidently this which has been figured by Daubenton and Levaillant, and in the "Centenaire du Muséum d'Historie Naturelle." From the latter plate my figure has been taken.

The example in Vienna is unfortunately semi-albinistic, there being some white feathers on the back, wings and tail. Another normal individual, however, lived formerly in the Menagerie of the King of Bavaria, where it was depicted by Hahn in 1835. Unfortunately this specimen has not been preserved.

*" *Psittacus* brachyurus fuscus, facie nigra, cauda albente. Habitat in Mascarina. Rostrum incarnatum. Caput caerulescens."

PALAEORNIS EXSUL NEWTON.

(PLATE 19.)

Palaeornis exsul A. Newton, Ibis 1872, p. 33.

LEGUAT was the first to mention these parrots as "Perroquets verds et bleus," and that they were wonderfully good to eat and also delightful pets.

Professor Newton's description is as follows: "Female: Of moderate size. General appearance greyish-glaucous, darker above than beneath. From the corner of the mouth proceeds an ill-defined dull black chin stripe, which becomes broader as it passes backward and upward, ceasing somewhat abruptly on reaching the level of the ears. Head, nape and shoulders, upper wing-coverts, and rectrices above dull greyish-glaucous, the blue tinge in which predominates when the bird is seen against the light, and the green when seen in the contrary aspect; the outer rectrices paler. Rump verditer blue. Primaries with their outer, and most part of their inner, webs deep greenish blue, the former with narrow, lighter edges, and the latter broadly bordered with pitch black; shafts and lower surfaces greyish black. Secondaries much the same as the primaries, but of a still deeper shade. Breast dull greyish-glaucous, but lighter than the upper parts and passing on the belly into verditer, which becomes lighter and greener on the vent. Rectrices beneath yellowish grey, darker toward the tips of the longer feathers. Bill black."

The specimen was sent in spirits to Sir Edward Newton in 1871 by Mr. Jenner, the Magistrate of Rodriguez.

The male differs from the female in having the upper mandible crimson, fading into horn at the tip. Top of head more glaucous. Black stripe from nostril to eye. Black chin stripe prolonged almost to meet on nape of neck. Most of primaries with dull black patch on inner webs. Middle secondaries dusky black.

The male was sent to Sir Edward Newton in 1875 by Mr. J. Caldwell.

Total length	....	16 inches.
Wing	....	7·5 ,,
Tail	....	8·5 ,,

Probably almost if not quite extinct. Recent investigations about its status are very desirable.

Habitat: Rodriguez Island.

PALAEORNIS WARDI E. NEWTON.

(PLATE 20.)

Palaeornis wardi E. Newton, P.Z.S. 1867, p. 346 (Seychelles).

THE translation of Sir Edward Newton's diagnosis is as follows: "Similar to *P. alexandri*, but with a stouter bill, purple red shoulder patches, and the hind neck without a red band.

"*Adult Male.* Crown of head and throat bluish, cheeks ochraceous green, chin and line round base of mandible black, continued in a stripe from the gape to the hind neck; back and wings grass green; rump brighter; a single wide band (or patch) on the shoulders purplish red; remiges and rectrices deep green washed with blue, the latter yellowish, the former dusky below; belly yellowish green; bill vivid scarlet with paler tip; feet dusky. Total length 16 inches, wings 7·75, tail 9."

Female similar to the male but duller, and with the bill all black, and without the black mandibular stripe.

Formerly abundant on most of the islands in the Seychelles, especially Mahé, but now confined to the little islet of Silhouette, where it will in all probability become extinct. According to E. Newton its name was "Cateau vert."

Habitat: Seychelles Islands.

PALAEORNIS EQUES (BODD).

Psittaca borbonica torquata Briss., Orn. IV p. 328, pl. XXVII f. 1 (1760). (Bourbon.)
Psittacus alexandri var. γ Linnaeus, S.N. p. 142 (1766).
Perruche à collier de l'Isle de Bourbon Daubenton, Pl. enl. 215.
Perruche a double collier Buff., Hist. Nat. Ois. VI, p. 143 (1779).
Alexandrine Parrakeet var. C. Double Ringed Parrakeet Latham, Syn. I p. 326 (1781).
Psittacus eques Boddaert, Tabl. Pl. Enl. p. 13 (1783).
Psittacus semirostris Hermann, Obs. Zool. p. 125 (1804).
Psittacus bitorquatus Kuhl, Consp. Psitt. p. 92 (1820).
Rose Ringed Parrakeet var. B. Latham, Gen. Hist. II p. 161 (1822).
Psittacus bicollaris Vieillot, Enc. Meth. III p. 1385 (1823).
Palaeornis bitorquatus Vigors, Zool. Journ. II p. 51 (1825).
Palaeornis borbonicus Bp., Rev. and Mag. Zool. 1854, p. 152. No. 140.

THERE has been considerable confusion with regard to this parrot. It was first asserted that it occurred on both Bourbon and Mauritius. Then Professor Newton separated the Mauritius bird as *Pal. echo*. Salvadori, however, in Cat. Birds. Brit. Mus. XX, p. 442, reunited the Bourbon and Mauritius birds, while quite unaccountably stating only Mauritius as the habitat.

The Abbé Dubois describes this bird as follows: "Green Parrots as large as pigeons having a black collar."

Now the species of *Palaeornis* from Rodriguez, the Seychelles, and the mainland of Africa are all distinct, and the other land birds of Mauritius are and were different from those of Bourbon. I therefore feel quite certain that Professor Newton is right, and that his *Palaeornis echo* is distinct from *P. eques*, though, unfortunately, we do not know in which way the two forms differed.

Habitat: Bourbon or Réunion, but now extinct. No specimens known.

PALAEORNIS ECHO NEWTON.

Palaeornis echo Newton, Ibis 1876, p. 284.
Palaeornis eques Salvadori, Cat. Birds Brit. Mus. XX, p. 442 (1891).

DESCRIPTION of Male: Green, the occiput tinged with bluish; a narrow black stripe from the nostrils to the eyes; broad black mandibular stripes passing down and across the sides of the neck where they meet a pink collar, which is interrupted on the hind neck; under wing-coverts yellowish green; central tail feathers scarcely tinged with bluish; tail below dark yellowish grey; upper mandible red, under mandible almost black with only a brownish tinge in places. Iris yellow. Naked skin round eyes orange. Wing 7·5 inches, tail 8·75 inches, bill 9 inches. The female differs by the absence of the collar, no bluish tint on occiput, and the bill entirely blackish.

It differs from *P. torquatus* in the incomplete collar, darker green colour and broader tail feathers. This bird is still found in the interior of the island, but is rare and apparently on the verge of extinction.

Habitat: Mauritius.

Three specimens at Tring, four in the British Museum.

CYANORHAMPHUS ZEALANDICUS

(LATHAM.)

Red Rumped Parrakeet Latham, Syn. I, p. 249, No. 50 (1781).
Psittacus novae seelandiae Gmelin (nec. Sparrm.), S.N. I, p. 328, No. 83 (1788).
Psittacus zealandicus Latham, Ind. Orn. I, p. 102, No. 58 (1790).
Psittacus novae-zealandiae Kuhl, Consp. Psitt. p. 44, var. 1 (1820).
Psittacus erythronotus Kuhl, Consp. Psitt. p. 45, No. 67 (1820).
Psittacus pacificus var. No. 3, Vieillot, Enc. Méth., p. 1387 (1823).
Platycercus pacificus, part. Vigors, Zool. Journ. I, p. 529 (1825).
Platycercus erythronotus Stephens, Gen. Zool. XIV., p. 129, No. 9 (1826).
Conurus phaeton Des Murs, Rev. Zool. 1845, p. 449.
Platycercus phaeton Des Murs, Icon. Orn. pl. 16 (1845).
Cyanorhamphus pacificus Bonaparte, Rev. et. Mag. 1854, p. 153, No. 184.
Cyanorhamphus erythronotus Gray, Hand-list II, p. 140, No. 8029 (1870).
Cyanorhamphus forsteri Finsch, Papag. II, p. 270 (1868).

THIS bird has received a variety of names owing to the adult bird being very different to the younger and quite young birds. *Adult*, forehead black; stripe from lores passing through eye almost to hind-neck scarlet; rump scarlet; back and breast dull green; cheeks, head, neck, belly, under-tail coverts and wing coverts, bright green. Flight-feathers blue on outer, brown on inner, webs; bend of wing blue; tail feathers blue, edged with green.

Young differs in having a dull bluish-black forehead, brownish head, back mixed brown and green, rump and eye stripe chestnut red, and the underside greyish green.

This species was confined to the Society Islands, where it was obtained during Cook's Voyage by Ellis and by Forster, and lastly by Lieutenant de Marolles in 1844. We only know for certain at the present day of the existence of two specimens, one in the British Museum, ex Massena collection, whose origin is doubtful, and one in Paris, collected by Lieutenant de Marolles. What became of the other two specimens of the latter's collecting, and of Forster's and Ellis' specimens, I cannot say.

Habitat: Society Islands.

Evidently extinct.

CYANORHAMPHUS ULIETANUS (GM.)

Society Parrot Latham, Syn. I p. 250 (1781).
Psittacus ulietanus Gmelin, S.N. I p. 328, n. 85 (1788).
Platycercus ulietanus Vig., Zool. I p. 533, Suppl. pl. 3 (1825).
Cyanorhamphus ulietanus Bonaparte, Rev. et Mag. de Zool. 1854, p. 153, n. 188.
Platycercus tannaensis Finsch, Papag. II, p. 272 (1868).
Psittacus fuscatus Pelz., Ibis 1873, p. 30.

ADULT: "Olive brown, the head brown-black; rump and basal upper tail-coverts brown-red, the longest upper tail-coverts olive brown like the back; underparts olive-yellow; quills, primary-coverts, under wing coverts and tail-feathers grey; bill black, base of upper mandible grey; feet brown." (Salvadori, Cat. B. XX p. 579). Wing 5·3 inches, bill 0·8 inches, tarsus 0·8 inches, tail 5 inches.

Habitat: Ulietea, Society Islands (fide Latham).

The type from the Leverian Museum is in Vienna, and a specimen from Bullock's collection is in the British Museum. These are the only two specimens known, and as it is now more than a hundred years since anyone has procured a specimen, we may suppose that this is an extinct species. The specimen in Vienna, which I have recently been able to examine, has the head, back, wings, and tail deep umber-brown, the rump dark-crimson, upper tail-coverts olive, underside brownish yellow.

CYANORHAMPHUS SUBFLAVESCENS SALVADORI.

Parrot from Lord Howe Island Phillips, Bot. Bay, p. 225 (1789).
Cyanorhamphus subflavescens Salvadori, Ann. & Mag. (6) VII, p. 68 (1891).

VERY similar to *C. cooki* and *C. saisseti* and intermediate in size. Above more yellowish than *C. saisseti*, below more greenish, tail shorter than in either of the latter.

This species is believed to be extinct. Last year I received some specimens of a *Cyanorhamphus* from an inhabitant of Lord Howe's Island, but from subsequent letters these appear to have been collected on Norfolk or Philip Island, and they certainly are *C. cooki*.

Habitat: Lord Howe's Island.

A pair in the British Museum appear to be the only known specimens.

BUBO (?) LEGUATI NOM. NOV.

Strix sp. Milne-Edwards, Ann. Sci. Nat. (5) XIX p. 13 (art. 3.) 1874.

MILNE-EDWARDS had only a single tibio-tarsus of this form and described this bone, but refrained from giving it a specific name, though he stated it was probably a small *Bubo*, in the hopes of getting more material.

As, however, we have no further specimens, I think I am justified in naming it after Leguat, who first mentions Owls on Rodriguez. Milne-Edwards' description of this tibio-tarsus is that it equals in length that bone in *Asio accipitrinus*, but was distinguished from the latter by the strong inward curvature and the great development in width of its distal extremity.

Tibio-tarsus.

Total length	77	mm.
Length from the proximal extremity to the top of the peronial ridge	25	,,
Width at distal extremity	10·5	,,
Width at proximal extremity	9	,,
Width of shaft	3·7	,,

Habitat : Rodriguez.

SCOPS COMMERSONI OUST.

Scops commersoni Oustalet, Ann. Sci. Nat. (8) III, p. 35 fig 3 (1896).

THIS owl, I believe, is not a true *Scops*, being much too big, but we must leave it in that genus for the present, as there are no specimens or bones extant, and only Jossigny's drawing to guide us as to its appearance. The first mention of owls on Mauritius was in the year 1606, when Admiral Matlief says that owls were common in the Island. Monsieur Desjardins, in 1837, gave the first accurate description of the bird, of which I here reproduce the translation. "The digits and even the tarsi are not feathered, only on the front portion of these latter one sees some short, stiff feathers running down to a point nearly to the centre. The digits are very strong, they being armed with hooked nails.

The beak is very stout, arched from its base; the upper mandible, which is much longer than the other and covering it, is as if cut square at the point. The nostrils pierce the bill pretty high up in the horny portion. The eyes, of which I could not see the colour, are round, and placed, like in the entire family, in front. They are surrounded by a circle or disc of stiff, thread-like feathers, which is interrupted at the sides. A sort of collar is perceptible on the throat. Two tufts, similar to those of the Eagle Owls and Eared Owls, and very apparent, are behind the eyes and towards the top of the occiput.

The wings are a little longer than the tail, the fourth and fifth primaries being the longest, the third and sixth are shorter, and the second still shorter, being equal to the eighth, and the first is shortest of all. The tail reaches to the end of the digits; it is rounded and not much lengthened: all the retrices are equal in length. The ear-tufts are brown, with some slight buff shading, the discal plumes being white marked with buff. All the upper side is of a dark brown colour, the feathers of the head, the neck and the back are edged with rufous, but not very distinctly so; this rufous colour is more apparent on the scapulars, and some of these even have on the outer web one or two whitish patches surrounded with brown.

The large tail feathers are less brown and more rufous in colour, with lighter rufous marbling mixed with brown.

The tertials and secondaries have a darker brown bar towards the centre, and their outer web is pleasantly marked with somewhat square ocelli or irregular bands of white, pale buff, and brown. The large primaries or flight feathers present the same ornamentation, but more strongly developed, and the blotches are buffy white on the inner web, which produces a regular spotting on a brown ground colour; the tip of these large feathers is finely stippled with brown on a fairly pale ground; and there is a large patch of white on the wings in addition.

The throat and abdomen are nicely adorned with dark buff feathers, which have a black brown centre and two to four large round white spots. The large feathers on the flanks are whitish, with a brown shaft line and marked with buff. All the well feathered parts, underneath the feathers are covered by a very thick black down."

The colour of bill and feet is reddish brown. Total length, 13¾ inches = 365 mm. Desjardins says the specimen he described was killed at the end of October, 1836, in the forest crowning the hills close to "Bamboo Creek." In 1837 several were still seen near "La Savane," and one was killed at Curepipe by Dr. Dobson of the 99th Regiment. This latter is believed to have been one of, if not the last of this species, so we have to thank that excellent naturalist, Desjardins, and Monsieur Jossigny, the companion of Commerson, that we know what this extinct species was like.

Habitat: Mauritius.

ATHENE MURIVORA MILNE-EDWARDS.

Strix (Athene) murivora Milne-Edwards, Ann. Sci. Nat. (5) XIX p. 13 (Art. 3.) (1874).

PROFESSOR MILNE-EDWARDS described this bird from a tibio-tarsus and a tarso-metatarsus collected in Rodriguez by Sir Edward Newton, and says that he considers it to belong to the genus *Athene*, because the proportions of the tibio-tarsus and tarso-metatarsus agree with those of that genus. The most remarkable specific characters appear to be that the ridge to which the fibula is articulated is stout, and extends very far along the outer edge of the bone. The diaphysis is large and nearly straight; the distal extremity is furnished with two equal condyles separated by a deep channel.

Tibio-tarsus.

Total length	71 mm.
Length from proximal extremity to end of peronial ridge	25 ,,
Width of distal extremity	10 ,,
Width of proximal extremity	9 ,,
Width of shaft	4 ,,

Tarso-metatarsus.

Total length	46 mm.
Width at proximal extremity	10 ,,
Width at distal extremity	15 ,,
Width of shaft	5 ,,

Habitat : Rodriguez.

SCELOGLAUX RUFIFACIES BULLER.

Sceloglaux rufifacies Buller, Ibis 1904, p. 639; id. Suppl. B. New Zealand II, p. 65, pl. VII (1906).

ORIGINAL description: "Adult female: Similar to *Sceloglaux albifacies*, but appreciably smaller; face dull rufous brown, instead of being white; crown and nape blackish brown; entire upper surface strongly suffused with rufous; quills marked with regular transverse bars and a terminal edging of rufous brown; tail-feathers uniform yellowish brown, obscurely barred with pale brown; bill lemon-yellow; feet dull yellow."

"Wairarapa district, near Wellington, North Island, in the summer 1868-9."

This supposed "species" is a very doubtful one. A close examination in the Tring Museum of the type (which was offered me for such a high price that I did not feel justified in buying it, fond as I am of possessing extinct forms, types and varieties) by Messrs. Hartert, Hellmayr and myself proved beyond doubt to all three of us that the specimen was not fully adult, but showed signs of immaturity. If I said to Sir Walter Buller that it was an "extremely young, hardly fledged *Sceloglaux*," this was certainly incorrect, and was perhaps just an exclamation after a hasty preliminary examination, for the bird is of course fully fledged and has passed, at least partially, through one moult of the feathers. On the other hand, both Professor Newton's and Dr. Sharpe's reputed statements that the owl in question is fully adult are not correct. It certainly shows unmistakable signs of immaturity, as noticed at once by Dr. Gadow (cf. Newton's letter on p. 66, l.c.), by Hartert, Hellmayr and myself. Moreover Professor Newton—though Buller says he "pronounced it to be an adult bird"—also admits that the bird "had moulted, though not necessarily to be in adult plumage," and he continues that he thinks the "character of the markings continues to be juvenile."

Having thus discussed the age of this owl, the question must be considered if it is different from *S. albifacies* from the South Island. This is less easily done. Buller described it as a "new species," and mentions among the distinctive characters (see above) the colour of the tail. The tail, however, is "skillfully" (as Buller calls it, though I should use a less complimentary adverb) stuck in, and does not belong to a *Sceloglaux*, but to an Australian *Ninox*, and also some feathers on the neck are foreign. The wings being abraded, its slightly smaller length is not very significant. Certainly, however, the colouration in general is slightly more rufous than in *S. albifacies*, though some of my specimens approach it almost completely, and the face is more rufescent. Professor Newton cautiously warned Sir Walter Buller, suggesting that *S. albifacies* might possibly have a red "phase," like *Syrnium aluco*, and this North Island specimen represented the latter. As for myself, I do not think that *S. albifacies* has two phases, as I have seen too many specimens, and found them to vary but little. I have now in my collection eight specimens from the South Island. On the other hand, I have not seen juvenile examples; but it is very likely that the rufous face of the North Island specimen is a character peculiar to the North Island form, which would then be a sub-species of *S. albifacies* from the South Island, and should be called *S. albifacies rufifacies*. The type from Wairapara is said to have been killed in the summer of 1868-9, and, since no further evidence of its existence has come forth, I presume that the North Island race of this owl must be extinct by this time.

STRIX NEWTONI NOM. NOV.

Strix sp. Newton and Gadow, Trans. *Zool. Soc.* XIII, p. 287 (1893).

MESSRS. NEWTON AND GADOW give the measurements of, and describe a pair of metatarsi procured with the remains described as *Strix sauzieri*, and state that they do not fit in with that species. For, as they are fully adult bones, it is impossible to attribute their much smaller size to youth. They then add a sentence of which this is the first part: "Unless we assume, what is unlikely, that the Island of Mauritius possessed two different species of *Strix*, we have to conclude that the short pair of metatarsals belonged to a small individual of *Strix sauzieri*, ———." Evidently Messrs. Gadow and Newton, when they wrote this, did not remember the fact that throughout a very large portion of the range of *Strix flammea*, its various geographical races are found side by side with another species of the group of *Strix*, namely, *S. candida* and *S. capensis*, popularly called "*Grass owls*"; these in nearly every case have the legs considerably longer than in the true "*Barn Owls*" (*Strix flammea* and its races).

Therefore I consider it not in the least unlikely that two species of *Strix* inhabited Mauritius, and that *Strix sauzieri* was the Mauritian representative of the "Grass Owls," while these two short metatarsals belonged to the representative of the "Barn Owls." I therefore have much pleasure in naming this form after the collector of these bones, the late Sir Edward Newton.

Length of tarso-metatarsi, 56 mm.

Habitat : Mauritius.

STRIX SAUZIERI NEWT. & GAD.

Strix sauzieri Newton & Gadow, Trans. Zool. Soc. XIII, p. 286, pl. XXXIII, figs. 11-18 (1893).

MESSRS. NEWTON AND GADOW describe this species from four metatarsi, three tibiae, and two humeri. They state that the relative length of the tibia to the metatarsus is very constant and characteristic of the various families and genera of owls. In the present instance this comparison indicates a species of *Strix*.

The longer and higher cnemial process of the tibia and the shortness of the humerus serve amply to justify the specific separation of this Mauritian owl.

The following are the measurements:—

Humerus, length	71 mm.
Tibia-tarsus, length	90—93 ,,
Tarso-metatarsus, length	63—66 ,,

Habitat: Mauritius.

"CIRCUS HAMILTONI" FORBES.

Circus hamiltoni Forbes, Trans. N.Z. Inst. XXIV, p. 186 (1892—no proper description).

A VERY large harrier, much larger than *Circus gouldi*, but not so big as *Harpagornis*.

Habitat: Middle Island, New Zealand.

"CIRCUS TEAUTEENSIS" FORBES.

Circus teauteensis Forbes, Trans. N.Z. Inst. XXIV, p. 186 (1892—no proper description).

ANOTHER very large harrier from Teaute, which has never yet been properly described.

Habitat: Middle Island, New Zealand.

ASTUR ALPHONSI NEWT. & GAD.

Astur sp. Milne-Edwards, Ann. Sci. Nat (5) XIX, Art. II, pp. 25, 26, pl. 15 fig 2. (1874).
Astur alphonsi Newton and Gadow, Trans. Zool. Soc. XIII p. 285, pl. XXXIII, figs 9, 10 (1893).

MESSRS. NEWTON AND GADOW bestowed the name *Astur alphonsi* on a pair of tibiae, a pair of metatarsals, and the metacarpals of the left side of a goshawk apparently of the same size and relative proportions as *A. melanoleucus* of South Africa. They justified their description of this goshawk as a distinct species, first of all by the fact that most of the Mascarene extinct species were distinct; and then because the bony ridge for the *M. flexor digitorum communis* was more strongly developed, the fibula reached further down the tibia, the peroneal crest was straighter and longer, and the cnemial crest slanted more gradually into the anterior inner edge of the shaft of the tibia.

Milne-Edwards gives the measurements of the solitary tarso-metatarsus of this bird which he had for examination as follows:—

Total length	80 mm.
Width at proximal extremity	11 ,,
Width at distal extremity	13 ,,
Width at smallest part of shaft	6 ,,

Messrs. Gadow and Newton give the length of their tarso-metatarsi as 81 mm., of their tibiae as 117 mm., and of the metacarpals as 55 mm.

Habitat : Mauritius.

Seven tarsi in the Tring Museum.

HARPAGORNIS HAAST.

ALLIED to *Aquila*, from which it is distinguished by the ulna being relatively shorter and the tarso-metatarsus stouter.

HARPAGORNIS MOOREI HAAST.

Harpagornis moorei Haast, Trans. N.Z. Inst. IV, p. 192 (1872).

DESCRIPTION of femur (from Haast): The cylindrical shaft bent forward, and above the distal extremity it is slightly curved back. The hollow on the top of the head is very large and measures ·42 inch across.

The trochanteric ridge is well developed and the outer side is very rough, showing that muscles of great strength and thickness must have been attached to it.

The inter-muscular linear ridges are well raised above the shaft, of which the one extending from the fore and outer angle of the epitrochanteric articular surface to the outer condyle is the most prominent. The pits for the attachment of the ligaments in the inter-condyloid fossa are strongly marked. The femur is pneumatic, the proximal orifice is large and ear-shaped, resembling in form most closely that of the Australian Sea Eagle.

Total length .... 6·66 inches.
Circumference at proximal end .... 4·66 „
Circumference at distal end .... 5·58 „
Circumference at thinnest part of shaft .... 2·50 „

Ungual phalanx (probably of left hallux):
Length .... 2·92 inches.
Circumference at articular end .... 3·17 „

Ungual phalanx (probably of right second toe):
Length .... 2·75 inches.
Circumference .... 2·92 „

Type locality: Glenmark Swamp.

Habitat: New Zealand.

Type bones: 1 left femur, 2 ungual phalanges, and 1 rib.

For a more detailed description my readers must refer to the Transactions of the New Zealand Institute VI, pp. 64-75 (1874).

CARBO PERSPICILLATUS (PALL.)

(PLATE 39.)

Phalacrocorax perspicillatus Pallas, Zoogr. Rosso.-Asiat. II, p. 305 (1827—Berings Island); Gould, Zool. Voy. Sulphur, p. 49, pl. XXXII (1844); Stejneger, Bull. U.S. Nat. Mus., No. 29, p. 180 (1885); id. Proc. U.S. Nat. Mus. XII, pp. 83-94, pls. II-IV (1889—Osteology); Grant, Cat. B. Brit. Mus. XXVI, p. 357 (1898).

Graculus perspicillatus Elliot, New and heret. unfig. sp. N. Amer. B. II, part 14, No. 3, text and plate (1869).

Pallasicarbo perspicillatus Coues, Osprey III, p. 144 (1899).

PALLAS gives the first recognizable description of this bird, which, as translated from the Latin, is as follows: "Of the size of a very large goose. Of the shape of the former (sc. Cormorants), which it also resembles in the white patches on the flanks. The body is entirely black. A few long, white, narrow pendant plumes round the neck, as in Herons. Occiput with a huge tuft, doubly crested. Skin round the base of the bill bare, red, blue and white, mixed, as in a turkey. Round the eyes a thick, bare white patch of skin, about six lines wide, like a pair of spectacles. Weight 12 to 14 pounds. Female smaller, without crest and spectacles. (From Steller.)"

Steller, who was shipwrecked on Bering Island in 1741, was the discoverer of *C. perspicillatus*, and Pallas took his diagnosis from Steller's notes.

The Spectacled or Pallas's Cormorant is one of the rarest of all birds. It is generally said that four specimens are known, but five are really in existence: Two in the St. Petersburg Museum, one in Leyden, and two in London. One of these latter is perfect, while the other has no tail. Probably all five have been obtained by Kuprianoff, the Russian Governor at Sitka, who, in 1839, gave one to Captain Belcher, and sent some others to St. Petersburg. The careful researches of Stejneger and others on Bering Island have clearly shown that this Cormorant exists no longer. Formerly it is said to have been numerous, but the natives were fond of its flesh, which formed their principal diet when other meat was difficult to obtain. Probably it would not so soon have become extinct if it had not been that their rather short wings resulted in a certain slowness of locomotion on land and in the air. A good description is given in the Catalogue of Birds, and a still more detailed one by Stejneger (Proc. U.S. Nat. Mus. 1899, p. 86) from Brandt's manuscript.

Habitat: Bering Island.

CARBO MAJOR (FORBES).

"*Phalacrocorax novaezealandiae var. major*" Forbes, Trans. N.Z. Inst. XXIV, p. 189 (1892—no proper description).

DR. FORBES only informed us that this shag was of greater dimensions than *Ph. novaezealandiae* (a very closely allied form of *Ph. carbo*). It would be interesting to know more about it, and, especially, if this extinct form was incapable of flight, like *Ph. harrisi* of the Galápagos Islands.

Habitat: New Zealand.

PLOTUS NANUS NEWT. & GAD.

Plotus nanus Newton and Gadow, Trans. Zool. Soc. XIII p. 288, pl. XXXIV figs 1-5. (1893).

THE humerus, the pelvis with sacrum, and the tibia were the materials on which our authors founded this new species. They state that all the strongly developed characters in these bones leave no possible doubt as to its being a species of *Plotus*, and its diminutive size at once distinguishes it from the three known species—*P. anhinga*, *P. melanogaster*, and *P. novaehollandiae*.

The measurements are as follows :—

Left humerus, length .... 89 mm.
Left tibia, length .... 61 ,,

Distance from acetabular axis to anterior end of sacrum 30 mm.

Distance between ventral inner margins of the acetabula 14·5 mm.

Habitat : Mauritius. (Also recorded from Madagascar.)

"CHENOPIS SUMNERENSIS" FORBES.

Chenopis sumnerensis Forbes, Trans. N.Z. Inst. XXIV, p. 188 (1892) (Nomen nudum).

THIS appears to have been a very large species, with not very great powers of flight, if not flightless.

Habitat: New Zealand and Chatham Islands.

Bones from Chatham Islands in my collection.

CHENALOPEX SIRABENSIS ANDREWS.

Chenalopex sirabensis Andrews, Ibis 1897, p. 355, pl. IX, figs 1-3.

THIS species of which skull, sternum, pelvis, the bones of fore and hind limbs, &c., are preserved, appears to be closely allied to *Chenalopex aegyptiacus*, but has such a number of small differences that Mr. Andrews is, I think, quite justified in separating it; I do not, however, agree with him when he suggests that perhaps it is the same as Newton and Gadow's *Sarcidiornis mauritianus*, although many of the bones agree. Of course, his line of comparison was strengthened by the fact of subfossil bones of *Plotus nanus* occurring both in Mauritius and Madagascar; but it does not follow that because in one family of birds the same species occurred in two places the others must do likewise, and, therefore, one must not necessarily regard a certain similarity of osteological characters as proof of identity. I must here again refer my readers to Mr. Andrews' very full description.

Habitat: Sirabé in C. Madagascar.

The measurements are:—

Coracoid	67— 75 mm.
Humerus	132—147 ,,
Radius	126—134 ,,
Ulna	129—142 ,,
Metacarpus	76— 85 ,,

The smaller bones, undoubtedly, belonged to female, and the larger to male individuals.

CENTRORNIS ANDREWS.

ALLIED to *Chenalopex* and *Chenopis*, but differs from *Chenalopex* in the form and proportion of its metatarsus, and from all other Anserine forms by the extreme length and slenderness of the shaft of the tibio-tarsus and the relative shortness of the fibular crest. From *Chenopis* it differs in several respects, and the very long fibular crest of the latter at once separates them.

CENTRORNIS MAJORI ANDREWS.

Centrornis majori Andrews, Ibis 1897, p. 344, pl. VIII.

THIS species was discovered by Dr. Forsyth Major and Monsieur Robert in the bed of an old lake at Sirabé, Central Madagascar, in 1896-1897. It was similar in many respects to *Sarcidiornis* and *Chenalopex* but differed in its large size and the great length of its legs. Indeed, judging from the slenderness of the metatarsus and femur and the slight degree of inflection of the lower end of the long tibia, it seems probable that this bird was ill adapted for swimming, though a good runner. The wings were long and powerful and armed with a long spur. I must refer my readers for a fuller description to Mr. Andrews, as quoted above.

The measurements are:—

Tibia.

Length (exclusive of cnemial crest)	213—215 mm.
Width of upper articular surface	20— 21 ,,
Width of middle of shaft	11—11·5 ,,
Thickness of shaft	8·5— 9 ,,
Width of distal extremity	20— 21 ,,

Femur.

Length	103—107 mm.
Width of proximal extremity	25— 26 ,,
Width of distal extremity	26 ,,
Width of shaft	11 ,,

Metatarsus.

Length	130	mm. approx.
Width of shaft	8·5	,,
Width of middle trochlea	10	,,

Coracoid.

Length	31	mm.
Width of glenoidal surface	13	,,

Scapula.

Width at proximal extremity	23	mm.

Radius.

Length	24	mm.

Ulna.

Width at middle of shaft	10	mm.

Metacarpus.

Greatest width at proximal extremity	31	mm.
Length of spur	26	,,
Width of second metacarpal	9	,,

Habitat: Madagascar.

CNEMIORNIS OWEN.

SKULL short and massive, with beak rounded and stout. Carina of sternum aborted. Limb-bones short and very stout, the ulna being shorter than the humerus, and having very prominent tubercles for the secondaries; cnemial crest of tibia greatly developed. No foramen between third and fourth trochleae of tarso-metatarsus. Spines of dorsal vertebrae tall. The power of flight was absent. The chief differences from *Cereopsis* were the presence of extra pre-sacral vertebrae, so that two only instead of three ribs articulate with the sacrum; and an elevated pent-roof arrangement of the *ossa innominata*, which indicate more decided cursorial habits.

CNEMIORNIS CALCITRANS OWEN.

Cnemiornis calcitrans Owen, Trans. Zool. Soc. V, p. 396 (1865).

"THE type species. Very considerably larger than the existing *Cereopsis novaehollandiae*, with the limbs relatively much stouter and shorter" (Lydekker).

Height of back from ground .... 26 inches.
Length from beak to tail.... .... 34 ,,

Habitat: Middle Island, New Zealand.

For full description see Trans. N. Z. Inst. VI, pp. 76-84, pls. X-XII (1874).

"CNEMIORNIS GRACILIS" FORBES.

Cnemiornis gracilis Forbes, Trans. N.Z. Inst. XXIV, p. 187 (1892) *(Nomen nudum)*.

"A MOST elegantly moulded goose from the North Island." Unfortunately this is all that has been published about this form!

Habitat: North Island, New Zealand.

CNEMIORNIS MINOR FORBES.

Cnemiornis minor Forbes, Trans. N.Z. Inst. XXIV, p. 187 (1892); vide also Trans. N.Z. Inst. VI, pp. 76-84 (Hector).

THIS species appears to be distinguished from *Cnemiornis calcitrans* by its very small size, being hardly bigger than *Cereopsis novaehollandiae*.

Habitat: Middle Island, New Zealand.

CEREOPSIS NOVAEZEALANDIAE FORBES.

Cereopsis novaezealandiae Forbes, Trans. N. Zealand Inst. XXIV, *p.* 188 (1892).

THIS species was founded on an incomplete skull, and differed from *C. novaehollandiae* by its slightly larger size.

Habitat: New Zealand.

SARCIDIORNIS MAURITIANUS NEWT. & GAD.

Sarcidiornis mauritianus Newton & Gadow, Trans. Zool. Soc. XIII, p. 290, pl. XXXIV, figs. 9-10.

THE evidence on which this species is founded is a single left metacarpal and an incomplete left half of the pelvis. Its specific character is the very large size as compared to the two existing species.

Habitat: Mauritius.

In an old work entitled "Memorandums concerning India" by J. Marshall (1668) in the article on the Island of Mauritius, there occurs this passage: "They are many Geese; the halfe of their wings towards the end are black and the other halfe white; they are not large, but fat and good. Plenty of Ducks." As there is no mention of the caruncle on the bill here or in other authors alluding to geese in Mauritius, Oustalet doubted that these geese were this *Sarcidiornis*, but I believe this merely to have been an oversight of Marshall's and that his description goes far to prove the distinctness of Newton and Gadow's species.

The allusion to the small size also points to the geese of Marshall being the *Sarcidiornis*. L'Abbé Dubois in "Les Voyages du Sieur D. B." records the fact that on Bourbon were some wild geese slightly smaller than the geese of Europe but having the same plumage. Their bill and feet were red. It is also probable that wild geese were found on Rodriguez. There is nothing to show what these Bourbon geese were, and as no osseous remains of such birds have been found as yet it is impossible to do more than mention the fact of such birds having been recorded.

ANAS FINSCHI VAN BENEDEN.

Anas finschi Van Beneden, Journ. Zool. IV, p. 267 (1875); Ann. de la Soc. Geol. Belg. II, p. 123 (1876).

THIS duck is most peculiar, as it stands intermediate between *Querquedula* and *Dendrocygna* in structure, and its nearest known ally seems to be the extinct *A. blanchardi* of Europe, and of living forms apparently *Clangula clangula.*

Skull nearest to that of *Clangula clangula* but wider, nostrils more elongated, eye-sockets smaller, and the whole skull more regularly rounded off. *Sternum* differs from that of *C. clangula* by having the notch lower, more faint behind and shorter in front. Clavicle and coracoid resemble those of *Fuligula marila.* Humerus larger and stronger than in *F. marila* and *C. clangula*, as are the femur, tibio-tarsus and tarso-metatarsus, which are almost double as long and thick.

Judging from the shape of its leg-bones this bird must have been a strong runner, and probably at the same time was a poor flyer.

Habitat: Middle Island, New Zealand.

ANAS THEODORI NEWT. & GAD.

Anas theodori Newton & Gadow, Trans. Zool. Soc. XIII, p. 291, pl. XXXIV, figs 11-17 (1893—Mauritius).

MESSRS. NEWTON AND GADOW founded this species on a fragment of a sternum, a pair of coracoids, eight humeri, and a pair of tarso-metatarsi. These are referable to a duck of larger size than *Nettion bernieri*, and somewhat intermediate between *N. punctata* and *Anas melleri.*

The sternum differs from that of *A. melleri* by the lesser height of the keel and by the shape and direction of the anterior margin of the latter. The coracoid is longer and larger than in *N. bernieri*, but is much shorter than in *A. melleri*, though agreeing with that of the latter in shape, and by the plain almost ridgeless ventral surface of the shaft. The seven humeri vary in length from 70-78 mm., and agree in size with those of *N. punctata*, thus proving our species to be smaller than *A. melleri.*

The two tarso-metatarsi are in poor condition ; the right one measuring 42 mm. in length, thus indicating that *A. theodori* was a bird with a shorter foot than *A. melleri.*

Habitat : Mauritius.

CAMPTOLAIMUS LABRADORIA (GM.)

(PLATE 36.)

Anas labradoria Gmelin, Syst. Nat. I, 2, p. 537 (1788—"Habitat gregaria in America, boreali." Ex Pennant and Latham.)

Anas labradora Latham, Ind. Orn. II, p. 859 (1790).

Rhynchaspis labradora Stephens, in Shaw's Gen. Zool. XII, 2, p. 121 (1824).

Fuligula labradora Bonaparte, Ann. Lyceum N.Y. II, p. 391 (1826).

Somateria labradora Boie, Isis 1828, p. 329.

Kamptorhynchus labradorus Eyton, Mon. Anat. p. 151 (1838).

Fuligula grisea Leib, Journ. Acad. Sc. Philad. VIII, p. 170 (1840—young bird).

Camptolaimus labradorus Gray, List. Gen. B. ed. 2, p. 95 (1841); Dutcher, Auk. 1891, p. 201, pl. II; 1894, pp. 4-12; Hartl. Abh. naturw. Ver. Bremen XVI, p. 23 (1895).

Camptolaemus labradorius Baird, B.N. Amer. p. 803 (1858); Baird, Brewer and Ridgway, Water—B. N. Amer. II, p. 63 (1884); Milne-Edw. and Oustalet, Centen. Mus. d'Hist. Nat., Notice Ois. éteint. p. 51, pl. IV (1893); Salvadori, Cat. B. Brit. Mus. XXVII, p. 416 (1895).

THE adult male and a young male, both in my museum, are represented on plate 36, but the young bird became too rufous, through the colour type reproduction, and should be somewhat more mouse-gray. Though first technically named by Gmelin in 1788, this duck was first described in 1785 by Pennant, in the Arctic Zoology II, p. 559, as follows:—

"Pied Duck. With the lower part of the bill black, the upper yellow, on the summit of the head is an oblong black spot; forehead, cheeks, rest of the head and neck, white; the lower part encircled with black; scapulars and coverts of wings white; back, breast, belly, and primaries, black; tail cuneiform, and dusky; legs black. The bill of the supposed female? resembles that of the male, head and neck mottled with cinereous brown and dirty white; primaries dusky; speculum white; back, breast, and belly clouded with different shades of ash-colour; tail dusky and cuneiform; legs black. Size of a common Wild Duck.

"Sent from Connecticut, to Mrs. Blackburn. Possibly the great flocks of pretty Pied Ducks, which whistled as they flew, or as they fed, seen by Mr. Lawson in the western branch of Cape Fear inlet, were of this kind."

The Labrador-Duck is one of those birds, the disappearance of which is not easily explained. As Mr. Dutcher truly said, "we can speculate as to the cause of its disappearance, but we have no facts to warrant a conclusion." Formerly *Camptolaimus* was of regular occurrence along the northern Atlantic shores of North America, in winter south to New Jersey and New York. It has often been sold on the markets of New York and Baltimore, and nobody anticipated even fifty years ago that they might become extinct, but they appear never to have been very numerous, at least we have no proof of this. It is true that Professor Newton tells us that this duck used to breed on rocky islets, and that "its fate is easily understood," since "man began yearly to visit its breeding haunts, and, not content in plundering its nests, mercilessly to shoot the birds." This, however, seems to be mere conjecture, as we do not know for certain where the breeding haunts of this Duck have been, and that anyone has ever visited them. All information known about the breeding of this bird is that of Audubon, who says that his son was shown empty nests on the top of bushes, which a clerk of the fishing establishment told him were those of the Labrador Duck. This information is certainly too uncertain to draw any conclusions from, but the breeding places might just as well have been much further to the north, and probably were.

The number of specimens extant is 48.

Amiens, Town Museum: 1 ♂ ad. (Auk. 1897, p. 87).

Berlin Museum: 1, bought from Salmin (Hartl. p. 23).

Paris: ♂ adult, presented 1810 by M. Hyde de Neuville.

London, British Museum: 2, a ♂ ad. and a ♀ ad., neither of them with exact locality or date.

Liverpool: 2 ♂ ad., 1 ♀, 1 ♂ jun.

Cambridge: 1 ♂

Dublin: 1 fine mounted ♂ (Dr. Scharff in litt.)

Tring: 1 ♂ ad., 1 ♂ jun. (See below.)

Brussels: 1 ♂ ad.

St. Petersburg: 1 ♂ ad., purchased from Salmin.

Heine Museum in Germany: 1 poor specimen.

Munich: The Museum possesses a male from the collection of the Duke of Leuchtenberg.

Dresden: 1 ♂ and two doubtful eggs—the latter doubtless wrong I should say.

Vienna: 1 ♂ ad., exchanged from Baron von Lederer in 1830. Locality New York; 1 ♀ ad., bought from Brandt in Hamburg in 1846, for 4 Gulden!

Leiden Museum: ♂ ♀, from the Prince of Wied.

American Museum, New York: 7, three of which formerly belonged to George N. Lawrence.

Long Island Historical Society, Brooklyn: 1 ♂ ad.

Vassar College, Poughkeepsie, N. York: 1 ♂ ad.

New York State Museum, Albany: ♂ ♀ ad.

Cory collection: ♂ ♀ ad.

University of Vermont, Burlington, Vermont: 1 ♂ ad.

Philadelphia: 2 ♂ jun., 1 ♀

U.S. National Museum, Washington: 2 ♂, 1 ♀, 1 ♂ jun.

Collection of Mr. William Brewster: 1 ♂ jun., 1 ♀

Boston Society of Natural History: 1 ♂ jun.

Collection of Dalhousie College, Halifax: ♂ ♀

This makes a total of 48 known specimens.

The last specimens killed were those shot in May, 1871, at Grand Manan Island, the date of which is absolutely certain, and the specimen bought from a Mr. J. G. Bell in 1879, for the Smithsonian Institution, which is said to have been shot in 1875, but this date seems not quite certain (Cf. Auk, 1894, p. 9). That several other specimens were shot later than 1852 is perfectly certain. As the specimen of 1875, or thereabouts, is a young male, Mr. Lawrence's question about the old birds is certainly justified. As, however, no Labrador Duck has been recorded later than 1871 or 1875 we may suppose that it is now extinct.

My young male was bought in the Fulton Market, New York, about 1860, and probably came from Long Island. It was mounted by John Bell, a bird-stuffer, through whose hands several Labrador Ducks have gone, and is in the finest possible condition. I bought this bird from the late Gordon Plummer, shortly before his death. He died at his home in Brookline, Mass., in November, 1893. (Cf. Auk, 1891, p. 206.)

My adult male is the one of which the history is given in Auk, 1894, p. 176. It is described there in detail and then added : "Shot in the bay of Laprairie this spring (1862) by a habitant, and purchased by Mr. Thompson of this city, who has kindly placed it at my disposal for examination." Mr. William Dutcher of New York City bought this specimen from the widow of the Mr. Thompson, mentioned in the above note as the original owner, and I purchased it from Mr. William Dutcher, who informs me that "the Bay of Laprairie" is simply a name given to a wide part of the River St. Lawrence, just south of Montreal, Quebec. The name is found on good maps of Quebec.

"BIZIURA LAUTOURI" FORBES.

Biziura lautouri Forbes, Trans. N.Z. Inst. XXIV, p. 188 (1892—nomen nudum).

DR. FORBES, unfortunately, gives no description whatever of this bird. It would be interesting to know something about it, and especially if its powers of flight were impaired, as it seems to have been the case in so many extinct birds.

ARDEA MEGACEPHALA MILNE-EDWARDS.

"*Butors*" Leguat, Relation du Voyage (1708).
Ardea megacephala Milne-Edwards, Ann. Sci. Nat. (5) XIX, 1874, p. 10.

LEGUAT'S description, here translated, is as follows:—"We had Bitterns as big and as fat as capons. They are tamer and more easily caught than the 'gelinotes.'" He also says, "The lizards often serve as prey for the birds, especially for the Bitterns. When we shook them down from the branches with a pole, these birds ran up and gobbled them down in front of us, in spite of all we could do to prevent them; and even if we only pretended to do so they came in the same manner and always followed us about."

Milne-Edwards remarks, among other notes, that "This bird is not a true Bittern, but its head is so large and its feet so short that it is easy to understand that Leguat should have called it so.

The bony structure of the head is remarkable on account of its massive and thick proportions; the skull itself is strongly enlarged posteriorly, and the temporal fossae are bordered by very pronounced ridges, especially those on the occipital region. The upper side of the skull is hardly convex, and the interorbital region is large, but only slightly depressed along its middle line. The bill is stout, almost straight, a good deal enlarged at its base and rounded beneath. The nostrils are large and preceded by a large groove, which extends very far towards the tip.

It is impossible to confound this skull with that of any Bittern, the latter having the beak relatively slender and only barely exceeding the skull in length. These also have the skull much constricted at the temporal region. The fossil skull from Rodriguez therefore presents characters essentially those of a Heron, but differs from all known species in its massive appearance. In the Grey, Purple and Goliath Herons, as well as in the Egrettes, the head is narrower, more elongated, the bill less conical and less strong. In *Ardea atricollis*, now inhabiting Madagascar, the beak much resembles that of our extinct species, but it is longer and less enlarged at the base. The interorbital area is much wider, while on the other hand the hinder portion of the skull is narrower and more elongated, which gives to the skull a totally different aspect.

The feet relatively to the head are extremely short, and from this I conclude that we know no species of Heron which can be compared to that of Rodriguez. Nevertheless, the tarso-metatarsus presents all the characters of *Ardea*, and is far removed from that of *Botaurus*. The tibia is big and short; it surpasses in length the tarso-metatarsus by about a third, as is usual in the Herons; but the femur on the contrary is strongly developed, being quite as large as in the *Ardea cinerea;* which shows us that the body of this creature was of large size, and that the reduction in size of the feet had only taken place at their extremities.

The sternum is puny and small as compared with the creature's size. It is clearly that of a bird not furnished with powerful wings, and is even much less elongated than in the Bittern, but the coracoidal bones are very long and slender. The wings also were short and feeble, the humerus being hardly as big as in *Butorides atricapilla*. It is conspicuously slenderer and shorter than in the Bittern. The main body of the bone is slightly curved on the outside, and the lower articular condyle is large and flattened. I have not been able to examine any bone of the "manus," but the metacarpal bone shows exactly the same proportions for the wing as does the humerus, as it also barely reaches the size of that of *Butorides atricapilla*. The measurements are as follows:—

Skull.

Total length	154	mm.
Length of upper mandible	94	,,
Width of upper mandible at base	22	,,
Width of interorbital region	22	,,
Space between the mastoid apophyses	40	,,
Width of skull at level of postorbital apophyses	40	,,
Length of lower mandible	147	,,

Tarso-metatarsus.

Total length	95—162	mm.
Width at proximal extremity	14	,,
Width at distal extremity....	0135—14	,,
Width of shaft	0062—7	,,

Tibio-tarsus.

Total length	140—210	mm.
Width at distal extremity	12—13	,,
Width at proximal extremity	13—14	,,
Width of shaft	6—0065	,,

Femur.

Total length	90—92	mm.
Width of distal extremity	15—16	,,
Width of proximal extremity	14—16	,,
Width of shaft	0062—7	,,

Sternum.

Total length	64—88	mm.
Width in front	35—48	,,
Width behind costal facets	26—36	,,
Width at posterior border	27—35	,,

Coracoidals.

Total length	59—67	mm.
Width at lower extremity	17—18	,,

Humerus.

Total length	118—180	mm.
Width of proximal extremity	20—27	,,
Width of distal extremity	0165—24	,,
Width of shaft	7—11	,,

Metacarpals.

Total length	62—98	mm.
Width of proximal extremity	12—17	,,
Width of distal extremity	7—11	,, ”

The anonymous author of the manuscript “ Rélation de l’île Rodrigue ” (see Ann. Sci. Nat. (6) II p. 133 et seq. 1875) about the year 1830 mentions this bird as follows :—“ There are not a few Bitterns which are birds which only fly a very little, and run uncommonly well when they are chased. They are of the size of an Egret and something like them.”

Habitat : Rodriguez Island.

2 Humeri, 2 Femora, 2 Tibiae, and 2 Metatarsi in the Tring Museum.

ARDEA DUBOISI NOM. NOV.

Butors ou Grands Gauziers Dubois, Les Voyages faits par le Sieur D.B. (1674) p. 169.

L'ABBÉ DUBOIS is the only author who has, as far as I can ascertain, told us that the Island of Réunion also had a large almost flightless Heron as well as Mauritius and Rodriguez; and so feeling sure that it, like most other birds of this island, was distinct I name it after him.

The translation of his original description is as follows:—"Bitterns or Great Egrets, large as capons, but very fat and good. They have grey plumage, each feather spotted with white, the neck and beak like a Heron, and the feet green, made like the feet of Poullets d'Inde (*Porphyrio*, W.R.). This bird lives on fish."

Habitat: Réunion or Bourbon.

ARDEA MAURITIANA (NEWT. & GAD.)

Butorides mauritianus Newton & Gadow, Trans. Zool. Soc. vol. XIII, p. 289 (1893).

THE bones on which this species is founded are a pair of ulnae, one radius, four metatarsi, and one coracoid. The description is as follows :—"The bones in question are all considerably shorter than the corresponding bones of *A*. (*Nycticorax*) *megacephala*. The metatarsi agree otherwise in every detail with those of the latter species ; this relative stoutness indicates that they belonged to a Night-Heron or Bittern like *A. megacephala*. The two ulnae cannot, unfortunately, be compared with those of *A. megacephala;* their length, 110 mm., compared with the length of the humerus of *A. megacephala*, 119 mm., shows, however, likewise that they were those of a considerably smaller bird. The single left coracoid agrees in all the features of its dorsal or scapular half with *A. megacephala*, but its ventral or sternal half differs considerably, first by the much more strongly marked ridge of the *linea intermuscularis* on its ventral surface, secondly by the almost straight instead of inwardly curved margin between the *processus lateralis* and the lateral distal corner of the sternal articulation, thirdly by a very low but very distinct and sharp ridge, which arises from the median margin of the coracoid, a little above its median articulating corner. This roughness or prominent ridge is entirely absent in *A. megacephala* and in all other Herons which we have been able to examine, but at least a slight indication of it occurs in an individually varying degree in *Nycticorax* and *Botaurus*. That this coracoid bone belonged, however, to an Ardeine bird is clearly indicated by its whole configuration, notably by the shape and position of the precoracoid process, the various articulating facets at the dorsal end, and the prominent lip on the visceral or internal surface of the median portion of the sternal articulating facet."

The following are the measurements :—

Length of ulna	111—112 mm.
Length of metatarsus	81—87 ,,
Length of coracoid	48 ,,

Habitat : Mauritius.

Although *megacephala* and *mauritiana* have been placed in *Ardea* and *Butorides* respectively, from the short, stout legs and general build, I am inclined to think that all three of these Herons belong to the genus *Nycticorax*.

PROSOBONIA BP.

THIS genus is, in the Catalogue of Birds, placed in a section with somewhat long tarsus, the latter being longer than the culmen, containing in addition to *Prosobonia* the genera *Tringites*, and *Aechmorhynchus* (see afterwards), and it differs from the latter by its long hind toe, from the former by its square tail. The position of this singular bird is, however, not quite certain. The late Henry Seebohm placed it in the genus *Phegornis*, though the latter has no hind toe whatever, and it has even—but doubtless wrongly—been suggested that it belonged to the *Rallidae*, rather than to the *Charadriidae*. We know only one species. It is true that Dr. Sharpe bestowed a new name on the figure of Ellis, which is said to have been taken from an Eimeo-specimen, but it is hardly creditable that it belongs to a different species. Latham appears to have had three specimens, which were all three different from each other. Both Forster and Ellis, in their unpublished drawings in the British Museum, as well as Latham, evidently considered all three to belong to the same species, and it is not advisable now to over-rule their verdict, given with the specimens before them, merely on account of the different plumages, since we all know that most waders, and especially brightly-coloured ones, differ considerably in plumage, according to age and seasons. We are convinced that "*P. ellisi*" has been a younger bird. Sharpe attaches importance to the different habitat, but this is no argument in this instance, because Eimeo is, at the nearest point, not more than seven and a half miles from Tahiti,* and it is quite against all precedents among *Charadriidae* and beyond all plausibility that two such closely situated islands have closely allied forms of a Wader.

*See Findlay's South Pacific Ocean Directory, p. 642.

PROSOBONIA LEUCOPTERA (GM.)

(PLATE 35.)

White-winged Sandpiper Latham, Gen. Syn. III, pt. 1, p. 172, pl. LXXXII (1785—Otaheite and Eimeo).

Tringa leucoptera Gmelin, Syst. Nat. I, p. 678 (1788—ex Latham !); Westermann, Bijdr. Dierk. I, p. 51, pl. 15 (1854—Figure of the type).

Totanus leucopterus Vieillot, Nouv. Dict. d'Hist. Nat. (Ed. II) VI, p. 396 (1817).

Calidris leucopterus Cuvier, Règne Anim. I, p. 526 (1829).

Tringa pyrrhetraea Lichtenstein, Forster's descr. anim. p. 174 (1844—Otaheiti).

Prosobonia leucoptera Bonaparte, Compt. Rend. XXXI, p. 562 (1850); Sharpe, Cat. B. Brit. Mus. XXIV, p. 525 (1896).

Tringoides leucopterus Gray, Handl. B. III, p. 46 (1871).

Phegornis leucopterus Seebohm, Geogr. Distrib. Charad. p. 452 pl. 18 (1888).

Prosobonia ellisi Sharpe, Bull. B.O.C. XVI, p. 86 (1906—" Eimeo ").

DR. SHARPE'S description, made from the type in the Leyden Museum, is as follows: " Adult. General colour of upper surface blackish brown; the lower back and rump ferruginous; centre tail-feathers blackish, the rest rufous, banded with black, less distinctly on the two next the middle pair; wing-coverts blackish, with a white spot near the carpal bend of the wing, formed by some of the lesser coverts; crown of head blackish, the hind-neck browner, mixed with black; sides of face brown, the lores and ear-coverts slightly more reddish, behind the eye a little white spot; cheeks and under surface of body ferruginous red, the throat buffy white. Length 6·7 inches, culmen 0·9, wing 4·45, tail 2·15, tarsus 1·3 (Mus. Lugd.)"

We know nothing of this bird, but the one specimen in the Leyden Museum, which is the type, or at least one of the types. As no other specimens have been obtained for nearly a century and a quarter, there is every reason to fear that this bird is extinct. My plate has been made up by Mr. Lodge from the unpublished drawings of Ellis and Forster in the British Museum.

Habitat: Tahiti, and the adjacent islet of Eimeo.

AECHMORHYNCHUS COUES.

THIS genus appears to be closely allied to *Prosobonia*, but has a much shorter hind toe. Its colouration is very different, and quite that of a Sandpiper, while the pattern of *Prosobonia* is most singular. Seebohm placed *Aechmorhynchus*, together with *Prosobonia*, in the genus *Phegornis*.

We know only one species.

AECHMORHYNCHUS CANCELLATA (GM.)

(PLATE 35.)

Barred Phalarope Latham, Gen. Syn. III. pt. 1, p. 274 (1785—Christmas Island in the Pacific Ocean).

Tringa cancellata Gmelin, Syst. Nat. I, p. 675 (1788—ex Latham).

Tringa parvirostris Peale, U.S. Expl. Exp., Birds p. 235, pl. LXVI, 2 (1848—Paumotu) Cassin, U.S. Expl. Exp. p. 321, pl. 38, 2 (1858—Paumotu).

Totanus (Tryngites ?) cancellatus Gray, Cat. B. Trop. Islands Pac. Ocean, p. 51 (1859).

Phegornis cancellatus Seebohm, Geogr. Distrib. Charadr. p. 451, pl. 17 (1888).

Aechmorhynchus cancellatus Sharpe, Cat. B. Brit. Mus. XXIV, p. 525 (1896).

"BILL short, straight, and slender; wings long, first, second, and third quills very nearly equal; tertiaries but very little longer than the secondaries; tail rather long, wide, rounded; legs and toes long, the former robust; tibia feathered for more than half its length. A distinct stripe over and behind the eye ashy-white. Entire upper parts umber-brown, unspotted on the top of the head, but on the other upper parts edged and tipped with ashy-white and reddish fulvous. Tail-feathers umber-brown, with irregular and imperfect transverse narrow bands of ashy and pale reddish-white, and tipped with the same. Underparts white, with a tinge of ashy; throat and middle of the abdomen unspotted; breast, sides, and under coverts of the tail spotted, and with irregular transverse bars of brown, the latter most apparent on the sides, flanks, and under tail-coverts. Under wing-coverts ashy-white, irregularly spotted with brown. Bill greenish, darker at the tip; legs dark green. Sexes very nearly alike, female slightly paler." (Cassin.)

I have here given the synonymy of this bird, as it has now been generally accepted by Seebohm, Sharpe, and others. An actual comparison of the types would, however, be very desirable, but, unfortunately, we do not know where the type of Latham is, and if it still exists. Christmas Island lies much to the north of the Paumotu group ! As no specimens have been obtained since the U.S. Exploring Expedition, we may safely suppose that the species has ceased to exist for some reason.

Habitat : " Christmas Island in the Pacific Ocean and Paumotu Islands."

GALLINAGO CHATHAMICA FORBES.

Gallinago chathamica Forbes, Ibis 1893, p. 545.

EVIDENTLY a species allied to *G. pusilla*, but very much larger. Bill three inches long.

Habitat: Chatham Islands.

Several skulls and a few bones in the Tring Museum. This is a snipe only a little larger than the existing *Gallinago aucklandica*.

HYPOTAENIDIA (?) PACIFICUS (GM.)

(PLATE 26.)

Pacific rail Latham, Gen. Syn. III, pt. 1, p. 255 (1785).
Rallus pacificus Gmelin, Syst. Nat. I, p. 717 (1788).

FORSTER'S description is as follows, in translation: "Black with white spots or bars; abdomen, throat, and eyebrow white; hind neck ferruginous; breast grey; bill blood-red; iris red. Bill straight, compressed, narrowed at the top, thicker at the base, and blood-red. The mandibles subequal, pointed; the upper slightlv curved, with the tip pale fuscous; gape medium. Nostrils almost at the base of bill, linear. Eyes placed above the gape of the mouth. Iris blood-red. Feet four-toed, split, built for running, flesh coloured. Femora semi-bare, slender, of medium length.

"Tibiae slightly compressed, shorter than the femora. Four toes, slender, of which three point forward (are front toes). The middle one almost as long as the Tibia, the side ones 'of equal length shorter, the back one short, raised from the ground. Nails short, small, slightly incurved, pointed, and light coloured. Head oval, slightly depressed, fuscous. A superciliary line from bill to occiput whitish. Throat white. Hindneck ferruginous. Neck very short. Back and rump black, sparsely dotted with minute white dots. Breast bluish grey. Abdomen, crissum, and loins white. Wings short, wholly black, variegated with broken white bands. Remiges short. Rectrices extremely short, black spotted with white, hardly to be distinguished from the coverts.

Total length from bill to tail	9	inches.
Total length to middle toe	$12\frac{3}{4}$	,,
Bill	$1\frac{1}{10}$	,,
Tibiae	2	,,
Middle toe	$1\frac{3}{10}$	,, ,,

Mr. Keulemans' plate was done from Forster's unpublished drawing in the British Museum, and no specimen is in existence. The legs should, however, be less bright red, more flesh-colour.

Habitat: Tahiti, but evidently long extinct.

This bird, according to Forster, was called "Oomnaa" or "Eboonaa," on Otaheite, and the neighbouring islands.

NESOLIMNAS ANDREWS.

DIFFERS from *Cabalus* by the relatively shorter bill ; by having the whole culmen convex with the tip sharply decurved, by having a close instead of a loose plumage, and a much less reduced sternum, with a well-developed instead of almost obsolete keel. Type of genus *Nesolimnas dieffenbachi* (Gray).

NESOLIMNAS DIEFFENBACHII GRAY.

(PLATE 27.)

Rallus Dieffenbachii Gray, Dieffenb., Trav. N.Z. II App. p. 197 (1843).
Ocydromus dieffenbachi Gray, Voy. Ereb. and Terr., Birds p. 14, pl. 15 (1846).
Hypotaenidia dieffenbachi Bonaparte, C.R. XLIII, p. 599 (1856).
Cabalus dieffenbachi Sharpe, Voy. Ereb. and Terr., Birds p. 29, pl. 15 (1875), id., Cat. B. Brit. Mus. XXIII p. 47 (1894).
Nesolimnas dieffenbachi Andrews, Novit. Zool. III. p. 266, pl. X, figs 3-15 (1896).

ADULT: "General colour above, brown, banded on the mantle and scapulars, and spotted on the upper back with ochreous buff, these buff markings being margined with black, which takes the form of broad bars on the mantle; lower back and rump uniform brown; upper tail coverts brown, barred across with light rufous and black ; lesser wing coverts like the back ; median and greater coverts, as well as the primary coverts and quills, light chestnut, barred with black, the inner secondaries spotted and barred with ochre and black, like the back ; tail feathers brown, mottled with chestnut near the base ; crown of the head and nape uniform brown, followed by an indistinct patch of chestnut on the hindneck ; lores dull rufous, surmounted by a broad line of bluish grey, extending from the base of the nostrils to the sides of the nape; rest of the sides of the face bluish grey, extending on to the lower throat ; this grey area of the face separated from the grey eyebrow by a broad band of dark chestnut, which extends from the lores through the eye along the upper part of the ear-coverts ; chin and upper throat white ; lower throat black, barred across with white ; fore neck and chest ochreous buff, banded rather narrowly with black, this pattern of colouration extending up the sides of the neck to the chestnut on the ear coverts; lower breast and abdomen black, banded with white, the light bars on the flanks and vent feathers being tinged with ochreous; under-tail coverts broadly banded with black and ochre; under-wing coverts and axillaries blackish, barred with white; under surface of quills chestnut, with broad black bars.

Wing 4·8 inches, culmen 1·35, tail 2·7" (Sharpe).

Habitat: Chatham Islands.

The type and only known specimen is that in the British Museum.

CABALUS HUTTON.

Cabalus Hutton, Trans. N.Z. Inst. Vol. VI p. 108, pl. XX (1874—Type and unique species *Cabalus modestus*).

CAPTAIN HUTTON characterized his new genus as follows: "Bill longer than the head, moderately slender and slightly curved, compressed in the middle and slightly expanding towards the tip; nostrils placed in a membranous groove which extends beyond the middle of the bill, openings exposed, oval, near the middle of the groove. Wings very short, rounded; quills soft, the outer webs as soft as the inner, fourth and fifth the longest, first nearly as long as the second; a short, compressed claw at the end of the thumb. Tail very short and soft, hidden by the coverts. Tarsi moderate, shorter than the middle toe, flattened in front, and covered with transverse scales; toes long and slender, inner nearly as long as the outer, hind toe short, very slender, and placed on the inner side of the tarsus; claws short, compressed, blunt.

"The bird is incapable of flight, and the stomach of the specimen, dissected by Dr. Knox, contained only the legs and elytra of beetles."

Captain Hutton also adds, l.c., a valuable description of the skeleton.

One species known.

CABALUS MODESTUS (HUTTON).

(PLATE 28.)

Rallus modestus Hutton, Ibis 1872, p. 247. (Mangare, Chatham Islands.)

Cabalus modestus Hutton, Trans. New Zeal. Inst. VI p. 108. (The genus *Cabalus* established.)

"*Rallus dieffenbachii* juv." Buller, B. New Zealand, Ed. I pp. 179, 180; Ed. II p. 121 (1888).

Cabalus dieffenbachii (part., juv.!) Sharpe, Cat. B. Brit. Mus. XXIII p. 47 (1894); corr. p. 331.

Cabalus modestus Forbes, Bull. Brit. Orn. Club. No. IV. p. XX (Dec. 1892); Salvadori, op. cit. V p. XXIII (Jan., 1893); Forbes, Ibis 1893, pp. 532, 544, pl. XIV, fig. 4, egg; Sharpe, Cat. B. Brit. Mus. XXIII p. 331 (1893); Buller, Suppl. B.N.Z. I p. 45, pl. III (1905).

Ocydromus pygmaeus Forbes, Nature XLVI, p. 252 (1892—nomen nudum! cf. Ibis 1893, p. 544).

CAPTAIN HUTTON (Ibis 1872, p. 247) described this interesting species as follows: "Olivaceous brown, bases of the feathers plumbeous; feathers of the breast slightly tipped with pale fulvous, those of the abdomen and flanks with two narrow bars of the same colour;

throat dark grey, each feather slightly tipped with brown. Quills soft brown, the first three faintly barred with reddish fulvous, fourth and fifth the longest. Tail very soft and short, brown. Irides light brown, bill and legs light brown. Length 8·75 inches, wing 3·15, bill from gape 1·4, tarsus 1, middle toe and claw 1·4.

Young. Uniform brownish black.

A single specimen and young from Mangare ; also a specimen in spirits."

The author knew perfectly well what he was doing when he described this excellent species. Sir Walter Buller afterwards (B. New Zealand, Ed. I, pp. 179, 180) declared "after carefully comparing it with the type of *Rallus dieffenbachii*, and submitting the matter to the judgment of other competent ornithologists, I have no hesitation in considering it the same species, in an immature state of plumage." (*Sic !*) Unfortunately, Dr. Sharpe, in the Catalogue of Birds XXIII, repeated Buller's error, and, on Plate VI, figured *Cabalus modestus* under the name of *Cabalus dieffenbachii*, though the latter is not congeneric with *C. modestus*, and must be called *Nesolimnas dieffenbachii*, while the third form included in *Cabalus* by Dr. Sharpe, viz. *sylvestris* of Lord Howe's Island, must also be separated generically from *Cabalus*.

Formerly *Cabalus modestus* inhabited Great Chatham Island, as Dr. Forbes proved by bones found by himself at Warekauri, but when the species was discovered it existed there no more, though being plentiful on the little outlying island of Mangare. Unfortunately even there it is evidently extinct now, this island being overrun with cats and rats, besides which, according to Buller, the original vegetation has been ruthlessly burnt down for the purpose of sowing grass-seed, as even this bleak little island has been claimed by an enterprising sheep-farmer. Fortunately a good many specimens have been secured by the late W. Hawkins. I have fifteen in my museum, and there are specimens in the British Museum, in Liverpool, and one in Cambridge. Henry Palmer failed to get specimens when he visited Mangare.

I have also the egg described and figured in the Ibis by Dr. Forbes. It measures 40 by 21·4 mm., and is creamy white, with faint pale reddish and purplish roundish spots.

Habitat : Chatham Islands, east of New Zealand.

OCYDROMUS MINOR HAMILTON.

Ocydromus sp. Hamilton, Trans. N.Z. Inst. XXV, p. 103 (1893).
Ocydromus minor Hamilton (nec. Forbes) l.c.

THIS species is nearest allied to *sylvestris* Scl., which has quite erroneously been placed in the genus *Cabalus* by Dr. Sharpe ; *sylvestris* will have to form the type of a new genus, but until the skull of *minor* is known I prefer to leave the latter temporarily in *Ocydromus*.

The present species is known from two pelves, seven femora, six tibiae, and five metatarsi, as well as the front portion of a sternum. The measurements all show that *minor* was a slightly larger form than *sylvestris*, but owing to having a much shorter tibio-tarsus it must have been a much stumpier bird.

	Minor.	*Sylvestris.*
Pelvis extreme length	.... 65 mm.	.... 62·5 mm.
Pelvis extreme breadth....	.... 28 ,,	.... 25 ,,
Femur length	.... 64 ,,	.... 63 ,,
Tibio-tarsus length	.... 93 ,,	.... 98 ,,
Tarso-metatarsus length	.... 53 ,,	.... 51 ,,
Sternum greatest width	.... 24·5 ,,	.... 24·5 ,,

Habitat : Middle Island, New Zealand. Extinct.

OCYDROMUS INSIGNIS FORBES.

Ocydromus insignis Forbes, Trans. N.Z. Inst. XXIV, p. 188 (1892—insufficient description).

THIS bird "far exceeded in size any of the existing species of *Ocydromus*." That is all that is published about this bird.

Habitat: Middle Island, New Zealand.

APHANAPTERYX FRAUENFELD.

BILL produced, not cut short, rather curved. The nostrils are exposed and situated at the base of the bill. Halluces of the naked fowl-like legs of moderate length. Front of legs apparently scutellated. Wings abortive, no rectrices apparent.

APHANAPTERYX BONASIA SELYS.

(PLATE 29.)

A Hen Sir Thomas Herbert, A relation of some years' Travaile (1626).

Velt-hoenders Reyer Cornelisz, Van der Hagen's voyage (1646).

Poules rouges au bec de Becasse Cauche, Rélations véritables et curieuses de l'Isle de Madagascar (1651).

Apterornis bonasia Edm. de Sélys-Longchamps, Revue Zoologique, p. 292 (1848).

Didus herberti Schlegel, Vers. Med. Ak. Wetensch., II, p. 256 (1854).

Didus broecki Schlegel, l.c.

Aphanapteryx imperialis Frauenfeld, Neu aufgef. Abbild. Dronte, p. 6 (1868).

Aphanapteryx broeckii Milne-Edwards, Ann. Sci. Nat. (5), X, pp. 325-346, pls. 15-18 (1868).

Pezophaps broeckii Schlegel, Mus. Pays-Bas, Struthiones, p. 4 (1873).

I HERE give a translation of Frauenfeld's original diagnosis: "Of the size of a fowl, of a uniform brown red all over. Bill and legs dark, Iris yellowish. Feathers decomposed, as in the *Apteryx*, somewhat lengthened on the nape."

This description was made by Frauenfeld from a drawing by G. Hoefnagels, in the Imperial Library, Vienna, executed about the year 1610, and, together with that of the Dodo, apparently drawn from life in the Imperial Menagerie at Ebersdorf. This drawing proves Van den Broecke, Herbert, and Cauche's descriptions to have been correct, though their drawings are somewhat startlingly different in shape. Only known from these four drawings and osseous remains. 18 fragments of beaks, 5 pelves, 35 tibiae, 1 sacrum and fragments, and 1 vertebra in the Tring Museum.

Habitat: Mauritius.

DIAPHORAPTERYX FORBES.

THIS genus is closely allied to *Aphanapteryx* and *Erythromachus*, but, on the whole, is nearer to *Aphanapteryx*. It differs from both these genera and *Ocydromus* in the large protuberances on the basi-temporal region of the skull, and the tarso-metatarsus was much shorter than in *Aphanapteryx*. For complete diagnosis of this genus see Andrews in Novitates Zoologicae, Vol. III, pp. 73-76 (1896).

DIAPHORAPTERYX HAWKINSI (FORBES).

Aphanapteryx hawkinsi Forbes, Nature XLVI, p. 252.
Diaphorapteryx hawkinsi Forbes, Bull. B.O.C.I. p. XXI, 1893.

THE remains of this bird were first sent to Dr. H. O. Forbes in 1892 by the late W. Hawkins, from the Chatham Islands, 500 miles E.S.E. of New Zealand. It appears to have been confined to the Island of Wharekauri. Dr. Forbes subsequently went to the Chathams himself and collected a large number of bones of various extinct birds, including those of *Diaphorapteryx*. In 1895 I received a consignment of bones through the agency of Mr. Dannefaerd, from the Chathams, such as has never been equalled from any deposit elsewhere, for literally there were many hundreds of thousands of bones of a considerable number of species of birds. From this collection Mr. C. W. Andrews was able to draw up a most minute description of the skeleton of *Diaphorapteryx*, founded on several practically complete skeletons, some thirty or more skulls, and several thousand individual bones of various portions of the skeleton. This description, published in "Novitates Zoologicae," Vol. III, pp. 73-84, is too long for reproduction here, and so I must refer my readers to it.

This bird, as well as the *Palaeolimnas*, shows an apparent relationship between the Chatham Islands and the Mascarene Islands; but I believe that

this is not a real relationship, as has been asserted, due to a former land-connection, but merely a case of parallel development owing to similar conditions of existence.

Habitat : Wharekauri Island, Chatham Islands.

In the Tring Museum are two complete skeletons, more than a thousand bones, and about fifteen skulls.

One almost complete skeleton, and the type, skull, and bones, are in the British Museum.

ERYTHROMACHUS MILNE-EDWARDS.

"LEGS stout, made for running, and from a quarter to one-fifth shorter than in *Ocydromus*, the three anterior digits well developed and the hallux very small. Body less massive than in *Ocydromus*, with the wings slightly more developed, but not serviceable for flight. Head small; bill red, straight, pointed, and about 60 mm. = 2·4 inches. A red naked patch round the eye; plumage pale grey."

ERYTHROMACHUS LEGUATI MILNE-EDWARDS.

Gelinote Leguat, t. II p. 71 (1708).

Erythromachus leguati Milne-Edwards, Ann. Sci. Nat. (5) XIX, pp. 6, 7, pls. XI, XII (1874).

Aphanopteryx leguati Günther & E. Newton, Phil. Trans. Vol. 168, pp. 431-432, pl. XLIII (1879).

OF the older writers only Leguat appears to have described the Rodriguez flightless rail. There are several references to "*Hens*," "*Veld Hoenders*," &c., but all appear to refer to the Mauritius bird *Aphanapteryx bonasia*. Leguat's description is as follows:—

"Our 'gelinotes' are fat all the year round and of a most delicate taste. Their colour is always of a bright grey, and there is very little difference in plumage between the two sexes. They hide their nests so well that we could not find them out, and consequently did not taste their eggs. They have a red naked area round their eyes, their beaks are straight and pointed, near two and two-fifths inches long, and red also. They cannot fly, their fat makes them too heavy for it. If you offer them anything red, they are so angry they will fly at you to catch it out of your hand, and in the heat of the combat we had an opportunity to take them with ease."

Quite extinct. Only known from descriptions and osseous remains. One tibia in the Tring Museum.

Habitat: Rodriguez Island.

PENNULA DOLE.

Pennula Dole, Hawaiian Alman. 1879 p. 54 (Reprint in Ibis 1880 p. 241).

I BELIEVE that the genus ***Pennula*** should be placed near ***Porzanula***, but its wings are softer, the rectrices are next to invisible, but can be felt, as they have stiff shafts and are about 13 mm. long, though being entirely hidden by the soft tail-coverts. The tibia is bare for about 7 mm., the metatarsus covered in front with nearly a dozen transverse, very distinct scales, and distinctly reticulated behind. The bill much as in ***Poliolimnas*** and ***Porzanula***.

Two species can be recognized : ***Pennula millsi***, with a uniform upper surface, and ***Pennula sandwichensis***, with a distinctly spotted upper side. Both forms are now extinct.

PENNULA MILLSI DOLE.

MOHO OF THE NATIVES.

(PLATE 26, FIG. 3.)

Pennula millei (misprint for *millsi*) Dole, Hawaiian Almanac 1879 p. 54 (reprint in Ibis 1880 p. 241. "Uplands of] Hawaii : named in honour of Mr. Mills, spec. in Mills's Coll., nearly extinct") ; Rothsch., Avif. Laysan, etc., p. 241 pl. LXXVI.

"*Pennula ecaudata*" apud Wilson & Evans, Aves. Hawaii., part V, text and plate.

ALL we know of this bird are the five specimens caught by an old native bird-catcher named Hawelu for the late Mr. Mills of Hawaii. Two of these are now in my Museum, one in Cambridge, and two in the Bishop-Pauahi Museum in Honolulu. There can be no doubt that this bird is now extinct. All recent attempts to find specimens have been futile. Mr. Palmer, whom I sent a specially trained dog, also failed to find even traces of it. It lived formerly in the country between Hilo and the volcano Kilauea, in places where thick grass, *Vaccinium* and *Dianella*, forms the thickest cover possible. In former times the "Moho" was a dainty on the tables of the Hawaiian kings, but its disappearance is probably due to the introduction of the obnoxious mongoose and to bush fires.

PENNULA SANDWICHENSIS (GM.)

(PLATE 26, FIG. 2.)

Rallus Sandwichensis Gmelin, Syst. Nat. I p. 717 (1788—ex Latham! "Habitat exilis in insulis Sandwich").

Pennula Wilsoni Finsch, Notes Leyden Mus. XX p. 77 (1898—Finsch explains that the specimen in the Leyden Museum is not the type of Latham—and therefore of Gmelin's name—and therefore renames it).

For full synonymy and explanations of name, etc., cf. Avifauna of Laysan, p. 239, 240 and 243, also plate LXXVI.

LATHAM'S description—from which Gmelin's diagnosis was taken—distinctly says that the feathers were "darkest in the middle," and in the Index Ornith. "supra maculis obscuris." Moreover, the unpublished drawing of Ellis, well reproduced in Mr. Scott Wilson's book, shows beyond doubt the identity of the bird of the old authors with the specimen in the Leyden Museum.

The Leyden specimen is all we are acquainted with, and of the history of this bird we know nothing but Latham's statement that it came from the "Sandwich Islands."

TRIBONYX ROBERTI ANDREWS.

Tribonyx roberti Andrews, Ibis 1897, p. 356, pl. IX, figs 4-7.

THIS bird is described from an imperfect pelvis, a perfect left tibio-tarsus and a femur. The pelvis differs from that of *T. mortieri* in not having the deep depression in the ilia in front of the acetabulum and above the pectineal process. It also differs in having a rather wider pelvic escutcheon and wider renal fossal, and the supra-acetabular ridges of the ilia are smaller than in the Australian bird. The beautifully-preserved left tibia differs from that of *T. mortieri* in having the intercondylar groove wider and shallower, the inner condyle less massive, thus making the difference between the inner and outer condyle more marked ; *T. roberti* also has the shaft immediately above the extensor bridge wider, the bridge itself less oblique, and the fibular crest is longer.

The measurements are :—

Pelvis.

Length of Ilium	82 mm.	approx.
Least width of acetabular region of Pelvis	14 ,,	
Width at Antitrochanter	40 ,,	
Width at anterior angle of Pelvic Escutcheon	36 ,,	
Width at Posterior angle of Pelvic Escutcheon....	40 ,,	
Length of Sacrum	68 ,,	

Tibia.

Length	143 mm.
Width at distal extremity....	12 ,,
Width at middle of shaft	7 ,,

Femur.

Length	83 mm.
Width at distal extremity....	17 ,,
Width at middle of shaft	7 ,,

Habitat : Sirabé in C. Madagascar.

NOTORNIS OWEN.

DIFFERS from *Porphyrio* by the secondaries being nearly as long as the primaries, and the wing-coverts more or less elongated, sometimes nearly hiding the quills.

Type: *Notornis mantelli.*

NOTORNIS MANTELLI OWEN.

Notornis mantelli Owen, Trans. Zool. Soc. III, p. 377, pl. LVI, figs. 7-11 (1848).

THIS species was founded on a nearly entire skull, collected by Walter Mantell at Waingongoro, North Island, New Zealand. This skull is more than twice the size of that of *Porphyrio melanotus*. The basisphenoidal surface, however, is flatter, the anterior angle projects below the base of the presphenoid, and there is a slender ridge continued from each paroccipital to the lateral angles of the platform, the posterior angles being hemispheric tubercles as in *Palapteryx*.

The occipital region inclines forwards as it rises, while the same is more vertical in *Porphyrio*. The post-frontal is broader than in *Porphyrio*. The chief distinction from that of *Porphyrio* is, however, the almost regular four-sided figure of the skull. The breadth of the anterior part is almost exactly that of the occipital region, and the extent of the sides is not much more than that of the front and back part. The parieto-frontal region of the skull is very unlike that of *Porphyrio*, being convex and oblong, and *Notornis* also lacks cerebral or hemispheric convexities. Owen gives a large number of other differences, but I refer my readers to the original article as above, pp. 366-371. I, however, must state here, as is already mentioned by Mr. Hamilton, Trans. N.Z. Inst. XXIV, p. 176, 1892, that the *Dinornis* skull, with which Professor Owen compared *Notornis*, referred by him to *D. casuarinus* is really that of *Aptornis defossor* (*vide* Trans. Zool. Soc. III, pl. 52, figs. 1-7), and, therefore, it is quite natural that Professor Owen found a great likeness to *Dinornis* in *Notornis*, as the skull he compared it with was really that of the Ralline *Aptornis*, and not the Struthious *Dinornis* at all.

Habitat: North Island, New Zealand.

Dr. H. O. Forbes, Trans. N.Z. Inst., discusses at length measurements of tibiae and femora of *Notornis*, provisionally naming the skeleton in the Otago Museum *Notornis parkeri*, as a new species, but I consider we must wait for confirmation till we get an associated skeleton of *N. mantelli*.

NOTORNIS HOCHSTETTERI A.B.M.

(PLATE 34.)

Notornis Hochstetteri A. B. Meyer, Abbild. Vogelskelett, Lief. IV & V, p. 28, pl. XXXIV-XXXVII (1883—South Island, New Zealand); Zeitschr. ges. Orn. II, p. 45, pl. I (1885—figures of the bird).

Notornis mantelli (non Owen 1848!) Gould, P.Z.S. London, 1850, pl. 21; Trans. Zool. Soc. London IV, pl. 25 (1850); Gould, B. Austr. Suppl., pl. 76 (1869); Buller, B. New Zealand, pl. (1873); Sharpe, Cat. B. Brit. Mus. XXIII, p. 208 (1894).

THE name *Notornis mantelli* having been based on a cranium and some leg-bones from the North Island, and the bones of a specimen from the South Island, showing marked differences, Dr. A. B. Meyer was fully justified in describing the latter form as different, under the name of *N. hochstetteri*.

According to the describer there are considerable differences in the cranial bones, but the comparison of the leg-bones shows such differences in size that these alone would be sufficient to separate the North and South Island forms. The femur of *N. hochstetteri* measures 109, that of *N. mantelli* 122, the tibia of the former 165, the tarso-metatarsus 109, the tibia of the latter 200, the tarso-metatarsus 129 mm. For further measurements see A. B. Meyer, Abbild. Vogelskelett I, p. 30.

The upper surface is olive-green with some slaty-blue shading, the quills are black with purplish blue outer webs; rectrices blackish, green on the outer webs. Head, neck, and under surface purplish blue, thighs more blackish. Under tail-coverts white, frontal plate and bill bright red, yellow towards the tip of both mandibles. Feet red.

Although this bird is evidently not extinct, a specimen having been captured as late as 1898, it seems that not many examples live at present in New Zealand, as they have been sought after a good deal, and yet only four have been taken so far, *i.e.*, the two in the British Museum, one in the Dresden Museum, and the last-mentioned one.

Full accounts of the capture of this last specimen have been given in the Trans. New Zealand Institute, XXXI, pp. 146-150, and in Sir Walter Buller's Supplement to the Birds of New Zealand, I, pp. 66-74, where, however, the year of the capture is not mentioned, though one can guess that it must have taken place shortly before the articles on it appeared.

Habitat: Middle Island, usually called South Island, apparently nearly extinct.

NOTORNIS STANLEYI (ROWLEY).

White gallinule, Voy. of Gov. Phillip to N.S.W., p. 273, cum tab. (1789).
Porphyrio stanleyi Rowley, Orn. Misc. I, p. 36, pl. IX (1875).
Porphyrio melanotus (part.) Sharpe, Cat. Birds Brit. Mus. XXIII, p. 205 (1894).
Porphyrio alba G. R. Gray, List Birds N.Z., &c., Ibis 1862, p. 214.

THE first to point out the differences between the bird now in the Liverpool Museum and the specimen in Vienna was Mr. Dawson Rowley. The original description of the anonymous author of Phillip's Voyage is as follows :—

"This beautiful bird greatly resembles the purple Gallinule in shape and make, but is much superior in size, being as large as a dunghill fowl. The length from end of bill to that of the claws is two feet three inches. The bill is very stout, and the colour of it, the whole of the top of the head and the irides red; the sides of the head round the eyes are reddish, very thinly sprinkled with white feathers; the whole of the plumage is, without exception, white. The legs the colour of the bill. This species is pretty common on Lord Howe Island, Norfolk Island, and other places, and is a very tame species. The other sex, supposed to be the male, is said to have some blue on the wings."

Gray states under *Porphyrio alba*, in Ibis 1862, p. 214: "It is stated that a similar kind was found on Lord Howe Island which was incapable of flight. The wings of the male were beautifully mottled with blue."

Dr. H. O. Forbes, in the Bulletin of the Liverpool Museums, Vol. III, No. 2, pp. 62-68 (1901), gives an exhaustive account of Rowley's type, in which he comes to the conclusion that the bird is not a *Porphyrio* but a *Notornis*, and that it is also probably a specimen of *Notornis alba*. That it is a *Notornis* I equally believe; but I think the length of the wing-coverts in the type of *N. alba*, puts it out of the question that the two birds could be the same. Moreover, the two original pictures of Phillip and White show this difference of the wings very well. I have therefore kept the two separate, and I feel sure if we had other specimens with exact data we should find this a parallel case to that of *Nesonetta aucklandica* of the Auckland Islands and *Anas chlorotis* of New Zealand, and that *Notornis alba* of Norfolk Island was a still further degenerate form to the already flightless *N. stanleyi* of Lord Howe Island. Wing nine inches.

Habitat: Lord Howe Island.

NOTORNIS ALBA (WHITE).

(PLATE 33.)

? *White gallinule* Callam, Voy. Botany Bay (1783 ?) (teste Gray).
Fulica alba White, Journ. Voy. N.S.W., p. 238 and plate (1790).
Gallinula alba Latham, Ind. Orn. I, p. 768 (1790).
Porphyrio albus Temminck, Man. d'Orn. II, p. 701 (1820).
Porphyrio melanotus var. alba Gray, Voy. Ereb. and Terror, Birds, p. 19 (1144).
Porphyrio melanotus Gray, Voy. Ereb. and Terror, Ed. II (1846), p. 14.
Notornis ? alba Pelzeln, Sitz. k. Akad. Wiss. Wien. XLI, p. 328 (1860).
Notornis alba Salvin, Ibis 1873, p. 295, pl. X.

THERE has been considerable confusion in connection with this bird and the following species, owing to the fact of White not having given any locality for the specimen on which Latham founded his *Gallinula alba*, and which is now in the Vienna Museum. That the Vienna specimen is really White's bird is proved because it was bought at the sale of the Leverian Museum, and White expressly states that all his birds were deposited in the Leverian Museum.

It is quite impossible to say with *certainty* which of the two forms, *Notornis alba* or *N. stanleyi*, came from Norfolk Island, as we have no indication of the origin of the Liverpool specimen. But seeing that in the anonymous work, "The Voyage of Governor Phillip to Botany Bay," the first mentioned habitat is Lord Howe Island, and the figure shows a bird with the shorter wing-coverts of *N. stanleyi*, I think I am justified in taking the bird with longer wing-coverts—viz., *Notornis alba*, to be the bird from Norfolk Island.

White's description is as follows :—" White Fulica, with bill and front red, shoulders spined, legs and feet yellow." White's figure clearly shows the long wing coverts characteristic of the genus *Notornis*. Von Pelzeln says in his account of this bird that there is a label on it bearing the number 102, and giving as place of origin Norfolk Island, but White makes no mention of this. There are traces of a bluish shade, and two or three dark spots on the plumage, which has led many ornithologists to consider *N. alba* an albino. Gray, in "A List of Birds from New Zealand, &c.,"* remarked that some Norfolk Island specimens had blue between the shoulders, and the back spotted with the same colour. He also states that the young are said to be black, then become bluish grey, and afterwards pure white. From these and other authors' similar remarks I believe we have not here a case of albinism, but a bird which was in a stage of evolution towards becoming a fixed white species. Wing 9 inches (measured by myself in the Vienna Museum).

Habitat : Norfolk Island.

---

* Ibis 1862, p. 214.

APTERORNIS SELYS.

"DIFFERED widely from *Didus* and *Pezophaps* in its long beak, which resembles a little that of a woodcock, but is much stronger. These birds were high on the leg, ran swiftly, and were far removed from pigeons like the Dodo and the Solitaire, but to which they had a certain resemblance, owing to their rudimentary wings, apology for a tail, and the disposition of their digits."

The above is a translation of de Selys-Longchamps' diagnosis of the genus, but owing to his inclusion therein of *Didus solitarius* and *Aphanapteryx bonasia*, it does not fit when restricted to the "Oyseau bleu" of Le Sieur D.B. It might be described as: Resembling *Aptornis*, but with shorter bill and feet, thus more approaching *Notornis*.

One species.

APTERORNIS COERULESCENS SELYS.

(PLATE 32.)

"*Oyseaux bleus*" Le Sieur D.B., Les Voyages aux Isles Dauphine and Bourbon, pp. 170, 171 (1674).

Apterornis coerulescens Selys-Longchamps, Rev. Zool. 1848, p. 294.

THE original description of the Sieur D.B. (Dubois) is as follows (translated):—"*Oyseaux bleus*: As big as the Solitaires; they have the plumage entirely blue, the beak and the feet red and made like those of fowls; they do not fly at all, but run extremely quickly, so that a dog can hardly catch them; they are very good."

Habitat: Bourbon or Réunion.

Dubois gives the size of these birds as the same as that of a big goose and the feet as being like those of a fowl: I have, therefore, in reconstructing the plate of this bird, had it made intermediate in structure between the New Zealand *Notornis* and *Aptornis*, which were evidently its nearest allies.

APTORNIS OWEN.

DIFFERS from *Dinornis*, *Palapteryx* and *Notornis* in having an articular surface for a very strong hind toe, and the tarso-metatarsus of a conformation more nearly resembling that found in the *Dodo*, but shorter and thicker than in the latter. In addition, the strong calcaneal process, perforated by a complete bony canal for the tendon at the back part of the proximal end of the tarso-metatarsus ; the perforation above the interspace between the condyles for the middle and outer toes; and the more posterior position for the condyle for the inner toe all prove the distinctness of this genus.

Type: *Aptornis otidiformis*.

APTORNIS OTIDIFORMIS (OWEN).

Dinornis otidiformis Owen, Trans. Zool. Soc. III, p. 247, pls. XXV and XXVI, fig. 5 (1844).
Aptornis otidiformis Owen, ibidem p. 347 (1848).

THIS is the North Island form, and I must refer my readers to Owen's description, only remarking that Mr. Hamilton, Trans. N.Z. Inst. XXIV, p. 179, says the vertebrae assigned by Owen to *Cnemiornis* all belong to *Aptornis*.

Locality of type tibia: Poverty Bay, North Island, New Zealand; collected by Rev. Wm. Williams in 1842.

APTORNIS DEFOSSOR OWEN.

Aptornis defossor Owen, Trans. Zool. Soc. VII, pp. 353 to 366, pls. 40-44 (1871).

THE skull differs from that of *A. otidiformis* by the vertical surface of the descending part of the occiput being less deeply concave, the occipital foramen relatively smaller. The hind part of the base of the alisphenoid is more produced and tuberous outside the end of the hyoid process of the paroccipital in *A. defossor*.

The chief other differences in size, according to Owen, are as follows :—

	A. defossor.		*A. otidiformis.*
Skull.			
Length	7·2 inches.		6·2 inches.
Breadth across paroccipitals	3·3 ,,	....	2·9 ,,
Breadth across postfrontals	3·2 ,,	....	2·10 ,,
Breadth across temporal fossae	2·3 ,,	....	1·1 ,,
Breadth of base of upper mandible	1·6 ,,	....	1·3 ,,
Breadth of middle of upper mandible	1·4 ,,	....	1·1 ,,
Breadth of fore end of upper mandible	0·7 ,,	....	0·6 ,,
Length of premaxillary	5·0 ,,	....	4·3 ,,
Femur.			
Length	7·6 ,,	....	6·2 ,,
Breadth of proximal end	2·2 ,,	....	1·9 ,,
Breadth of distal end	2·2 ,,	....	1·9 ,,
Circumference of middle of shaft	2·9 ,,	....	2·3 ,,
Tibia.			
Length	10·3 ,,	....	8·9 ,,
Breadth of proximal end	2·3 ,,	....	1·9 ,,
Breadth of distal end	1·10 ,,	....	1.3 ,,
Circumference of middle of shaft	2·6 ,,	....	1·11 ,,
Metatarsus.			
Length	4·4 ,,	....	3·10 ,,
Breadth of proximal end	1·8 ,,	....	1·5 ,,
Breadth of distal end	1·9 ,,	....	1·6 ,,
Breadth of middle of shaft	1·6 ,,	....	1·4 ,,

Locality of type: Oamaru.

Habitat : South Island.

A nearly perfect skeleton in the Tring Museum, collected by Mr. W. S. Mitchel in limestone cave on Oreti River, Southland.

PALAEOLIMNAS FORBES.

DIFFERS from *Fulica* by the much more curved shape of the skull, the deeply marked glandular impressions over the eyes, and the great pneumaticity of the frontal bones.

PALAEOLIMNAS CHATHAMENSIS (FORBES).

Fulica chathamensis H. O. Forbes, Nature, vol. XLVI p. 252 (1892).
Fulica newtoni H. O. Forbes, l.c. (non Milne-Edwards).
Palaeolimnas newtoni H. O. Forbes, Ibis 1893, p. 544.
Palaeolimnas chathamensis Milne Edwards, Ann. Sci. Nat. (VIII) 2, 1896 p. 130.

DR. FORBES says in Nature "I procured from the same beds which contained *Aphanapteryx* a certain number of bones of a *Fulica* which much resemble those of *Fulica newtoni;* like the bones of *Aphanapteryx* (should be *Diaphorapteryx*, W.R.) they vary much in size, some being equal to, while others were considerably larger than similar bones of *Fulica newtoni*. This variation is so great that I am inclined to consider them as belonging to different species, or at least different races. I have given the name *Fulica chathamensis*" to the larger species.

Later, in the Ibis, Dr. Forbes says, "The limb-bones and pelvis correspond so closely to those of *F. newtoni* that I am not able to separate them. The head of the type is, however, unknown."

Professor Milne-Edwards, however, points out numerous differences. In the humerus the sub-trochanterial groove is bigger, and particularly wider than in typical *Fulica*. The iliac grooves are larger than in *Fulica newtoni*, the pelvic knob is more extended, and the sciatic foramen is larger. The first sacral vertebrae are stunted below the median sinus, while in the Mauritius species one observes a very stout one, occupying the four first vertebrae of the pelvis. The feet were also larger and stronger than in the latter.

Habitat: Chatham Islands.

An almost complete skeleton and numerous bones in the Tring Museum, and an almost complete skeleton in the British Museum.

PALAEOLIMNAS NEWTONI (MILNE-EDWARDS).

Poules d'eau Sieur D.B., Voyages 1674.
Fulica newtoni Milne-Edwards, Ann. Sci. Nat. (5) VIII pp. 194-220, pls. 10-13 (1867).

THE translation of the Sieur D.B.'s (Abbé Dubois) description is as follows :—" Waterhens which are as large as fowls. They are always black, and have a large white crest on the head." For the anatomical description I must refer my readers to Professor Milne-Edwards.

Habitat : Bourbon.

Milne-Edwards gives so many details in which *Fulica newtoni* agrees with *Palaeolimnas chathamensis* that I feel convinced that the former is not a true *Fulica*, and, until we know its skull and can decide for certain, I think it is best to include it in the genus *Palaeolimnas.* 16 tibiae, 30 metatarsi, 8 humeri, 2 sternums, 4 fragments and an entire pelvis and sacrum, and 3 cervical vertebrae in the Tring Museum.

PALAEOLIMNAS PRISCA (HAMILTON).

Fulica prisca Hamilton, Trans. N.Z. Inst. XXV, p. 98 (1893).

THIS bird was nearly as large as *Notornis*, but with a very small head and with a frontal shield. It was probably a poor flier, though not flightless, as *Fulica chathamensis* was. It was smaller than the latter. Measurements, according to Hamilton :—

	prisca.	*newtoni.*	*chathamensis.*
Femur: Length	78—93 mm.	—	85 mm.
Tibio-tarsus: Length	143—162 ,, ...	144 mm.	152—163 ,,
Tarso-metatarsus: Length	81—98 ,, ...	88 ,, ...	96 ,,

Habitat: Middle Island, New Zealand.

LEGUATIA SCHLEGEL.

BODY not larger than that of a goose ; wings rather short but still fitted for flight ; feathers of the legs reaching down almost to the top of the tarso-metatarsus ; toes long and completely free, middle toe almost as long as tarso-metatarsus. Bill with a naked shield reaching back beyond the eye. Height about 6 feet.

LEGUATIA GIGANTEA SCHLEGEL.

(PLATE 31.)

Le Géant Leguat, Voyages (1708), p. 171, English edition.
Leguatia gigantea Schlegel, Versl. Med. Akad. Wetensch. Amst. VII, p. 142 (1858).

LEGUAT'S description is as follows : ". . . and many of those birds called giants, because they are six feet high. They are extremely high mounted, and have very long necks. Their bodies are not bigger than that of a goose. They are all white, except a little place under their wings, which is reddish. They have a goose's bill, only a little sharper ; their claws are very long and divided." This bird was apparently confined to the island of Mauritius.

Professor Newton asserts that Leguat's "Géants" were Flamingos, principally because bones of Flamingos have been found in Mauritius and not a single bone has ever been got of the "géant." This argument is, in my opinion, insufficient, and no evidence at all. We know that a Didine bird and a gigantic rail existed on Réunion, but no bones are yet known of these. I think, like Professor Schlegel, that Leguat's figure and description cannot be meant for a Flamingo and that they prove the former existence of a gigantic ralline bird in Mauritius.

The figure is made up from Leguat's description. The bill is drawn like that of a gigantic moorhen, and so are the feet.

Habitat : Mauritius.

ALCA IMPENNIS L.

THE GREAT AUK.

(PLATE 38.)

"*Penguin*" Hore, in Hakluyt's Coll. Voyages III p. 129 (Ed. 1600—ex Hore).

Anser Magelanicus s. Pinguinus Worm, Museum Wormianum, Lib. III, Cap. 19, p. 300, 301 (1655—Figured from a specimen from the Faröe Islands).

"*Penguin*" Willoughby, Orn. Lib. III p. 242 pl. 65 (1676).

"*Northern Penguin*" Edwards, Nat. Hist. Uncommon B. etc., III p. 147 pl. 147 (1750—First good coloured plate, from a specimen from Newfoundland).

"*Geyervogel*" Linnaeus, Fauna Suecica p. 43 no. 119 (1746).

Alca impennis Linnaeus, Syst. Nat. Ed. X p. 130 (1758—Ex fauna Sueciva no. 119, Mus. Worm. l.c., Willoughby l.c., and Edwards l.c.); Linnaeus, Syst. Nat. Ed. XII, I, p. 210 (1766); Naumann, Nat. Voy. Deutschl. XII p. 630 pl. 337 (1844); Dresser, B. Europe VIII p. 563, pl. 620 (1880); Seebohm, Hist. Brit. B. III p. 371 (1885).

Alca borealis Forster, Syn. Cat. Brit. B. p. 29 (1817—nomen nudum).

Plautus impennis Brünnich, Zool. Fundamenta p. 78 (1772); Baird, Brewer and Ridgway, Water Birds N. Amer., II p. 467 (1884); Grant, Cat. B. Brit. Mus. XXVI p. 563 (1898).

FOR FULL DESCRIPTIONS, LITERATURE, HISTORY, LIST OF REMAINS, SEE:—

Japetus Steenstrup: Bidrag til Geirfuglens Naturhistorie etc., Kjöbenhavn (Copenhagen) 1857 (In Naturh-Forening. Vidensk. Meddel. 1855, nos. 3-7).

Alfred Newton: Abstract of Mr. Wolley's Researches in Iceland respecting the Gare-fowl. (In Ibis, 1861, pp. 374-399).

William Preyer: Ueber Plautus impennis. (In Journal f. Orn. 1862 pp. 110-124, 337-356.

Alfred Newton: The Gare-fowl and its Historians. (In Natural History Review XII, 1865 pp. 467-488); id. in Encycl. Britannica Ed. IX vol. III; id. Dict. B. p. 220-221.

Wilhelm Blasius: Zur Geschichte von *Alca impennis*. Journ. f. Orn. 1884 pp. 58-176.

Symington Grieve: The Great Auk, or Garefowl. Its History, Archaeology, and Remains. London 1885; Supplem. note on the Great Auk; in Trans. Edinburgh Field Nat. Soc. (1897) p. 238-273.

Wilhelm Blasius: Der Riesenalk, Alca impennis L. In the New Edition of Naumann "Naumann, Naturg. d. Vögel Mitteleuropas") Vol. XII p. 169-208, plates 17, 17a-17d (1903).

PROBABLY the first mention of Great Auks is that in André Thevet's book "Les singularitéz de la France antarctique . . . ," Anvers 1558, where a large bird was mentioned under the name of "Aponars," "Apponatz" or "Aponath." But evidently this name covered several other sea-birds, and it is at least doubtful if it was solely applied to the Great Auk. The same applies to the remarks by Jacques Cartier, as translated in R. Hakluyt's collection of voyages. On the other hand there is no doubt that the "Penguin" mentioned by Robert Hore in 1536 (Hakluyt, Collection of Voyages III, p. 129—1600, and other Editions) was actually the Great Auk. In fact "Penguin" has been the name usually applied to the Great Auk and is even now used for it by the French, while in most other languages it has been transferred, from an early date, to the Antarctic flightless birds, the *Spheniscidae*.

All the first reports are from Newfoundland and thereabout, and even Clusius (Exoticorum libri decem, Lib. V, p. 103—1605), who gives a rather poor but perfectly recognizable figure, describes it first (p. 103) as a native of America, under the name of "Mergus Americanus." Later on, however, in the "Auctarium," on p. 367, he mentions it, on the authority of Henricus Hojerus, as found in the Faröe Islands, under the name "Goirfugel." Hojerus was also the authority for the account given in Nieremberg, Hist. Nat., etc., p. 215 (1635). The first comparatively good figure was published in 1655, in the "Museum Wormianum," on p. 301, from a specimen brought alive from the Faröe Islands. Curiously enough the figure shows a white ring round the neck, which no Great Auk, of course, possesses.

Linnaeus, when first bestowing a scientific name on the Great Auk, in 1758, l.c., gave the following short diagnosis and references:—

> "Alca rostro compresso—ancipiti sulcato, macula ovata utrinque ante oculos. Fn. Svec. 119.
>
> Anser magellanicus. Worm. mus. 300 t. 301.
>
> Penguin. Will. ornith. 244 t. 65 Edw. av. 147 t. 147.
>
> *Habitat in* Europa *arctica*."

From referring to the literature he quotes, there can, of course, be no doubt as to what species he refers.

The most detailed descriptions are probably those given in the New Edition of Naumann (see above), where also a list of literature and figures is given, fully seven folio pages long! As regards the difference in the sexes little is known, because very few specimens exist of which the sex has been ascertained. We find, however, some with the grooves and ridges on the bill more marked, and the grooves purer white, while others have the grooves of a dirtier white and less strongly developed; as these latter are apparently mostly smaller, I think they must be females, the former males In this case my two specimens would be females, and the one now in Professor Koenig's possession an adult male. Probably somewhat similar seasonal changes took place as in *Alca torda*, and Professor Blasius (l.c.) has described them. It must, however, be remembered, that the date of capture is known of but a few examples, and that by far the majority of all those that exist in collections have been killed in spring, on their breeding-places.

Nobody can doubt that the Great Auk is extinct. The last specimens were obtained on Eldey, near Iceland, in 1844, and the seas and islands where the great bird used to live are frequented by vessels every year. It is true that a certain Lorenz Brodtkorb told that in April, 1848, he saw four Great Auks, of which he shot one, near the Varanger Fjord, east of the North-Cape, but Professor Newton and Wolley have, in 1855, had an interview with Brodtkorb, and came to the conclusion that he saw and shot the Great Northern Diver. This is the more likely to be the case, as the occurrence north of the Arctic Circle is as yet uncertain, the finding of Great Auks both on the island of Disco (west-coast of Greenland) and on Grimsey and Mevenklint on the north coast of Iceland being open to doubt.

From sub-fossil and prehistoric finds, we know that the Great Auk formerly inhabited Norway and Sweden, Denmark, with Seeland, Sejerö and Havnö, the British Islands (Cleadon Hills in County Durham, Scotland, Ireland), the east coast of North America from Labrador to Florida.

In historic times we know of the occurrence on the islands near Labrador, Greenland—where it certainly used to breed on the east coast, but was probably only of rare and exceptional occurrence on the west coast—Iceland, the Faröe Islands, Fair Island between the Orkney and Shetland Islands (doubtful), Orkneys (Papa Westra), St. Kilda, Skye, and Waterford Harbour in Ireland. But as breeding stations within historic times the following only are absolutely certain:—

1. Funk Islands near Newfoundland.
2. Iceland (Geirfuglasker, Grimsey, Eldey).
3. Faröe Islands.
4. St. Kilda.
5. Orkney Islands.

While we know of regular occurrence and may assume that the bird has been breeding on the north and west side of Newfoundland, and in east Greenland (opposite Iceland).

The remains of the Great Auk and its eggs in collections are more numerous than one would think, considering the enormous prices paid for mounted specimens and eggs. There are at present known 79 or 80 skins, 26 or 27 skeletons, a great quantity of detached bones, and about 73 eggs.

I HAVE IN MY MUSEUM:

1. One adult female, formerly in the collection of the late Comte de Riocour at Vitry-le-François, in France. I bought this specimen from the late Alphonse Boucard, together with the bulk of the birds of the Riocour collection. It is evidently an adult female, having the white lines on the bill not very much developed, and showing a distinct grey tinge on the flanks. This shade is present in both my Great Auks; the feathers of the flanks, just under the wing, are nearly white, with a conspicuous, very light grey border. This grey tinge is present in all females, but appears to be absent in adult males. My bird is apparently in worn breeding plumage. As it was not very well mounted and the feet slightly damaged, I had it reduced to a "skin."

2. Another adult female. I purchased this from Mr. Rowland Ward, who had it from Mr. Leopold Field in London, in 1897. According to a letter, dated Paris le 20 Jan., 1890, written by the late A. Boucard, who sold it in that year to Mr. Field, the history is as follows: "This bird was captured in Iceland in 1837, did first belong to Mr. Eimbeck of Brunswick and afterwards in the collection of Mr. Bruch from Mayence." We must accept this information by the late A. Boucard as correct, though it is difficult to understand that in the most painstaking and exact list of remains of the Great Auk, by Prof. Wilhelm Blasius of Braunschweig, or anywhere else, no mention is made of a specimen in the possession of the late Eimbeck, or the late Bruch. Moreover, we have no explanation where this Auk has been between the time of Bruch's death and 1890, when Boucard sold it to Mr. Field in London.

This specimen has been described as "immature," but this is a mistake. Evidently it arose from some white speckles being visible on the neck *in the photograph* (see Symington Grieve, Trans. Edinburgh Field Nat. and Micros. Society, explanation to plate III, on page 269). The specimen itself, however, shows no white speckles, but only worn feathers, out of which the illusion arose in the photograph. This error has also been transferred to the admirable treatise on the Great Auk in the New Edition of Naumann. The grey shade "on the body lower than the wing," mentioned by Mr. Symington Grieve, is not a sign of immaturity, but appears in all adult females, though it is said to be absent in males.

Some years ago an extraordinary rumour was current in Germany about the Great Auk in the Brehm collection; it was said to have been exchanged by the widow of Pastor C. L. Brehm for a rare Dresden cup, and that its present resting-place was unknown. I do not know who invented this story, or how it arose, but suffice it to say, that the Auk which was in the Brehm collection was sold to the late King of Italy, in 1868 or 1869. The business was concluded by Dr. Otto Finsch, and the money was used for the benefit of a brother of the late Dr. A. E. Brehm, as it had been the wish of his father, Pastor Brehm. The specimen was re-stuffed by the late taxidermist Schwerdtfeger in Bremen and forwarded to a professor in Florence. It was kept for years at the "Veneria Reale," and recently, when the collection at that castle was dissolved, was placed in the Museum at Rome. It is one of the finest Great Auks known.

AESTRELATA CARIBBAEA (CARTE).

(PLATE 37.)

Procellaria jamaicensis Bancroft, Zoological Journal V, p. 81 (1835—Nomen nudum !).

Pterodroma caribbaea Carte, P.Z.S. 1866, p. 93, pl. 10 ("Blue Mountains in insula Jamaica").

Aestrelata caribbaea Giglioli & Salvadori, Ibis 1869, p. 66.

Fulmarus caribbaeus Gray, Handlist B. III, p. 107 (1871).

Aestrelata jamaicensis Ridgway, Man. N. Am. B., p. 67; Cory, Cat. West-Indian B., p. 84 (1892).

Oestrelata jamaicensis Salvin, Cat. B. Brit. Mus, p. 403 (1896).

IT is surprising that the name *jamaicensis* has generally been adopted for this species, as Bancroft gave no description whatever. The first description is that of Carte, in 1866, which is as follows:—"Head, neck, back, and wings of a uniform dark sooty brown; vertex and external webs of the primaries a shade or so darker; abdominal feathers and under tail-coverts a shade or two lighter than those of the back; upper tail-coverts and basal portion of tail-feathers of a light grey or dirty white. The light-coloured patch on the rump is conspicuous when the wings are expanded, but completely concealed when they are closed. Irides dark hazel. Tarsi, toes, webs, and nails jet-black.

"Length about 12¾ inches; expanse of wings 34 inches; length from carpal joint to tip of first primary 10¾ inches; length of bill, measured from gape, 1⅝ inches; length of nasal tubes $\frac{5}{16}$ inch; length of interval between nostrils and commencement of apical curve of upper mandible ¼ inch; length of tarsi 1$\frac{5}{16}$ inches; length of toes, outer and middle, sub-equal 2 inches; length of inner toe 1⅝ inches. First and second primaries sub-equal, and about ½ inch longer than the third. Tail about 4½ inches long and round at extremity. The closed wings extend about 1½ inches beyond the tail. Hallux small, and in shape triangular."

"With respect to the habits of the bird, Mr. March has most kindly furnished me with the following interesting details:—

"It is a night-bird, living in burrows in the marly clefts of the mountains at the east and north-east end of the island. The burrows form a gallery 6 to 10 feet long, terminating in a chamber sufficiently commodious to accommodate the pair; from this they sally forth at night, flying over the sea in search of food (fishes), returning before dawn. It is often seen on moonlight nights and at sunrise running about the neighbourhood of its domicile, and sometimes crossing the road, regardless of the labourers going to their work. I know nothing of its nidification."

The type of "*Pterodroma caribbaea*" is preserved in the Dublin Museum, and three specimens are in the British Museum. This bird is one of the rarest in collections, and all modern collectors have failed to obtain specimens. Quite recently (1906) Mr. B. Hyatt Verrill published a pamphlet entitled "Additions to the Avifauna of Dominica." In this unpaginated essay he said under the heading "*Aestrelata jamaicensis*": "Not uncommon (on Dominica), but seldom seen during the day. Breeds at La Bime, Pointe Guignarde, and Lance Bateaux, as well as at Morne Rouge and Scott's Head. In many of the above localities the musky odour of these birds is very pronounced when passing the cliffs, wherein they breed, on a calm evening. At dusk they may often be seen flying about the cliffs in company with myriads of bats that spend the day in the fissures and crevices. They are very difficult to procure, and although shot at repeatedly only two specimens have been obtained."

From all former evidence we might have well considered this species to be extinct, but if Mr. Verrill's statement is correct it would be far from exterminated. I do not, however, know if the Dominica specimens have been compared with Jamaica examples, and if Mr. Verrill's determination (apparently made on Dominica) is therefore correct.

Habitat : Jamaica.

AESTRELATA HASITATA (KUHL).

Procellaria hasitata (sic) Kuhl, Beitr. z. Zool. Temminck, Pl. Col. 416 (1826); Gould, B Australia VII, pl. 47 (1845).

Procellaria diabolica Lafresnaye, Rev. Zool. 1844, p. 168.

Procellaria meridionalis Lawrence, Ann. Lyceum N.Y. IV, p. 475 (1848—), V, pl. 15, p. 220 (1852).

Procellaria rubritarsi Newton, Zoologist 1852, p. 3692 (ex Gould's MS., descr. nulla).

Aestrelata haesitata Bonaparte, Compt. Rend. XLII, p. 768 (1856), Elliot, B. N. America II. pl. 60, fig. 1 (1868); Rothsch. & Hart, New Edition of "Naumann" XII, p. 20 (1903).

Aestrelata diabolica Bonap., Consp. Av. II, p, 189 (1855).

Oestrelata haesitata Newton, Ibis 1870, p. 277; Dresser, B. Europe VIII, p. 545, pl. 618 (1880); Stevens, B. of Norfolk, III, p. 361, pl. 4 (1890); Salvin, Cat. B. Brit. Mus. XXV, p. 403 (1896).

MR. SAUNDERS describes this bird as follows: "The adult has the crown and nape dark brown, hind-neck white, cheeks and ear-coverts greyish; mantle dark brown; upper tail-coverts white; central tail-feathers chiefly brownish-black, the rest more or less white on their basal portions but broadly edged with brown; forehead and under-parts white; bill black; legs and feet dusky-yellow. Length 16 inches, wing 11·3 inches. The immature bird is believed to be mottled with brown on the forehead and to be duller in tint on the upper parts."

Though evidently not quite extinct, it seems certain that the fate of this bird is sealed. In former times it used to breed in great numbers on several of the West Indian Islands: Hayti, Guadeloupe, and Dominica. Its last breeding place was the Morne au Diable or Morne Diablotin on Dominica. There it was searched for in vain by Colonel Feilden, in 1889, who wrote a lengthy article about it in the "Trans. Norfolk and Norwich Nat. Society V. p. 24-39. Mr. Selwyn Branch again, ten years later, ascended La Morne au Diable, and found the old breeding places deserted. The "Manicou," evidently an introduced North-American Opossum, Mongoose and rats had entirely extirpated the "Diable."

Two-and-a-half centuries ago Père du Tertre found this Petrel breeding on Guadeloupe, and Père Labat, about forty years later, found it in great numbers, and gave a long, graphic description of it in his "Nouveau Voyage aux isles de l'Amérique" (Edit. I, Vol. II, pp. 349-353). These birds were then known as the "Diable" or "Diablotin," and their flesh was highly esteemed, and they were even salted and exported to Martinique and other French islands in great numbers.

In 1876 Mr. F. A. Ober searched already unsuccessfully for our birds.

It seems that the disturbance and destruction on their breeding places has scattered these Petrels about, for specimens have at various times been taken on the coast of Florida and Virginia, and even as late as 1893 and 1895, inland of the State of New York on Oneida Lake, in Ulster County, Vermont and Ontario; moreover, a specimen has been killed in 1850 in Norfolk, England, and an example in the Museum of Boulogne is said to have been killed in the neighbourhood of that town.

In an undated and unpaginated pamphlet, received last year in Europe, Mr. A. Hyatt Verrill informs us that this bird is "not uncommon on the fishing grounds and in Martinique and Guadeloupe channels," and that he took a specimen in September, 1904. This statement requires confirmation.

In collections this bird is very rare. I have the male (in moult) which was caught on August 28th, 1893 on Oneida Lake, in the State of New York.

Habitat : West Indian Islands.

HEMIPHAGA SPADICEA (LATH.)

(PLATE 21.)

Chestnut-shouldered Pigeon Latham, Gen. Syn. Suppl. II, add. p. 375 (1802—Norfolk Island).

Columba spadicea Latham, Ind. Orn., Suppl. p. LX, No. 7 (1802—Norfolk Island); Temminck and Knip, Pigeons, II, p. 1, pl. 1 (1808—" Friendly Islands."—Errore).

Columba gigas Ranzani, Elementi di Zool. III, 1, p. 223 (1821—" Friendly Islands."—Errore).

Columba princeps Vigors, P.Z.S. 1833, p. 78 (Australia—errore).

Columba leucogaster Wagler, Syst. Av., Columba spec. 12 1827—Norfolk Island).

Hemiphaga spadicea Salvadori, Cat. B. Brit. Mus. XXI, p. 238 (1893).

THE Norfolk Island Pigeon, *Hemiphaga spadicea spadicea*, is very similar to the New Zealand Pigeon, *Hemiphaga spadicea novaezealandiae*, but differs in having the hind-neck coppery or metallic green, sharply defined from the chestnut back, the wings and upper wing-coverts more greyish, less greenish, also the lower back and rump somewhat more greyish.

As 'far as we know this pigeon was only found on Norfolk Island, the locality " Australia " being doubtless erroneous. Like so many other birds it became extinct on Norfolk Island, probably more than half a century ago.

There are evidently quite a number of specimens in various museums, many of which have never been recorded. I am aware of the following examples :

1 in the British Museum (Cat. B. Brit. Mus. XXI, p. 238).
3 in the Liverpool Museum (Bull. Liverp. Mus. I, p. 35).
1 in my own collection (Proc. IV, Orn. Congress, p. 215).
1 in Philadelphia, U.S. America (Cassin, U.S. Expl. Exp. B, p. 225).
1 in Frankfurt a.M. (Hartert, Kat. Vogelsamml., p. 189).
1 in Wiesbaden (Lampe, Jahrb. Nassau Ver. 58).
1 in Bremen (Hartlaub, Verz. Museum, p. 98).
1 in Lisbon (Forbes and Rob., Bull. Liverp. Mus. II, p. 130).
1 in Leyden (Schlegel, Mus. Pays-Bas).
1 in Vienna (Ibis 1860, p. 422).
1 in Naples, seen by myself.
1 in Milan, examined by myself.

The specimen at Tring was bought at the auction of the "Cumberland Museum" at Distington.

ALECTROENAS NITIDISSIMA (SCOP.)

(PLATE 22.)

Pigeon hollandais Sonnerat, Voy. Ind. Orient. II, p. 175, pl. 101 (1782).
Hackled Pigeon Latham, Syn. B. II, 2, p. 641, No. 36 (1783).
Columba nitidissima Scopoli, Del. Flor. and Faun. Insubr. II, p. 93, No. 89 (1786) (ex Sonnerat).
Columba franciae Gmelin, Syst. Nat. I, 2, p. 779, No. 51 (1788). (ex Sonnerat).
Columba botanica Bonnaterre, Enc. Méth. I, p. 233 (1790).
Ramier périssé Levaillant, Ois. d'Afr. VI, p. 74, pl. 267 (1808).
Columba jubata Wagler, Syst. Av., *Columba*, sp. 22 (1827).
Alectroenas nitidissima G. R. Gray, List Gen. B., p. 58 (1840).
Alectroenas franciae Reichenbach, Syn. Av., *Columbariae*, p. 2, f. 1302 (1847).
Columbigallus franciae Des Murs, Encycl. d'Hist. Nat., Ois. VI., p. 31, (1854 ?).
Ptilopus nitidissimus Schlegel and Pollen, Rech. Faun. Madag., p. 159 (1868).
Alectroenas nitidissimus G. R. Gray, Hand-list II, p. 228, No. 9164 (1870).
Alectoroenas nitidissimus A. Newton, P. Z. S. 1879, pp. 2-4.

SONNERAT'S original description, translated into English, is as follows: "It is much larger than the European Woodpigeon ; the feathers of the head, neck and breast are long, narrow, and end in a point. These feathers are rather curiously constructed, they have the polish, brilliancy, and feel of a cartilaginous blade. I could not, with the aid of a lens, distinguish whether these blades were formed by the conglomeration of the barbules, but we may take it for granted that they are constituted in a like manner to the wing appendages of the Bohemian Waxwing and the cartilaginous blades of Sonnerat's Jungle Fowl. The eye is surrounded by naked skin of a deep red ; the back, the wings and the belly are of a dark blue ; the rump and tail are of a very bright carmine red ; the beak and iris are of the same colour, and the feet are black."

Undoubtedly quite extinct. Only three specimens are known of this bird : one in Edinburgh, one in Paris, and one in Mauritius. Some bones were collected by the Rev. H. H. Slater.

Habitat : Mauritius.

ALECTROENAS (?) RODERICANA (MILNE-EDWARDS).

Columba rodericana Milne-Edwards, Ann. Sc. Nat. (5) XIX art. 3, p. 16, pl. 12, ff. 1, 1a, 1b, 1c (1874).

THE original description of the sternum is as follows :—" It belongs to a species small in size, barely as large as *T. tympanistria*, but evidently much better built for flight. In fact the most striking characters of this sternum are the large size of the bouclier, the large size of the lateral notches, and the shape of the keel, whose anterior angle is not much produced in front. The coracoidal grooves are large and only slightly oblique. The lateral branches detach themselves from the bone in front of the costal facets—they are very widely spread, and stretch more directly outwards than in the remainder of the species of the family. The lower lateral branches are equally divergent, and the median blade of the posterior edge is remarkable from its enlargement. The keel is moderately prominent, its anterior angle is much rounded, and does not reach the level of the episternal apophysis, as is the case, as a rule, in the pigeons. All these peculiarities, to which must be added the general flattening of the bone which is hardly at all sloped like a roof, separate the pigeon of Rodriguez very widely, not only from *Erythroena* and *Turtur*, but also from *Vinago*. In its shape in general, by the little pronounced keel and the direction of the latter, this sternum presents certain analogies to the essentially arboreal species such as those of the genus *Carpophaga*, but they all differ in having the space for the costal facets on the sides of the sternum much more extended, the superior lateral branches larger, and the latter arising further back, so that the lateral notches are smaller. Up to the present I do not know any genus of the family of *Columbidae* in which the sternum can at all be likened to that found recently in Rodriguez, and therefore in all probability this fossil remainder is of yet another vanished species, which I propose to call *Columba rodericana*." (Translated.)

It is probable that Milne-Edwards's *C. rodericana* belonged to the genus *Alectroenas*, and was the representative on Rodriguez of the *Alectroenas nitidissima* of Mauritius. 1 humerus in the Tring Museum.

Habitat : Rodriguez.

NESOENAS SALVAD.

SOLES normal, not very broad, only the hind toe with the skin prominently expanded on the sides. First primary about equal to the sixth. Tail entirely rufous, composed of twelve feathers.

NESOENAS MAYERI (PREVOST).

(PLATE 3, FIG. 3.)

Columba mayeri Prévost & Knip, Pigeons II, pl. 60 (1843).
Columba meyeri Schlegel & Pollen, Rech. Faun. Mad. p. 111, pl. 36 (1868).
Peristera meyeri G. R. Gray, Gen. B. III App. p. 24 (1849).
Carpophaga meyeri G. R. Gray, fide Bp. Consp. Av. II p. 45 (1854).
Trocaza meyeri Bonaparte, Consp. Av. II p. 45 (1854).
Trocaza meijeri Pollen, N.T.D. I p. 318 (1863).
Nesoenas mayeri Salvadori, Cat. Birds Brit. Mus. vol. XXI p. 327 (1893).

THE following is the description by Salvadori in the "Catalogue of Birds":—"Head, neck and underparts pale pink, fading into whitish towards the forehead, cheeks and upper throat, and passing into rather darker pink on the mantle; remainder of the upper back and the entire wings brown, with a slight shade of olive and rufous; lower back and rump greyish, the latter mottled with chestnut; upper tail coverts and tail cinnamon, the outer tail feathers fading into buff on the outer webs and towards the tips; undertail-coverts pink, like the mantle; undersurface of the wings ashy brown, slightly pale on the axillaries, and under wing-coverts iris yellow; bill yellow, shaded with red towards the base; legs red (fide Shelley). Total length about 15·5 inches, wing 8·5, tail 6·5, bill 0·86, tarsus 1·3."

In the live bird the pink soon fades away almost entirely, and the olive shade on the wings is strongly developed.

This bird was not found by the Rev. H. H. Slater, during his visit to Mauritius. As observed by Mons. Paul Carié (Ornis XII, p. 127), the idea that it is extinct is, however, incorrect, as it can still easily be procured, though it is rare. M. Georges Antelme, of Mauritius, possesses the eggs of this pigeon. That it still exists is also evident from two specimens which were sent to the Zoological Gardens, London, last year, and are still living there.

Habitat: Mauritius.

NESOENAS DUBOISI SP. NOV.

"*Pigeons sauvages d'un rouge roussastre*" Le Sieur D.B., Voyages aux Iles Dauphine ou Madagascar, etc., p. 171 (1674—Bourbon).

TALKING of Wild Pigeons, "Le Sieur D.B." tells us that there were on the island of Bourbon "others of a russet red colour, a little larger than European pigeons, with the beak larger, red at base near the head, the eyes surrounded by a fiery colour, as in the pheasants. At a certain season they are so fat 'qu'on ne leur voit point de croupion;' they taste very good."

This passage cannot be meant for a turtle-dove, but the description of the bill and surrounding of the eyes shows that it refers to a form allied to *Nesoenas mayeri*. The latter, however, is not entirely russet red, but the head, neck, underside and back are creamy white, washed with a greyish-rose colour. Therefore the bird mentioned by Le Sieur D.B. was evidently a representative of *N. mayeri* or Bourbon. I name it in memory of Monsieur Dubois, who was the author of the Voyages of the "Sieur D.B."

Habitat: Bourbon or Réunion.

ECTOPISTES SWAINS.

Ectopistes Swainson, Zoological Journal III p. 362 (1827—Partim! *Columba speciosa* and *C. migratoria* mentioned as types, but ten years later the genus *Ectopistes* was restricted to *C. migratoria* by the same author).

TAIL very long and excessively cuneate, the central rectrices sharply pointed. First primary of the wing longest. Tarsus very short, in front half covered with feathers. Now, only the Passenger Pigeon is included in this genus, while formerly the *Zenaidura carolinensis* auct. used to be associated with it.

ECTOPISTES MACROURA (L.)

PASSENGER PIGEON.

Columba macroura Linnaeus, Syst. Nat. Ed. X p. 164 (1758—Ex Catesby, Carolina I p. 23, pl. 23 [1754]. "Habitat in Canada, hybernat in Carolina." Regarding the necessity of accepting this name see Bangs, Proc. Biol. Soc. Washington XIX p. 42, and Auk 1906, pp. 474, 475. The conclusions of Messrs. Bangs and Allen are perfectly correct).

Columba canadensis Linnaeus, Syst. Nat. Ed. XII, p. 284 (1766—Ex Brisson, Orn. I p. 118. "Habitat in Canada." Cf. note of Salvadori, Cat. B. Brit. Mus. XXI, p. 369).

Columba migratoria Linnaeus, Syst. Nat. Ed. XII p. 285 (Ex Frisch, pl. 142, Kalm., Brisson I, p. 100, Catesby. "Habitat in America Septentrionali copiosissima . . ."); Wilson, Amer. Orn. I p. 102, pl. XLIX (1808); Temminck & Knip, Pigeons I, seconde fam., pls. 48, 49 (1808-11); Andubon, Orn. Biogr. I, p. 319 (1831); Baird, Brewer & Ridgway, Hist. N.A.B., Land-Birds III, p. 368, pl. 57, 4 (1874).

Pigeon de Passage Buffon, Hist. Nat. Ois. II, p. 527 (1771).

Tourterelle du Canada Daubenton, Pl. Enl. 176.

Columba Histrio P.L.S. Müller, Natursyst. Suppl. p. 134 (1776—ex Buffon).

Columba ventralis id., l.c. p. 134 (1776—ex Buffon).

Ectopistes migratoria Swainson, Zool. Journal III, p. 362 (1827); Gould, B. Europe, pl. 247 (1848); Coues, B. North-West, p. 387 (1874); Maynard, B. E. North America, p. 335 (1881).

Trygon migratoria Brehm, Handb. Naturg. Vög. Deutschl., p. 495 (1831).

Ectopistes migratorius G. R. Gray, Gen. B. II, p. 471 (1844); Brewster, Auk 1889, pp. 286-291; Bendire, Life-History N. Amer. B., p. 132; Salvadori, Cat. B. Brit. Mus. XXI, p. 370; Proc. Delaware Valley Ornith. Club II, p. 17 (1898); A.O.U. Check-List (Ed. II) p. 120, No. 315 (1895); Wintle, B. Montreal, p. 51 (1896); Minot, B. New England, p. 395 (1895); Auk 1903, p. 66.

Trygon gregaria Brehm, Vogelfang, p. 258 (1855).

IT is true that Linnaeus' diagnosis of his *Columba macroura* is very short, reading, as it does, as follows: "Columba cauda cuneiformi longa, pectore purpurascente." These words, however, are clearly taken from Catesby, who gives an excellent figure and description, as is also the "Habitat," viz.:

"Habitat in Canada, hybernat in Carolina," though Linnaeus first quotes "Edwards 15, pl. 15," where an entirely different bird is described and figured. (Cf. Bangs, l.c.)

The Passenger Pigeon in former times occurred throughout North America in great abundance, from the Atlantic to the great Central Plains, and from the Southern States, where it rarely occurred, north to at least 62° northern latitude. Being a migrant, this bird used to migrate southwards after the breeding season, and to return to their homes in spring, but it also shifted its quarters according to the abundance or scarcity of food, like our Pigeons. Sometimes incredible numbers flocked together. Such stupendous flights have been described independently by Audubon, Wilson and others. In 1813 Audubon says that during his whole journey from Hardensburg to Louisville, fifty-five miles, countless masses of Pigeons continued to pass over, and also did so during the three following days. "At times they flew so low, that multitudes were destroyed, and for many days the entire population seemed to eat nothing else but Pigeons." Where they roosted in millions, the dung soon covered the ground and destroyed the grass and undergrowth, limbs and even small trees broke down from the weight of the birds. "One of the breeding places visited by Wilson, not far from Shelbyville, Kentucky, stretched through the forest in nearly a north and south direction. This was several miles in breadth, and upwards of forty miles in extent. In this immense tract nearly every tree was furnished with nests wherever there were branches to accommodate them. He was informed by those who sought to plunder the nests of the squabs, that the noise in the woods was so great as to terrify their horses, and that it was difficult for one person to hear another speak. The ground was strewed with broken limbs, eggs and young Pigeons. Hawks were sailing about in great numbers, while from twenty feet upwards to the tops of the trees there was a perpetual tumult of crowding and fluttering multitudes of Pigeons, their wings resounding like thunder, and mingled with the frequent crash of falling trees. In one instance he counted ninety nests in a single tree."

It is only natural that man took advantage of such vast multitudes, and that they were killed in great numbers, for food, and, maybe, sometimes wantonly destroyed. Yet it is difficult to understand what brought on their total destruction, as their power of flight was great, and their vision remarkably keen. In 1874 Messrs. Baird, Brewer and Ridgway considered them still common birds, though "their abundance in large extents of the country had been very sensibly reduced." At that time "in the New England States and in the more cultivated part of the country, these birds no longer bred in large communities. The instance near Montpelier, in 1849, is the only marked exception that has come within my knowledge. They now breed in isolated pairs, their nests being scattered through the woods and seldom near one another." In 1895, in the A.O.U. check-list, the authors say: "Breeding range now mainly restricted to portions of the Canadas and the northern borders of the United States, as far west as Manitoba and the Dakotas."

At the present time the Passenger Pigeon seems to have entirely disappeared, a small flock in an aviary apparently being all that is left of it alive. Mr. James H. Fleming, of Toronto, kindly sends me the following notes, which I think are of the greatest interest :—

"The disappearance of the Passenger Pigeon in Ontario dates back at least forty years, though as late as 1870 some of the old roosts were still frequented, but the incredible flocks, of which so much has been said, had gone long before that date, and by 1880 the pigeon was practically exterminated, not only in Ontario, but over the greater part of its old range. There are however occasional records of birds taken, for some years later. An immature bird taken September 9, 1887, in Chester County, Pennsylvania, is said to be the last for that part of the State[1]; a bird, also immature, is in my collection, taken in December, 1888, at Montreal, Quebec. There are other Montreal records of the same date,[2] but with the exception of one taken at Tadousac, July 26, 1889,[3] these are the last Quebec records of birds actually taken. In Ontario two were taken at Toronto in 1890, on September 20, and October 11, both immature females, the latter is in my collection, as is an adult female taken by Mr. Walter Brett, at Riding Mountain, Manatoba, May 12, 1892, one of a pair seen. I also have an adult male taken at Waukegon, Illinois, December 19, 1892. I was in New York in the latter part of November, 1892, and was then assured by Mr. Rowland, a well known taxidermist, that he had recently seen several barrels of pigeons that had been condemned as unfit for food; they had come to New York from Indian Territory, and I believe had had their tails pulled out to permit tighter packing. Mr. William Brewster has recorded the sending of several hundred dozens of pigeons to the Boston market in December of the same year, and in January, 1893; these were also from Indian Territory[4]; these are the last records we have of the Passenger Pigeon as anything more than a casual migrant. The records ceased after this till 1898, when three birds were taken at points widely apart, an adult male at Winnipegosis, Manatoba, on April 14,[5] an immature male at Owensboro, Kentucky, on July 27, now in the Smithsonian Institution, and another immature bird taken at Detroit, Michigan, on September 14, now in my collection; these are the last records that can be based on specimens.

"In 1903 I published a list including sight records, one as late as May, 1902; this latter is possibly open to doubt, but the ones I gave for 1900 are, I feel confident, correct, as the birds were seen more than once and by different observers. For all practical purposes, the close of the Nineteenth Century saw the final extinction of the Passenger Pigeon in a wild state, and there remained only the small flock, numbering in 1903 not more than a dozen, that had been bred in captivity by Prof. C. O. Whitman, of Chicago; these birds are the descendants of a single pair, and have long ago ceased to breed. It was in an effort to obtain fresh blood for this flock that I started a newspaper enquiry that brought many replies, none of which could be substantiated as records of the Passenger Pigeon, and many referred to the Mourning Dove. I am aware that there has been lately wide-spread and persistent rumours of the return of the pigeons, but no rumour has borne investigation, and I feel that Prof. Whitman's small flock, now reduced (in 1906) to five birds, are the last representatives of a species around whose disappearance mystery and fable will always gather."

---

1. Proceedings of the Delaware Valley Ornithological Club, II, 1898, 17.
2. Wintle, Birds of Montreal, 1896, 51.
3. In collection of Dr. J. Dwight, Jr.
4. Minot, Birds of New England, 1895, 395.
5. Auk, XX, 1903, 66.

FAMILY DIDIDAE.

INCLUDES very large and massively-built forms, agreeing with the *Columbidae* in the truncation of the angle of the mandible, but with the extremity of the cranial rostrum strongly hooked. They were totally incapable of flight, the wing-bones being small, the carina of the sternum aborted, and the caracoidal grooves shallow and separated from one another.

Two genera: *Didus* and *Pezophaps*.

DIDUS LINN.

SKULL with a very large and deeply hooked rostrum, and the nasal and maxillary processes of the praemaxilla converging anteriorly; the front region inflated into a sub-conical prominence of cancellous tissue. Neck and feet shorter than in the succeeding genus. Delto-pectoral crest of humerus distinct.

Two species: *Didus cucullatus and Didus solitarius*.

DIDUS CUCULLATUS (L.)

DODO.

(PLATES 24, 24A, 24B, 24C.)

Walchvoghel Van Neck, Voy., p. 7, pl. 2 (1601).
Walchvögel De Bry, Orient. Ind. pt. VIII, t. 11 (1606).
Gallinaceus gallus peregrinus Clusius, Exot. Libr. V p. 99 t. 100 (1605).
Dod-eersen or *Valgh-vogel* Herbert's travels 1st ed. (1634) t. page 212.
Cygnus cucullatus Nieremberg, Nat. p. 231 (with fig. ex. Clus.) (1635)
Dronte Bontius, Ind. Orient. t. p. 70 (1658).
Raphus Moehring, Av. gen. 57 (1752).
Dodo Edwards, Glean. Nat. Hist. III p. 179 pl. 296 (1757).
Struthio cucullatus Linn., S. N. I p. 155 No. 4 (1758).
Didus ineptus Linn., S. N. I p. 267 No. 1 (1766).

THE first description of this very remarkable bird was given in the account of the voyage of Admiral Jacob van Neck in 1598, which was published by Corneille Nicolas at Amsterdam in 1601. It is as follows:—"Blue parrots are very numerous there, as well as other birds; among which are a kind, conspicuous for their size, larger than our swans, with huge heads only half covered with skin as if clothed with a hood. These birds lack wings, in the place of which 3 or 4 blackish feathers protrude. The tail consists of a few soft incurved feathers, which are ash coloured. These we used to call 'Walghvögel,' for the reason that the longer and oftener they were cooked, the less soft and more insipid eating they became. Nevertheless their belly and breast were of a pleasant flavour and easily masticated."

In a large number of works on travel and voyages published in the 17th and 18th Centuries we find all sorts of notices about the Dodo, and numerous pictures of which I have given outline drawings. From these sources it appears that the Dodo became extinct about the end of the 17th Century, *i.e.*, 1680—1690. The causes of the extermination of this, perhaps the best known and most talked about of the recently extinct birds, are not far to seek. The total inability of flight, the heavy slow gait, and the utter fearlessness from long immunity from enemies, led to a continual slaughter for food by the sailors and others who came to and dwelt on Mauritius. But the final cause of the extermination of this and many other birds in the Mascarene Islands was probably the introduction of pigs, and also of the Ceylon Monkey. These animals increased enormously in numbers, ran wild in the woods, and soon destroyed all the eggs and young birds they could find.

It is strange that for many years after great attention had been paid to the *Dodo*, ornithologists differed conspicuously as to what family it and the other two Didine species belonged. Many asserted that it was a Struthious bird, in fact Linnaeus called it calmly *Struthio cucullatus*, while others just as forcibly declared it to be an abnormal Vulture. The truth is, that although the *Didunculus strigirostis* of Samoa, which was supposed to be its near representative, is not at all closely allied, yet the two species of *Didus* and *Pezophaps solitarius* form a group of very specialized pigeons.

THE FOLLOWING IS A LIST OF THE PAINTINGS REPRESENTING THE DODO.

1. *Vienna*, in the Library of the Emperor Francis. By Hufnagel, 1626, reproduced by von Frauenfeldt in his book, 1868.
2. *Berlin*. "Altes Museum," Cabinet 3, Division 2, No. 710. By Roelandt Savery, 1626.
3. *Sion House*. Duke of Northumberland. By John Goeimare, 1627.
4. *Vienna*. Kunsthistorisches Hofmuseum, formerly Belvedere. By Roelandt Savery, 1628.
5. *London*. Zoological Society, formerly Broderip. By Roelandt Savery, undated.
6. *Pommersfelden, Bavaria*. Count Schönborn, "Orpheus charming the Beasts." By Roelandt Savery, undated.
7. *Haag*. Mauritshuis. "Orpheus charming the Beasts." By Roelandt Savery.
8. *Stuttgart*. Formerly Dr. Seyffer, but sold at his death and since disappeared. By Roelandt Savery.
9. *London*. British Museum, formerly belonging to G. Edwards. Probably by Roelandt Savery.
10. *Emden*. Galerie der Gesellschaft für Bildende Kunst. "Orpheus charming the Beasts." By Roelandt Savery.
11. *Oxford*. Ashmolean Museum. By John Savery, 1651.
12. *Haarlem*. Dr. A. van der Willigen, Pz. By Pieter Holsteyn (1580-1662), not dated.
13. *Dresden*. Kgl. Gemälde-Galerie. "Circe and Ulysses." By C. Ruthart, 1666.
14. *Dresden*. Kgl. Gemälde-Galerie. "The Creation of the Animals." Supposed to be by Franz Francken (1581-1642), no date, and said to be by a different artist.

At least 2 *Mauritius Dodos* have been exhibited alive in Europe, one brought back by Van Neck in 1599, and which most likely served as the model for nearly all Roelandt Savery's pictures, and one exhibited in London in the year 1638, mentioned by Sir Hamon Lestrange. This is almost certainly the bird afterwards preserved in Tradescant's Museum (1656), and finally in Oxford (Ashmolean Museum), and probably served for the model of the supposed Savery picture in the British Museum.

The Dodo inhabited Mauritius.

NOTE.—*Didus nazarenus* Gmelin, based on the "Oiseau de Nazareth" of Cauche (Descr. de l'île de Madagascar, p. 130, ff, 1651) is evidently founded on a mistaken and partly fictitious description of a Dodo, or rather a mixture of that of the Dodo and a Cassowary. The name was, perhaps, also a mistake, derived from that of "*Oiseau de nausée*," which has a similar meaning as "Walghvogel."

Explanation of Plates of Dodo.

Plate 24.

This was taken from the picture by Roelandt Savery in Berlin, but the wings, tail and bill have been altered, partly from Pierre Witthoos' picture of the Bourbon Dodo, and partly from anatomical examination. The tail, however, appears to have been curled over the back in life, according to most authors.

Plate 24 (a).

Fig. 1. Reproduction in outline of the Dodo in Savery's Orpheus at Haag. Vide antea No. 7 in the List of Paintings.

Fig. 2. Outline of Dodo (and Pelican ?) in Ruthart's "Circe and Ulysses" at Dresden. Vide antea No. 13 in the List of Paintings.

Fig. 3. Outline of Dodo (and Pelican ?) in Frans Franckens (?) picture in Dresden. Vide antea No. 14 in the List of Paintings.

Plates 24 (b and c).

No. 1. Outline of Dodo in Roelandt Savery's picture at Berlin. Vide antea No. 2 in the List of Paintings.

No. 2. Outline of picture by Roelandt Savery in the British Museum. Vide antea No. 9 in the List of Paintings.

No. 3. Outline of Dodo in Jacob van Neck's Voyage, Plate 2 (1598).

No. 4. Outline of Roelandt Savery's Dodo, Vienna. Vide antea No. 4 in the List of Paintings.

No. 5. Outline of Dodo in Broeck's Voyage (Peter van Broeck's Voyage, 1617).

No. 6. Outline of Dodo in Piso's additions to Jacob Bontiu's Oriental Natural History, 1658.

No. 7. Outline of Dodo in Sir Thomas Herbert's Relation of some yeares Travels, 1626.

No. 8. Outline of Dodo in Clusius Exoticorum libri decem, 1605.

No. 9. Outline of Dodo in Joan Nievhof's Gedenkwaerdige Zee and Lantreize, 1682.

No. 10. Outline of Dodo in John Goeimare's picture at Sion House, 1627. Vide antea No. 3 in the List of Paintings.

No. 11. Outline of Dodo in Roelandt Savery's picture at Pommersfelden. Vide antea No. 6 in the List of Paintings.

No. 12. Outline of Dr. H. Schlegel's restoration of the Dodo in Transactions, &c., of the Amsterdam Academy, vol. 2, 1854.

No. 13. Outline of Dodo in Roelandt Savery's picture, Zoological Society, London. Vide antea No. 5 in the List of Paintings.

DIDUS SOLITARIUS (SELYS).

RÉUNION DODO.

(PLATES 25, 25A, 25B.)

Great Fowl Tatton, Voy. Castleton, Purchas his Pilgrimes, ed. (1625) I p. 331 (Bourbon or Réunion).

Dod-eersen Bontekoe, Journ. ofte gedenck. beschr. van de Ost. Ind. Reyse Haarlem(1646) p. 6.

Oiseau Solitaire Carré, Voy. Ind. Or. I p. 12 (1699).

Solitaire Voy. fait par Le Sieur D. B. (1674) p. 170.

Apterornis solitarius de Selys, Rev. Zool (1848) p. 293.

Didus apterornis Schlegel, Ook een Wordje over den Dodo p. 15 f. 2 (1854).

Pezophaps borbonica Bp., Consp. Av. II p. 2 (1854).

Ornithaptera borbonica Bp., Consp. Av. II. p. 2 (1854).

Didine Bird of the Island of Bourbon (Réunion) A. Newt. Tr. Zool. Soc. VI pp. 373-376, pl. 62 (1867).

Apterornis solitaria Milne-Edw., Ibis (1869) p. 272.

? Didus borbonica Schleg., Mus. P.B. Struthiones p. 3 (1873).

Solitaire of Réunion A. Newton, Enc. Brit. II p. 732 (1875).

THE Didine bird of Réunion was first mentioned by Mr. Tatton, the Chief Officer of Captain Castleton, in his account of their voyage given in "Purchas his Pilgrimes." His account is as follows:—

"There is store of land fowle both small and great, plenty of Doves, great Parrats, and such like; and a great fowle of the bignesse of a Turkie, very fat, and so short winged, that they cannot fly, being white, and in a manner tame: and so be all other fowles, as having not been troubled nor feared with shot. Our men did beat them down with sticks and stones. Ten men may take fowle enough to serve fortie men a day."

We then find frequent mention of this bird by Bontekoe in 5 separate treatises or editions, from 1646 to 1650, and by Carré in 1699. But the first more detailed description is given by the Sieur D. B. (Dubois) in 1674, which is as follows:—

"*Solitaires.* These birds are thus named because they always go alone. They are as big as a big goose and have white plumage, black at the extremity of the wings and of the tail. At the tail there are some feathers resembling those of the Ostrich. They have the neck long and the beak formed like that of the Woodcocks (he refers to the woodrails, *Erythromachus*—W.R.), but larger, and the legs and feet like those of Turkey-chicks. This bird betakes itself to running, only flying but very little. It is the best game on the Island."

It will be seen that, while Dubois says the wings and tail are black, Pierre Witthoos's picture, from which the accompanying plate was partly drawn, shows the wings yellow. This may either be due to Dubois' faulty description, or, what is much more probable, the bird brought to Amsterdam, which Witthoos painted, was somewhat albinistic. The bill in the picture by Witthoos shows a distinctly mutilated bill, evidently done by the bird's keeper to prevent being injured by the formidable hook of the untrimmed bill. In addition to two pictures (the one formerly in the possession of Mr. C. Dare, of Clatterford, in the Isle of Wight, and a second in Holland, both by Pieter Witthoos, painted about the year 1670), we know of this bird only the drawing given in Zaagman's edition of Bontekoe, 1646. In all these drawings the first four primaries point down and forward, which is probably owing to the injured condition of the specimen figured, so in the accompanying plate I had the wing drawn like the true Dodo's and the bill reconstructed.

Habitat: Island of Bourbon or Réunion.

Only known from the above-mentioned descriptions and two drawings. No specimens existing.

This bird became extinct between the years 1735 and 1801, because in the latter year Monsieur Bory St. Vincent made his scientific survey of the Island, and no such bird existed then ; while we know that Monsieur de la Bourdonnaye, who was governor of the Mascarene Islands from 1735 to 1746, sent one alive to one of the directors of the French East Indian Company. Of this, the second living specimen brought to Europe, we unfortunately have neither drawing nor history.

Explanation of Plates.

Plate 25.

Drawing of White Dodo from Pierre Witthoos' picture, the bill and tail being reconstructed from the model of the common Dodo.

Plate 25 (a).

Fig. 5. Outline of figure of White Dodo in the picture by Pieter Witthoos circa 1670 *vide supra.*

Fig. 8. Outline of Woodcut in Zaagman's edition of Bontekoe van Hoorn, 1646.

Fig. 7. Outline of figure of White Dodo in an edition of Plinius Secundus about 1643 but without date.

Fig. 4. Outline of Dr. H. Schlegel's reconstruction of the Réunion Dodo.

Plate 25 (b).

Drawing from description of the Sieur D.B. (Dubois), 1674.

PEZOPHAPS STRICKLAND & MELVILLE.

SKULL with a moderate rostrum, slightly hooked, and the nasal and maxillary processes of the praemaxillae diverging anteriorly; the frontal region flat with but little cancellous tissue. Coracoid stout. Manus armed with an ossified tuberosity. Neck and feet long. Delto-pectoral crest of humerus aborted.

This genus connects *Didus* with the *Columbidae*. The male is much larger than the female.

PEZOPHAPS SOLITARIUS (Gm.)

THE SOLITAIRE.

(PLATE 23, 25A, FIGS. 1, 2, 3.)

Solitaire Leguat, Voy. deux îles désertes Ind. Or. I pp. 98. 102 (1708).
Didus solitarius Gmelin, S. N. I p. 728, n. 2 (1788).
Pezophaps solitaria Strickland, the Dodo, &c., p. 46 (1848).
Didus nazarenus Bartl. (nec. Gmel.), P.Z.S. 1851, p. 284, pl. XLV.
Pezophaps minor Strickland, Contr. to Orn. 1852, p. 19 (♀).

THIS bird was first made known by Leguat in 1708, but some confusion seems to have arisen, owing to his applying the same name to them as the Sieur D.B. (Dubois) gave to the Bourbon Dodo in 1674. This is the original description:—

"The feathers of the males are of a brown-grey colour, the feet and beak are like a turkey's, but a little more crooked. They have scarce any tail, but their hind part covered with feathers is roundish, like the crupper of a hare. They are taller than turkeys. Their neck is straight, and a little longer in proportion than a turkey's when it lifts up his head. Its eye is black and lively, and its head without comb on cop. They never fly, their wings are too little to support the weight of their bodies; they serve only to beat themselves and flutter when they call one another. They will whirl about for twenty or thirty times together on the same side during the space of 4 or 5 minutes. The motions of their wings make then a noise very like that of a rattle, and one may hear it two hundred paces off. The bone of their wings grows greater towards the extremity, and forms a little round mass under the feathers as big as a musket ball. That and its beak are the chief defences of this bird. 'Tis very hard to catch in the woods, but easy in open places, because we run faster than they, and sometimes we approach them without much trouble. From March to September they are very fat, and taste admirably well, especially while they are young, some of the males weigh 45 pounds. The females are wonderfully beautiful, some fair, some brown. I call them fair, because they are the colour of fair hair; they have a sort of peak like a widow's, upon their breasts, which is of a dun colour. No one feather is straggling from the other all over their bodies, they being very careful to adjust themselves, and make them all even with their beaks. The feathers on their thighs are round like shells at the end, and being there very thick, have an agreeable effect. They have two risings on their craws, and the feathers are whiter there than the rest, which livelily represents the fine neck of a beautiful woman. They walk with so much stateliness and good grace that one cannot help admiring them and loving them, by which means their fine mien often saves their lives."

The unfortunate Solitaires, owing to the depredations by the pigs and monkeys introduced by the settlers, and the unceasing slaughter by the latter, became extinct between the years 1760 and 1780.

Of their habits we only have the accounts of Leguat :—

"Though these birds will sometimes very familiarly come up near enough to one, when we do not run after them, yet they will never grow tame, as soon as they are caught they shed tears, without crying, and refuse all manner of sustenance till they die.

When these birds build their nests, they choose a clean place, gather together some palm leaves for that purpose, and heap them up a foot and a half high from the ground, on which they sit. They never lay but one egg, which is much bigger than that of a goose. The male and female both cover it in their turns, and the young is not hatched till at 7 weeks end. All the while they are sitting upon it, or are bringing up their young one, which is not able to provide for itself in several months, they will not suffer any other bird of their species to come within two hundred yards round of the place. But what is very singular is, the males will never drive away the females, only when they perceive one they make a noise with their wings to call their own female—she drives away the unwelcome stranger, not leaving it till it was without her bounds. The female does the same as to males, which she leaves to the male who drives them away. We have observed this several times, and I affirm it to be true. The combats between them on this occasion last sometimes pretty long, because the stranger only turns about, and does not fly directly from the nest. However, the others do not forsake it till they have quite driven it out of their limits. After these birds have raised their young one, and left it to itself, they are always together, which the other birds are not, and though they happen to mingle with other birds of the same species, these two companions never disunite.

We have often remarked, that some days after the young one leaves the nest, a company of 30 or 40 bring another young one to it, and the new fledged bird, joining the band with its father and mother, they march to some bye place. We frequently followed them, and found that afterwards the old ones went each their way alone, or in couples, and left the two young ones together, which we called a marriage."

Leguat's, d'Heguerty's, and the Abbé Pingré's descriptions were all we had of this great ground pigeon down to 1866, except a few bones. When Mr. Strickland proved its distinctness from the Dodo of Mauritius in 1844, and up to 1852, these bones numbered 18. In 1864 Mr. E. Newton and Captain Barclay got 3 more bones, in 1865 Mr. Jenner, the resident magistrate, collected 8 bones, and in 1866 nearly 2,000 bones were collected, but during the Transit of Venus expedition in 1874, a thorough search was made, and a number of complete skeletons was collected.

Habitat : Island of Rodriguez.

Represented in Museums by a number of complete skeletons and a large number of bones.

Explanation of Plates.

Plate 23.

Coloured drawing made from Leguat's description and figure.

Plate 25 (a).

Fig. 1. Outline of figure in Leguat's Voyage, 1708.

Fig. 2. Outline of Schlegel's reconstructed figure of the Solitaire, 1854.

Fig. 3. Outline of Solitaire in Frontispiece to Leguat's Voyage, 1708.

TYMPANUCHUS CUPIDO (L.)

HEATH HEN.

Tetrao cupido Linnaeus, Syst. Nat. Ed. X, p. 160 (1758—ex Catesby, Carolina II, App. p. 1, pl. 1, 1743. "Habitat in Virginia"); Vieillot, Gal. Ois. II, p. 55, p. 219 (1825).

Pinnated Grouse Latham, Gen. Syn. II, 2, p. 740 (1783).

Bonasa cupido Stephens, in Shaw's Gen. Zool. XI, p. 299 (1819—New Jersey and Long Island).

Cupidonia cupido Baird, B. N. Am. p. 628 (1860—partim); Maynard, B. E. Massach. p. 138 (1870—Martha's Vineyard and Naushon Island); Brewster, Auk 1885, p. 82 (Massachusetts).

Cupidonia cupido var. cupido Baird, Brewer & Ridgway, N. Amer. B. III, p. 440 (1874).

Cupidonia cupido brewsteri Coues, Key N.A.B., App. p. 884 (1887).

Tympanuchus cupido Ridgway, Proc. U.S. Nat. Mus. VIII, p. 355 (1885); Bendire, Life-Hist. N. Amer. B. I, p. 93 (1892); Grant, Cat. B. Brit. B. XXII, p. 77; Check-List N. Amer. B. Ed. II, p. 115, No. 306 (1895); Hartlaub, Abh. Naturw. Ver. Bremen XIV, 1 (second ed. of separate copy, p. 15) (1896).

LINNAEUS' brief diagnosis is: "Tetrao pedibus hirsutis alis succenturiatis cervicalibus." After the habitat he adds: "Color Tetricis feminae; vertex subcristatus; a tergo colli duae parvae alae: singulae pennis quinque." This diagnosis is taken from Catesby, who gives a fairly good description and a recognizable coloured plate. He specially mentions that the neck-tufts are composed of five feathers, and in his figure they are shown to be much pointed. Catesby expressly states that he does not know exactly from which part of America his specimen came—yet Linnaeus says "Habitat in Virginia."

Formerly the Heath Hen inhabited New England and part of the Middle States (Southern Connecticut, Long Island, New Jersey, Nantucket, Eastern Pennsylvania), but in 1887 Ridgway stated already that it was then apparently extinct, except on Martha's Vineyard. About that time it was still common on that island, inhabiting the woods and chiefly haunting oak scrub and feeding on acorns. They were then "strictly protected by law," but this protection seems not to have been effectual, as from 1893 to 1897 a number were killed, skinned, and sold to various museums. This was, perhaps, fortunate rather than unfortunate, because Mr. Hoyle (the man who collected them) told us that in 1894 a fire destroyed many of them, and in the fall of 1897 they were practically gone. But almost worse than this, perhaps, two pairs of "Prairie Chicken" (*Tympanuchus americanus*) were liberated and broods of young (of the latter apparently) were seen, so that it is to be feared that birds shot now on Martha's Vineyards Island may have blood of *T. americanus* in them, the two forms being closely related, somewhat difficult to distinguish, and evidently sub-species of each other. Nevertheless, a bird taken in 1901 was pronounced to be typical *cupido* by Mr. Brewster.

From these facts it is pretty clear that the Heath Hen is among the birds the fate of which is sealed, and which, if not already exterminated or mixed with foreign blood, will soon have disappeared. The footnote in the Proceedings of the IV. International Ornithological Congress, p. 203, is herewith corrected.

COTURNIX NOVAEZELANDIAE QUOY & GAIM.

(PLATE 28, FIG. 2.)

Coturnix Novae-Zelandiae Quoy and Gaimard, Voy. Astrolabe, Zool. I. p. 242, pl. 24, fig. 1 (1830—"Il habit la baie Chouraki (rivière Tamise de Cook), à la Nouvelle—Zélande"); Gould, Syn. B. Austr., text and pl. fig 2 (1837-38); Buller, B. New Zealand, p. 161, pl. (1873); Hist. B. New Zealand, 2nd ed. I, p. 225, pl. XXIII (1888); Grant, Cat. B. Brit. Mus. XXII p. 245 (1893).

THIS Quail, though a typical *Coturnix*, is easily distinguished from all other species. The male has the upper-side almost black, each feather bordered and indistinctly barred with rufous-brown, and with a wide, creamy white shaft-line. The throat and sides of the head are rufous-cinnamon, the feathers of the chest and breast at their basal half buff with a broken black cross-bar, the distal half black, with two pale buff spots near the tip, or with a continuous white border.

This sole representative of the "gamebirds" in New Zealand was in former days very numerous in both islands, but especially so in the South Island, wherever there was open grass-land, but is now evidently extinct. Its disappearance is apparently not due to excessive shooting, but rather to the introduction of rats, cats, and dogs, and last, but not least, to bush-fires and to the regular burning of the sheep-runs, according to Sir Walter Buller. No doubt the establishment itself of extensive sheep-farms in the once, more or less, uninhabited grass-land was ominous for the future of the Quail.

It is not quite clear when the Quail disappeared. The last on the North Island was shot by Captain Mair at Whangarei in 1860. Specimens were recorded in 1867 and 1869, but were apparently not procured. In Haast's "Journal of Exploration in the Nelson Province" it is said to be still very abundant in 1861 on the grassy plains of the interior.

Sir Walter Buller mentions two specimens said to be from an island in Blue Skin Bay, shot in "1867 or 1868." In his Second Edition of the "Birds of New Zealand" he informs us that it was found occasionally in the South Island down to 1875, but in the "Supplement" he speaks of a specimen said to have been shot in 1871, but adds, "There is no absolute evidence of it," and "if true, this individual bird must have been about the last of its race." Therefore, evidently the note about 1875 was erroneous.

The statement of Mr. Cheeseman, that he took eggs on Three Kings Islands is erroneous. The eggs belonged to a *Synoecus*, and the egg given to Sir Walter Buller is now in my collection.

I have, however, also two eggs of *Coturnix novaezealandiae*, brought home by Dr. H. O. Forbes. They have a brownish-white shell, covered and washed all over with deep brown patches and lighter brown underlying markings. They show distinctly the character of Quails' eggs, but, besides being much larger, are easily distinguished from eggs of *Coturnix coturnix*. They measure 34·3 by 25 and 34·5 by 21·3 mm.

Of birds I have in my collection : One ♂ ad. Shot at Whangarei, North Island, by Major Mair, in 1860. (This is the specimen figured in the Second Edition of the "Birds of New Zealand." I bought it with Sir Walter Buller's collection eighteen years ago. By a curious *lapsus memoriae* Sir Walter Buller, in the "Supplement," p. 35, in 1905, states that this bird was in his son's collection.) One ♀ ad. and one ♂ in the first year's plumage, shot by Messrs. Walter Buller and E. French near Kaiapoi, South Island, in the summer of 1859.

Seven specimens are in the British Museum, the types in Paris, three in Cambridge, a pair in Christchurch in New Zealand, some in the Canterbury Museum, and doubtless many others, most of which have never been recorded.

DINORNITHIDAE.

MOAS.

THE first announcement of the former existence of large Struthious birds in New Zealand was made by Mr. J. S. Polack in 1838. In his book "*New Zealand*," he states that he found large bird bones near East Cape in the North Island. The first specimen, however, that came into the hands of a scientific man was the bone sent to Professor Owen in 1839 by Mr. Rule, who reported that the natives had told him that it was the bone of a large Eagle which they called "*Movie*." Professor Owen, with his extraordinary knowledge, at once saw that far from any connection with the *Raptores*, Mr. Rule's bone was a portion of a femur of a gigantic Struthious bird. He described it on November 12th, 1839, at a meeting of the Zoological Society, and it was figured on Plate 3 of Volume III of the Transactions of the Zoological Society.

The next notice of the Moas takes the form of a letter, received by Professor Owen from the Rev. W. C. Cotton, dated Waimate, near the Bay of Islands, New Zealand, July 11th, 1842; and in it the writer gives an account of his meeting with the Rev. Mr. Wm. Williams, a fellow missionary at East Cape. The latter had collected a lot of "Moa" bones and sent them to a Dr. Buckland. Mr. Williams also reported a conversation with two Englishmen, who declared they had been taken out by a native at night and had seen a Moa alive, but had been too frightened to shoot it.

On January 24th, 1843, Professor Owen exhibited a number of bones from Mr. Williams' collection, and described them, giving the bird the name of "*Megalornis novaezealandiae*," afterwards changing the generic title into *Dinornis*, as *Megalornis* was preoccupied. Afterwards, when describing these bones and those contained in the second box of Mr. Williams' collection more fully, he somewhat inconsistently changed the specific name to *struthioides*, which Captain Hutton, in his later classification, retained. Following the laws of priority, however (*novaezealandiae* has 10 months' priority over *struthioides*), we must reinstate the name *novaezealandiae*.

A number of other finds occurred between 1842 and 1847, but by far the largest and most important collections were made and sent home between 1847 and 1852 by the Hon. W. Mantell, who sent to Professor Owen many hundreds of bones and eggshells, from which the Professor was enabled to determine and describe a large number of species, and even as early as this to separate some genera.

The bulk of later finds were made by Sir Julius von Haast, Captain Hutton, and Mr. Aug. Hamilton, and the two most famous deposits were Glenmark Swamp and Te Aute; but it would take too much space to give here an account of all the other extraordinary discoveries of Moa deposits made by such men as Dr. Thomson, Mr. Earl, Mr. Thorne, Dr. H. O. Forbes, and many others. Besides many fragments of eggshell, a number of eggs have been found, which will be enumerated elsewhere.

Feathers have been found at Clutha River, near Roxburgh, and also in caves near Queenstown. Those from Clutha are mostly dark, being black with white tips; while the Queenstown ones resemble feathers of *Apteryx australis* in colours. Professor Owen has shown that *Megalapteryx huttoni* was feathered down to the toes, and in the plate I have represented it clothed with feathers similar to the Clutha ones, which I believe belong to this species. The Moas at one time must have been extraordinarily numerous, both in numbers and species, and they varied in height from 2½ feet to 12 feet. Professor Parker has shown that some of the species had crests of long feathers on the head, and, as some adult skulls of the same forms show no signs of this, he infers that the males alone had this appendage. There has been much discussion as to the time when the Moas became extinct, and we know for certain that the two species, *Dinornis maximus* and *Anomalopteryx antiquus*, belong to a much earlier geological epoch than the bulk of the other species. It would be too lengthy for my purpose to go into the arguments, but we can, by the study of the "*kitchen middens*" of Maoris and their traditions, fairly adduce that the Maoris arrived in the North Island some 600 years ago, that they hunted Moas, and that they exterminated them about 100 to 150 years after their arrival. In the South, or rather Central, Island, the Maoris appear to have arrived about 100 years later, and to have exterminated the Moas about 350 years ago. It is only fair to say, however, that Monsieur de Quatrefages adduces evidence in his paper which goes far to prove that Moas existed down to the end of the 18th or even beginning of the 19th century in those parts of the Middle Island not, or scantily, inhabited by Maoris.

The *Dinornithidae* form a separate group of the order *Ratitae*, in no way closely related to the Australian Emu (*Dromaius*), as many ornithologists have asserted, but nearer to the South American Nandu (*Rhea*) than any other living *Ratitae*, though exhibiting many characters in common with the *Apterygidae*. There have been a number of classifications set up of this family. The first by Reichenbach, in 1850, with 7 species and 7 genera !

The next was by Von Haast, in 1873, who enumerated 10 species, divided into 4 genera. The third was Lydekker's, in 1891, who acknowledged 23 species, divided into 5 genera. Then came Hutton's, in 1892, which left out *Megalapteryx*, with its then known 2 species, and acknowledged 26 species, divided into 7 genera. Lastly we have Professor Parker's, in 1895, in which again *Megalapteryx* is left out, and 21 species are acknowledged, divided into 5 genera. There has been a great amount of controversy as to the number of species of Moas which really ought to be distinguished, and of late years there has been a tendency to unite most of the species as synonyms, the authors declaring that bones vary to such a degree that all the characters relied on for the distinguishing of the various species were individual variations, and that, besides, it was impossible that so many distinct forms could have occurred in such a small area. The extreme of this lumping was reached when Professor Forbes, in the Bulletin of the Liverpool Museums, III, pp. 27 and 28 (1900), divided the Moas into six genera, each with a single species. He thus ignores the fact that by doing so he has united forms which were founded on FULLY ADULT bones, and yet some of them were only about half or two-thirds the size of the others. I personally think that too many species have been made, and at least 7 of Captain Hutton's forms must be sunk. On the other hand some have been described since 1895 and 1900, and I have been obliged to name others rather against my will, so that in spite of uniting so many species of others I find I am obliged to acknowledge more species than anyone else. I have divided these into genera according to Professor Parker's classification, only adding *Palaeocasuarius* of Forbes, with 3 species, and *Megalapteryx*, with 5, which brings my number up to 38 species, divided into 7 genera. My reasons for not uniting these into 7 species and 7 genera, as those of the "lumping school" do, are twofold,—first, the bones of the *Ratitae* are much more solid than those of other birds, and are not given to so much individual variation; and, secondly, in the face of the great number of species of Paradise Birds and Cassowaries found on New Guinea, the contention that there could not be so many species of Moa on so small an area is not easily maintained. Moreover, we have strong support in the present fauna and flora for the presumption that, when the Moas first came into existence and differentiated into species, New Zealand was a much larger area, stretching at least from the Macquarie Islands in the south to the Kermadecs in the north, and from Lord Howe's Island on the west to the Chatham Islands on the east. So that, like the giant tortoises on the Galápagos Islands, they only got driven so closely together after their specific differentiation, when the land gradually subsided, owing to volcanic action. The differentiation of the family is as follows :—

DINORNITHIDAE.

Skull with a short and wide beak. Pectoral girdle very small or absent, wing absent, only an indication in *Dinornis dromioides*. Hallux absent or present. An extension bridge to the tibio-tarsus, which is placed near the inner border of the bone. No superior notch to the sternum. Most of the species of very large size. The tarso-metatarsus is either long and slender or short and wide, and its anterior surface may or may not be grooved. The second trochlea is longer than the fourth, the third is not pedunculated, and there is no perforation in the groove between the third and fourth trochlea. In the tibio-tarsus the cnemial crest rises well above the head ; the extensor groove is separated by a considerable interval from the inner border of the bone. There is a well-defined intercondylar tubercle ; the intercondylar gorge is deep, and there is no deep pit on the lateral surface of the entocondyle. The femur may be either slender or stout, but is not markedly curved forwards. The popliteal depression is deep, and the summit of the great trochanter rises considerably above the level of the head. The pelvis approximates to that of the *Apterygidae*, but the pectineal process of the pubis is less developed, and the ischium and pubis may be longer and more slender. The coracoid and scapula are aborted and may be absent. The sternum, which may be either long and narrow, or broad and short, differs from that of the *Apterygidae* by the absence of the superior notch, the divergent lateral processes, and the reduction of the coracoidal grooves to small facets or their total disappearance. The cervical vertebrae are relatively short, an expanded neural platform as far as the sixth.

In *Anomalopteryx* and *Megalapteryx* the number of cervicle vertebrae is 21, and there are 2 cervico-dorsal and 4 free dorsal vertebrae, so it is fair to assume that this is the correct number throughout the family.

The feathers had after-shafts.

THE GENERA ARE AS FOLLOWS :

Dinornis Owen.

Palapteryx Owen, part.
Palapteryx Hutton.
Tylapteryx Hutton.

Megalapteryx Haast.

Anomalopteryx Lydekker, part.
**Mesopteryx* Hutton.

Cela Reichenbach.

Dinornis Owen, part.
Meionornis Haast.
Anomalopteryx Lydekker.
Mesopteryx Parker.

Emeus Reichenbach.

Euryapteryx Haast.
Syornis Hutton.
Dinornis Owen, part.

Pachyornis Lydekker.

Palapteryx Haast.
Dinornis Owen, part.
Euryapteryx Hutton.

Palaeocasuarius Forbes.

**Megalapteryx* Forbes, part.

Anomalopteryx Reichenbach.

Meionornis Haast.
Dinornis Owen, part.

I have adopted Professor Parker's classification in the genera, only substituting *Cela* Reichenbach for *Mesapteryx* Hutton, which is a synonym of *Megalapteryx* Haast. As to the species I have used my own judgment; I felt obliged to name a number of species acknowledged by Parker and Lydekker but not named, because this system of indicating species by the letters A, B, C, &c., which has crept into our nomenclature, will make all understanding impossible, as not always the same species is denoted by the same letter. A few of these species will naturally later have to be sunk, as some have been founded on skulls and others on leg bones, or so, which, when we get perfect individual skeletons may prove to be identical, but I do not think these will be many.

Besides a number of imperfect eggs, particulars of which will be found in Dr. A. B. Meyer's article in the Ibis, 1903, pp. 188-196, there are known two perfect Moa eggs and one almost perfect one.

1. Otago Museum. Molyneux River, 1901. *Pachyornis pondorosus.*
2. Tring Museum. Molyneux River, 1901. *Megalapteryx huttoni.*
3. Rowley Collection. South Island, 1859. *Dinornis novaezealandiae.*

DINORNIS.

THE skull is broad and much depressed, with a comparatively wide, somewhat pointed and deflected beak. Breadth at the squamosals twice the height at basi-temporal. It has a flattened frontal region, and a wide median ridge on the upper surface of the praemaxillae. The mandible is in the form of a narrow U, with the angle much inflected, no distinct anticular process, and the symphysis moderately wide, narrowing anteriorly, with a prominent and broad inferior ridge, widest in front. The quadrate is elongated, with a very large pneumatic foramen. The sternum is nearly as long as broad, very convex, with distinct coracoidal facets, 3 costal articulations, very small and reflected costal processes, the lateral processes very broad and widely divergent, and a wide xiphisternal notch. The pelvis is narrow with a high ilium, in which the inferior border of the postacetabular portion is flat, and does not descend as a sharp ridge below the level of the anterior postacetabular vertebrae. The pubis has a small pectineal process; and the ventral aspect of the true and postacetabular vertebrae is very broad and much flattened.

The distal extremity of the tibio-tarsus is not inflected. A hallux is present in some species. The tibio-tarsus and tarso-metatarsus are long and slender, the length of the latter equalling and more often exceeding the length of the femur, and also exceeding half the length of the tibio-tarsus. The femur is comparatively long and slender, with a short neck, the head rising but slightly and projecting only a small distance, the linear aspera in the form of a long irregular line, the outer side of the distal extremity moderately expanded, the popliteal depression small, deep, and sharply defined, the profile of the inner cordyle semi-ovoid and narrow, and the interior trochlear surface nearly flat. The phalangeals of the pes are long and comparatively slender, the proximal surface of the terminal segments not being trefoil-shaped. In the vertebral column the middle cervicals are long and narrow, with the postzygapophyses directed much outwardly and separated by a very deep channel, and the posterior face of the centrum low and wide. The dorsals have short transverse processes and neural spine, the anterior and middle ones (those with a haemal spine or carina) having a large anterior pneumatic foramen between the nib-facet, the foramen being triangular in shape. All the species of this genus are of comparatively large size, and include the tallest members of the family.

Type of the genus : *Dinornis novaezealandiae* (Owen).

Number of species : 7.

DINORNIS MAXIMUS OWEN.

Dinornis maximus Owen, Trans. Zool. Soc. VI. p. 497 (1868).
D. excelsus Hutton, Trans. N.Z. Inst. XXIV. p. 110 (1892).
D. giganteus Haast, Trans. N.Z. Inst. I p. 88, No. 20 part.

THIS is the largest species of Moa, the tibio-tarsus being from 37·5 to 39·2 inches in length, while that of the largest *D. giganteus* does not exceed 35 inches, but by far the largest number of the latter are considerably shorter.

The type bones were obtained in Glenmark Swamp, Middle Island of New Zealand, and were sent to Professor Owen by Major J. Michael of the Madras Staff Corps. Casts of these bones are in the British Museum, No. A 161 in the Palaeontological Department.

This bird was the tallest of all known birds, though it must have been considerably exceeded in bulk by *Aepyornis ingens* and *Aepyornis titan* of Madagascar.

Locality : Glenmark Swamp, Middle Island, New Zealand.

DINORNIS ALTUS OWEN.

Dinornis maximus Owen, Ext. Birds N.Z. p. 253 (Dr. Lillie's specimen) (1879).
D. altus Owen, Ext. Birds N.Z. (1879) p. 361.
D. giganteus var maximus Owen, Trans. Zool. Soc. VI p. 497 (1868).

ONLY known by a tarso-metatarsus, femur and tibio-tarsus from the Middle Island, New Zealand. The bones at once noticeable by their great length, and are more slender than the same bones in *D. maximus.* This form must therefore, till further material comes to hand, be treated as a separate species.

Locality: Middle Island, New Zealand. Collected by Dr. Lillie.

DINORNIS GIGANTEUS OWEN.

Dinornis giganteus Owen, Trans. Zool. Soc. III p. 237 (1843) and p. 307 (1846).
Moa giganteus Reichenbach, Nat. Syst. der Vög. p. XXX (1850).
Dinornis maximus (non *D. maximus* Owen of 1867!) Trans. Zool. Soc. X p. 147 (1877).
D. validus Hutton, Trans. N.Z. Inst. p. 111 (1892).

THIS is, as regards size, one of the more variable forms in the tarso-metatarsus, while the tibio-tarsus is remarkably constant. The tibio-tarsus is almost invariably 35 inches in length, while the tarso-metatarsus varies from 17·5 to 19 inches in length.

The type of *D. giganteus* Owen is from Poverty Bay; the type of *D. validus* is from Glenmark.

Habitat: North and Middle Islands, New Zealand.

Portion of skeleton in Tring Museum, from Kopua Swamps, Canterbury, New Zealand.

DINORNIS INGENS OWEN.

(PLATE 42.)

Dinornis ingens Owen, Trans. Zool. Soc. III p. 237 (1843).
Movia ingens Reichenbach, Nat. Syst. der Vög. p. xxx (1850).
D. ingens var. robustus Owen, Trans. Zool. Soc. III p. 307 (1846).
Palapteryx robustus Owen, Trans. Zool. Soc. III p. 345 (1848).
D. firmus Hutton, Trans. N.Z. Inst. XXIV p. 114 (1892).
D. potens Hutton, l.c. p. 115.

D. INGENS shows considerable variation in size, but the inter-gradation is so complete that it seems impossible to retain the four species *ingens*, *firmus*, *potens* and *robustus*, which Captain Hutton admits. This form was widely distributed over the North and Middle Islands. The type skull of *P. robustus* came from Timaru, the type of *firmus* from Wanganui, that of *ingens* from Poverty Bay, while that of *potens* is quoted from the East side of Middle Island, without specific type locality.

Habitat: North and Middle Islands.

The plate of this species was reconstructed by Mr. Frohawk from the skeleton and feathers in my museum, and the feathers found with the skeleton now in the York Museum. The only criticism that might be made in connection with this picture is that the feathers are drawn a little too much like those of *Apteryx australis*, but this is not of any consequence, as the Moa feathers in the Tring Museum and elsewhere vary considerably in appearance, though being more or less coloured like *Apteryx* feathers.

There is an almost perfect skeleton in the Tring Museum.

DINORNIS GRACILIS OWEN.

Dinornis gracilis Owen, Trans. Zool. Soc. IV (1855) p. 141.
D. torosus Hutton, Trans. N.Z. Inst. XXIV p. 117 (1892).

IF we acknowledge that *D. novaezealandiae* occurs both on the North and Middle Islands, then I feel sure that the distinctness of *D. gracilis* and *D. torosus* cannot be maintained, as the measurements intergrade completely.

The type of *D. gracilis* came from Wanganui, while that of *D. torosus* is a nearly perfect skeleton found in a cave at Takaka, near Nelson.

Habitat: New Zealand.

There is an imperfect skeleton in the Tring Museum, from a limestone cave at Takaka, near Motueka, Province of Nelson, New Zealand.

DINORNIS DROMIOIDES OWEN.

Dinornis dromioides Owen, Trans. Zool. Soc. III. p. 235 (1843).
Palapteryx dromioides Reichenbach, Nat. Syst. der Vög. p. XXX (1850).
Palapteryx plenus Hutton, Trans. N.Z. Inst. XXIV p. 122 (1892).

THIS form also inhabited both islands, but was probably one of the rarest. The type of *D. dromioides* came from Poverty Bay, and that of *P. plenus* from Glenmark.

Habitat: New Zealand.

DINORNIS NOVAEZEALANDIAE OWEN.

Dinornis novaezealandiae Owen, P.Z.S. (1843) p. 8.
D. struthioides Owen, Trans. Zool. Soc. III p. 244 (1844).
D. strennus Hutton, Trans. N.Z. Inst. XXV p. 8 (1893).

PROFESSOR OWEN changed the name of this form, but we cannot accept this change, as it is against the laws of nomenclatorial priority, though we all appreciate the motive the Professor had in making this change. The type came from Poverty Bay, but the bird inhabits both islands.

This species had wings.

Habitat: New Zealand.

A nearly perfect skeleton in the Tring Museum from Waitomo district, Auckland, New Zealand.

MEGALAPTERYX HAAST.

ORIGINALLY distinguished by Haast from the *Dinornithidae* as an ancient form of the *Apterygidae*, but afterwards united by Lydekker with the *Dinornithidae*. Mr. Lydekker's diagnosis of the genus is as follows :—

" Distinguished from *Dinornis* by the extreme slenderness and length of the femur and tibio-tarsus, and the relatively shorter tarso-metatarsus, of which latter the length is considerably shorter than that of the femur. The pelvis is much narrower than in *Dinornis*, with the ventral surface of the postacetabular sacrals ridged and narrower, and a more developed pectineal process to the pubis. The femur is markedly curved forwards, with the distal extremity moderately expanded, the popliteal depression larger and less defined, the linea aspera narrower and sharper, and a more distinct anterior inter-muscular ridge."

The following additional diagnostic characters are taken from Mr. Charles W. Andrews' description of the complete skeleton of *Megalapteryx tenuipes* in the Tring Museum (Nov. Zool. IV, pp. 188-194, fig. 1-2 in text and pl. VI) :—

Width of cranium at paroccipital processes less than half the length of the basis cranii. Length of premaxilla less than two-and-a-half times that of the basis cranii. Body of the premaxilla pointed and slightly decurved ; its length and breadth less than the basis cranii. The occipital plane slightly declined backwards. Occipital condyle projecting slightly beyond the paroccipital processes. Anterior and posterior lambdoidal ridges separated by a very narrow interval in their middle region only. Width at squamosals slightly more than double the length of the basis cranii. Mammillary tuberosities not very prominent. Margin of tympanic cavity evenly curved. Temporal fossae very large. The distance between the temporal ridges about four-fifths the width of the cranium at the fossae. The posterior temporal ridge confluent with the lambdoidal ridge. Post-temporal fossae very large.

The inferior temporal ridge is strongly marked, and there is a pretympanic process. The zygomatic process is well developed. Rostrum dilated towards its anterior end, compressed and carinate beneath the large presphenoid fossae. Mandible very slender. Posterior angular process small. Sternum very convex, and with a very nearly straight anterior border between the tuberosities for the coracoscapular ligaments. Costal processes short but large, with distinct coracoidal facets. The lateral processes are long and distally expanded. The sternum is just as wide as it is long. There are three costal articulations. The most notable character is the enormous length of the toes, the middle one being longer than the tarso-metatarsus. The ungual phalanges are peculiarly long, narrow and curved, instead of being comparatively short and broad, as in most other Moas.

Type of the genus *Megalapteryx hectori*, Haast.

Number of species 4.

MEGALAPTERYX HECTORI HAAST.

Megalapteryx hectori Haast, Trans. Zool. Soc. XII, p. 161 (1886); Lydekker, Cat. Fossil B. Brit. Mus., p. 252.

THIS form was described by Sir Julius von Haast as a gigantic *Apteryx*. This error arose from the absence of the skull. There is, however, no doubt now, since the skulls of *Megalapteryx* are known, that although sufficiently aberrant to form a distinct sub-family, the birds included in this genus are *Dinornithidae* and not *Apterygidae*.

Habitat : Middle Island, New Zealand.

MEGALAPTERYX HAMILTONI SPEC. NOV.

Lydekker, Cat. Fossil Birds in Brit. Mus., p. 252, under *M. tenuipes* (1891).

THE type is a left femur, No. 32145 in the British Museum. It is smaller and relatively narrower than the femur, of either *M. hectori* or *M. tenuipes*. This is most noticeable at the distal extremity.

Habitat : North Island, New Zealand. (Type locality Waingongoro.)

Named after Mr. A. Hamilton, who did so much in discovering deposits of extinct New Zealand birds.

MEGALAPTERYX TENUIPES LYD.

Megalapteryx tenuipes Lydekker, Cat. Foss. Birds Brit. Mus. p. 251 (1891).

THIS species was described from the tibio-tarsus, which is longer and relatively more slender than in *M. hectori*. Its distal width is about one-ninth of its length, while in *M. hectori* it is about one-seventh. The length of the tibio-tarsus is approximately 0·405 mm. = 16 inches, and width of distal extremity about 0·044 = 1·74 inches. Type specimens Nos. 49989 and 49990, British Museum.

Habitat : Middle Island, New Zealand, and perhaps North Island. (Type locality Lake Wakatipa, Queenstown, Otago.)

Complete skeleton in the Tring Museum.

Mr. Lydekker mentions also a right femur from the North Island, of the same proportions as those of *M. tenuipes* and 0·255 m. (= 10·1 inches) long. It may probably belong to a different form, as we know *M. tenuipes* otherwise only from the Middle Island.

MEGALAPTERYX HUTTONII (OWEN).

(PLATE 41.)

Dinornis huttonii Owen, Ext. Birds, N.Z., p. 430 (1879).
Dinornis didinus Owen, Trans. Zool. Soc. XI, p. 257 (1883).
D. didiformis Haast, (non Owen 1844) Trans. N.Z. Inst. I, p. 83, Nos. 5 & 6 (1869).
Mesopteryx didinus Hutton, Trans. N.Z. Inst. XXIV, p. 129 (1892).

THE synonymy of this form is somewhat confused, but I think it is clear that *huttonii* of Owen is its proper name. Professor Owen (Ext. B. p. 430) says :
" In the collection from the Glenmark Swamp, SOUTH ISLAND, are bones that scarcely differ, save in size, from the dimensions (? W.R.) of the type bones of *Dinornis didiformis* from the NORTH ISLAND. They are noted as of a large variety of that species." Captain Hutton remarks : " The bones that I have arranged under the name *D. didiformis* belong probably to a new species. The tibia is well marked and quite distinct, but the femur and metatarsus, that I have associated with it, pass almost into *D. casuarinus*, but are rather smaller. *D. casuarinus* is undoubtedly a good species, easily distinguished by its tibia." Possibly the *Dinornis* of the SOUTH ISLAND, with the tibia characteristic of *D. didiformis* of the NORTH ISLAND, may need to be noted for the convenience of naming the bones as *Dinornis huttonii*.

When describing his *D. didinus*, Professor Owen failed to recognise its identity with his previously named *D. huttonii*, doubtless owing to the leg bones being hidden by the dry integument. This being the case, it is necessary to reinstate the name *huttonii*, as it has four years' priority over *didinus*.

Captain Hutton says that a few bones of this form have been obtained in the North Island at Poverty Bay and Te Aute ; but I am convinced he is in error and that these bones are aberrant individual bones of *A. didiformis* and that *M. huttonii* is confined to the South or rather Middle Island. The plate of this species has been reconstructed by Mr. Lodge from the mummified remains which form the type specimen of *Didornis didinus*, and the feathers found in the alluvial sands of the CLUTHA RIVER. The type of *Dinornis didinus* was found at Queenstown by Mr. Squires.

Habitat : Middle Island, New Zealand.

Mr. C. W. Andrews, in his description of my complete skeleton of *Megalapteryx tenuipes* has shown that Owen's type specimens of his *Dinornis didinus* are certainly of a species of the genus *Megalapteryx*, and closely allied to *M. tenuipes*. Mr. Andrews, however, throws some doubt as to whether the pelvis and femora, referred to this species by Hutton, really belong to it.

A complete egg which I consider must be of this species is preserved in the Tring Museum. Its measurements are as follows :—

Large circumference, 21·4 inches = 535 mm.
Small ,, 17·5 ,, = 437·5 mm.

This egg was dredged up on the Molyneux River, near Otago, during gold dredging operations in 1901 ; a second perfect egg was dredged up a few months before in the same river, and was referred by Dr. Benham to *Pachyornis ponderosus*.

ANOMALOPTERYX REICHENBACH.

THE skull is narrow and vaulted, with a long, sharp and slightly deflected beak. Breadth at the squamosals 1½ times the height at basi-temporal, which has a constricted praemaxillary ridge, and the quadrate with a very small pneumatic foramen. The mandible is V-shaped, with a slight inflection of the angle, and a distinct postarticular process. The symphysis is very narrow and pointed, with a long and narrow inferior ridge, not expanding markedly at either extremity. The sternum is longer, flatter and narrower than in *Dinornis*, having no distinct xiphisternal notch, three costal articulations, long and narrow costal processes, slender lateral processes which are often elongated, and usually no coracoidal facets. The pelvis is wider and lower than in *Dinornis*, with the lower border of the postacetabular portion of the ilium descending as a sharp ridge much below the level of the sacral ribs, and without any distinct pectineal process. A hallux is present. The tibio-tarsus and tarso-metatarsus are relatively shorter and stouter than in *Dinornis*, the latter being shorter than the femur, which is usually stouter and relatively shorter than in *Megalapteryx*. The length of the tarso-metatarsus is less than half that of the tibio-tarsus. The femur, besides being usually relatively shorter is readily distinguished from that of *Dinornis* by its more expanded extremities, the rather longer neck, and the much larger and ill-defined popliteal depression.

The vertebrae are of the general type of those of *Pachyornis*, but the anterior pneumatic foramen commences in the third dorsal. The phalangeals are intermediate between those of *Dinornis* and *Pachyornis*. Haast considered that the coracoid was aborted and often absent in this genus, in *Emeus*, and *Pachyornis*. As additional characters of the skull it may be mentioned that there is a prominent supra-occipital protuberance, and a depression on the squamosal above the quadrate ; the par-occipital processes are pointed, and the basi-occipital processes only slightly prominent ; so that the posterior profile of the basi-occipital is nearly straight. The quadrate has a very short anterior process.

All the species of the genus are small, in fact *parvus* is the smallest but one of the family.

Type of the genus : *Anomalopteryx didiformis* (Owen).

Number of species : 4.

ANOMALOPTERYX DIDIFORMIS (OWEN).

Dinornis didiformis Owen, Trans. Zool. Soc. III, p. 242 (1844).
Anomalopteryx didiformis Reichenbach, Nat. Syst. der Vög. p. 30 (1850).
A. didiformis Lydekker, Cat. Fossil B. Brit. Mus., p. 275.

THE present form is confined to the North Island. Owen's type was collected by the Revd. Wm. Williams, and came from Poverty Bay.

Habitat: North Island, New Zealand.

Portion of skeleton in Tring Museum.

ANOMALOPTERYX PARVUS (OWEN).

Dinornis parvus Owen, Trans. Zool. Soc. XI, pp. 233-256, pls. LI-LVII (1883).
Anomalopteryx didiformis Hutton, Trans. N.Z. Inst. XXIV, p. 123 (1892), part.
A. parva Lydekker, t. c., p. 278.

THIS small form is confined to the Middle Island. The type, a skeleton in almost complete condition, was dug up in a cave at Takaka, near Nelson, and is now in the British Museum. A much less perfect skeleton is in my museum at Tring.

Habitat: Middle Island, New Zealand.

ANOMALOPTERYX ANTIQUUS HUTT.

"*Avian Remains*" Forbes, Trans. N.Z. Inst. XXIII, p. 369 (1891).
Anomalopteryx antiquus Hutton, Trans. N.Z. Inst. XXIV, p. 124 (1892).

A. ANTIQUUS was named by Captain Hutton from the photographs of bones described by Dr. Forbes in the above-quoted article. The evidence is very slight on which to found a species, but I prefer to treat it as one, for the bones were discovered in the Upper Miocene, a much older stratum than most remains of *Dinornithidae* occur in.

Locality: Timaru, Middle Island, New Zealand.

ANOMALOPTERYX FORTIS HUTT.

Anomalopteryx fortis Hutton, Trans. N.Z. Inst. XXV, p. 9 (1893).

THIS is the largest of the genus, and the type bones came from Glenmark. I append comparative table of Measurements:

	Tarso-metatarsus.	Tibio-tarsus.	Femur.
A. fortis	8·0 inches.	17·5 inches.	9·8 inches.
A. didiformis	6·3 ,,	13·3 ,,	8·0 ,,
A. parvus	6·3 ,,	13·7 ,,	8·5 ,,

Locality of Type: Glenmark.

Habitat : Middle Island, New Zealand.

CELA REICHENBACH.

SKULL convex, the temporal fossae very large. Breadth at the squamosals 1·6-1·7 times the height at the basi-temporal. Length from the supra-occipital to the nasals rather less than the breadth at the squamosals. Occipital condyle hidden by the supra-occipital. Ridge between temporal fossae and supra-occipital narrow. Beak short, slightly compressed and rounded at the tip, though more pointed than in *Anomalopteryx*. Lower mandible nearly straight and rather slighter than in *Anomalopteryx*, V-shaped. Sternum with coracoid pits faintly indicated or absent; length less than breadth. Costal processes well developed, lateral processes diverging at different angles.

Pelvis broader in proportion than in *Dinornis*, the acetabula set more forward. Tarso-metatarsus shorter than the femur, and less than half the length of the tibio-tarsus. Hallux present in some species. The smallest species of Moa is *Cela curtus*.

Type of the genus: *Cela curtus*.

Number of species: 5.

CELA CURTUS (OWEN).

Dinornis curtus Owen, Trans. Zool. Soc. III, p. 325 (1846).
Cela curtus Reichenbach, Nat. Syst. der Vög. p. 30 (1850).
Cela curta Hutton, Trans. N.Z. Inst. XXIX, p. 550, pl. XLVII, Fig. B.

THIS and the following are the two smallest species of *Moa*, having been about the size of a large turkey. It also is the most abundant species at Whangarei, and appears to have been most common in the North of the Island. The type is from Poverty Bay.

Habitat: North Island, New Zealand.

CELA OWENI (HAAST).

Dinornis oweni Haast, Trans. Zool Soc. XII, p. 171, pl. XXXI, XXXII (1886).
Cela curtus Hutton, Trans. N.Z. Inst., XXIV, p. 127 (1892), portion.

DR. VON HAAST (Sir Julius von Haast) took as his type of *Dinornis oweni* the almost complete skeleton collected by Mr. Cheeseman in a cave at Patana, Whangarei, and now in the Auckland Museum. While referring my readers to the original diagnosis for the specific characters, I wish to specially draw attention to the fact that Dr. von Haast says that in the collections he examined, made by Mr. Thorne and Mr. Cheeseman, there are bones belonging to at least 20 skeletons of his *D. oweni*, and that some were even smaller than the type, and the only difference was the constant average difference due to sex. I draw special notice to this, as Captain Hutton has united this form with *curtus*, saying Haast's type is only a small individual of that species. The fact of bones of at least 20 different individuals, showing the same characters and the same differences from *curtus*, is quite sufficient evidence for me to consider Dr. von Haast's *D. oweni* as a distinct species. I append measurements of the leg bones of the types of *Cela curtus* and *C. oweni* :—

	Tarso-metatarsus.	Tibio-tarsus.	Femur.
Cela curtus	5·0 inches	11·25 inches	5·65 inches
Cela oweni	4·4 ,,	9·6 ,,	6·5 ,,

Locality : Whangarei.
Habitat : North Island, New Zealand.

CELA GERANOIDES (OWEN).

Palapteryx geranoides Owen, Trans. Zool. Soc. III, p. 345 (1848)
Cela geranoides Hutton, Trans. N.Z. Inst. XXIV, p. 126 (1892).

THIS species is confined to the North Island. The type came from Waingongoro. It is most commonly found in the South of the Island.

Habitat : North Island, New Zealand.

CELA RHEIDES (OWEN).

Dinornis rheides Owen, Trans. Zool. Soc. IV, p. 8 (1850—partim).
Syornis rheides Hutton, Trans. N.Z. Inst. XXIV, p. 131 (1892).

THIS is a very difficult form to consider, as the type bones consisted of those of three different forms. Whether Professor Owen, were he now alive, would concur in Captain Hutton's treatment is very questionable, and I doubt if it ought not to be united to *Emeus crassus*, while Haast united it to *P. gravis*. I have kept it separate as no bones of a single individual united are known, and it might prove sufficiently distinct if a good skeleton were obtained. The type bones were sent from Waikawaite, Middle Island, by Colonel Wakefield, in 1849.

Habitat : Middle Island, New Zealand.

CELA CASUARINUS (OWEN).

Dinornis casuarinus Owen, Trans. Zool. Soc. III, p. 307 (1846).
Syornis casuarinus Reichenbach, Nat. Syst. der Vög, p. XXX (1850).
Meionornis casuarinus Haast, Trans. N.Z. Inst., VII, pp. 54-91 (1875).
Syornis casuarinus Hutton, Trans. N.Z. Inst., XXIV, p. 133 (1892).

C. CASUARINUS is found in both Islands, and is abundant in the Middle Island.

The type came from Waikowaiti.

Habitat: New Zealand.

Portions of one skeleton and two almost complete skeletons in Tring Museum ; one of the latter from Kapua Swamps.

EMEUS REICHENBACH.

THE skull is very short and wide, with a blunt and slightly deflected rostrum, and a very small pneumatic foramen to the quadrate. The mandible is in the shape of a wide U, with a slightly inflected angle, and a large post-articular process. The symphysis is very wide and deeply excavated, with a broad and slightly prominent inferior ridge narrowing in front. The sternum resembles that of *Anomalopteryx*, but the pelvis is much wider and approaches that of *Pachyornis*. The tibio-tarsus and tarso-metatarsus are relatively shorter and thicker than in *Anomalopteryx*, but less stout than in *Pachyornis*; the distal extremity of the tibio-tarsus is not inflected. A hallux is present. The length of the tarso-metatarsus is considerably less than that of the femur, and than half that of the tibio-tarsus, its width at the middle of the shaft being rather more than one-fourth of its length.

The vertebrae are of the type of *Anomalopteryx*. The species are larger than most of those of *Cela* and *Anomalopteryx*. Additional cranial characters are that the skull usually has very broad and blunt paroccipital processes; there is no distinct supraoccipital prominence, and no well-marked depression upon the frontal aspect of the squamosal above the head of the quadrate. The basi-occipital tubercles are prominent, and give an arched posterior profile to this bone. The quadrate is elongated with a long anterior bar; the cavity of the squamosal for the reception of its head is inclined much more outwardly than in either of the other genera.

Type of genus: *Emeus crassus* (Owen).

Number of species: 6.

EMEUS CRASSUS (OWEN).

Dinornis crassus Owen, Trans. Zool. Soc. III, p. 307 (1846—partim).
Emeus crassus Reichenbach, Nat. Syst. der Vög., p. XXX (1850).
Syornis crassus Hutton, Trans. N.Z. Inst. XXIV, p. 132 (1892).

THIS species has led to much confusion, owing to Professor Owen having associated with the real portions of *crassus* in his possession bones of *elephantopus*, *ponderosus* and *struthioides*. The type came from Waikouaiti.

Habitat: Middle Island, New Zealand.

Imperfect skeleton in Tring Museum.

EMEUS BOOTHI NOM. NOV.

Emeus, Species A, Parker, Trans. Zool. Soc. XIII, p. 379 (1895), pl. XVI.

EASILY distinguished by the shorter and narrower beak. Type specimen —the skull found by Mr. R. S. Booth at Stag Point—now in Otago University Museum, figured as above.

Habitat: Middle Island, New Zealand.

EMEUS GRAVIPES LYD.

Emeus gravipes Lydekker, Cat. Foss. Birds Brit. Mus., p. 298 (1891) Nos. A95, on p. 299, to 47444d, on p. 300.

Dinornis gravis (portion) Owen, Trans. Zool. Soc. VIII, p. 361 (1872).

Euryapteryx gravis Haast, Ibis 1874, p. 213.

THE present species is smaller than *E. crassus* and has the tarso-metatarsus relatively wider. Length, 198 mm. = 7·8 inches; width at middle of shaft, 51 mm. = 2 inches.

Habitat: Middle Island, New Zealand.

EMEUS HAASTI NOM. NOV.

Emeus species B, Parker, Trans. Zool. Soc. XIII p. 379 (1895).

Emeus gravipes Lydekker, Cat. Foss. Birds Brit. Mus. p. 301 Nos. 32017, 32016, a-e and c to 32044 e on p. 307 (1891).

SIR J. VON HAAST united this form with *Dinornis gravis*, and the skull which is the type of *E. haasti* is put on a skeleton of *D. gravis* in the Canterbury Museum. The measurements of this species are much smaller than those of the other species.

Habitat: Middle Island, New Zealand.

EMEUS PARKERI NOM NOV.

Emeus species Γ, Parker, Trans. Zool. Soc. XIII, p. 380 (1895).

THIS species is at once distinguished from the other species of the genus by having right-angled orbits. The type is a skull from Hamilton Swamp, named *Euryapteryx gravis*, by Prof. Hutton, in the Otago Museum.

Habitat : Middle Island, New Zealand.

EMEUS EXILIS (HUTT.)

Dinornis didiformis Owen, Trans. Zool. Soc. III, pl. 24 (1846), part.
Euryapteryx exilis Hutton, Trans. N.Z. Inst. XXIX, p. 552, pl. XLVIII, Fig. C (1897).

DIFFERS from *E. crassus* in the tibia being more convex on the anterior surface. The skull, among other differences, has a very slight frontal rising to the cranial roof, as opposed to the very conspicuous one in the remaining species. The type is a nearly complete skeleton in the Wanganui Museum. For full description see Hutton, l.c.

Habitat : North Island, New Zealand.

PACHYORNIS LYDEKKER.

THE skull is either vaulted or flattened, with a sharp and narrow beak. The paroccipital processes are shorter and more rounded, and the basi-occipital tubercles more prominent than in *Anomalopteryx*, while the quadrate and mandible resemble the same bones in that genus somewhat closely. The sternum is flat and very broad and short, with no coracoidal facets, a very small xiphisternal notch, broad and short costal processes, and widely divergent lateral processes; while there are only two costal articulations. The pelvis is extremely low and wide, with the anterior wall of the acetabulum very deeply concave, the ventral surface of all the vertebrae behind the true sacrals narrow and convex, and from which the very broad sacral ribs ascend to join the ilium, of which the inferior postacetabular border is very sharp, and descends far below the level of the ribs. There is no pectineal process to the pubis. The tibio-tarsus is very short, with the shaft curved outwards, the distal extremity markedly inflected, and the fibular ridge much shorter than in the other genera. The fibular border below the smooth space at the distal extremity of the fibular ridge is extremely rough ; and the distal extensor tubercle is very prominent, being situated partly on the line of the upper half of the extensor groove, instead of being altogether external to the same.

The tarso-metatarsus is still shorter and wider than in *Emeus*, the width at the middle of the shaft being usually rather more than one third of the length. The third trochlea is more prominent than in the other genera, and rises very abruptly from the shaft, the outer border of the anterior surface usually expanding suddenly at the proximal extremity, and the outer ridge of this surface being always more prominent than the inner, whereas in the other genera the opposite condition obtains. The femur, as compared with that of *Dinornis*, is very much shorter and thicker, with a longer neck, and the head rising and projecting very considerably, the linea aspera mainly forming a rough nodule near the distal end of the shaft, the outer surface of the distal extremity more suddenly expanded, and the popliteal depression larger, more open, and leading to the inner surface of the shaft by a more distinct channel. The profile of the inner condyle is wider antero-posteriorly, and more rounded, the anterior intertrochlear surface being deeply channelled.

The phalangeals of the pes are much shorter and stouter than in *Dinornis*, the proximal surface of the terminal segments generally presenting a trefoil-shaped contour. The length of the tarso-metatarsus is very much less than half that of the tibio-tarsus. In the vertebral column the cervicals are short with very stout centra, the prezygopophyses in the middle region being nearly horizontal and separated from one another by a wide channel. The posterior face of the centra is tall and narrow, and the neural spines of the last two vertebrae much inclined forward. In the dorsals there is usually no anterior pneumatic foramen till the fourth (or the last with a distinct haemal carina), this foramen being situated on the line of the anterior border of the rib-facet. The third and fourth dorsals are extremely compressed. Throughout the series also the neural spines and transverse processes are comparatively long. Additional characters of the skull are that the sphenoidal rostrum is expanded in a lance-like shape at the anterior extremity, in a manner unlike that of any of the other genera.

Then the supraoccipital never has a very strongly developed median prominence, and the temporal fossae are comparatively short. The mandible may be readily distinguished from that of the other genera by the low position of the inner aperture of the dental canal, which pierces the bone obliquely to join the small lateral vacuity.

Type of the genus: *Pachyornis elephantopus* (Owen).

Number of species: 8.

PACHYORNIS ELEPHANTOPUS (OWEN).

Dinornis elephantopus Owen, Trans. Zool. Soc. IV, p. 149 (1853).
Palapteryx elephantopus Haast, Ibis, Ser. 3, vol. IV, p. 212 (1874).
Euryapteryx elephantopus Hutton, Trans. N.Z. Inst. XXIV, p. 135 (1892).

UNTIL Mr. Lydekker described *Pachyornis immanis*, and Mr. Andrews *Aepyornis titan*, this was undoubtedly the most bulky and ponderous of all known Ratitae, extinct and living.

Type: Awamoa, near Oamanu.

Habitat: Middle Island, New Zealand.

Two imperfect skeletons in the Tring Museum; one from Kapua Swamps.

PACHYORNIS IMMANIS LYD.

Pachyornis immanis Lydekker, Cat. Foss. Birds Brit. Mus., p. 343 (1891).

THIS is the most bulky and largest member of the genus, and also of all *Dinornithidae*. Its living parallel to-day is *Casuarius philipi* Rothschild, which, though by no means the tallest species of *Casuarius*, is the most bulky, and has the shortest and stoutest legs—the tarso-metatarsus is specially short and stout.

The type tarso-metatarsus measures 228 mm. = 9·9 inches, and in width (shaft) 84 mm. = 3·3 inches, while the type tarso-metatarsus of *elephantopus* measures 239 mm. = 9·4 inches and 65 mm. = 2·55 inches.

The skull is much more depressed than in *elephantopus* and with deeper temporal fossae and a shorter post orbital region.

Type: No. A168 British Museum.

Habitat: Middle Island, New Zealand.

PACHYORNIS ROTHSCHILDI LYD.

Pachyornis rothschildi Lydekker, P.Z. S. 1891, pp. 479-482, pl. XXXVIII.

THE bones in the Tring Museum, which form the type of this species, unfortunately have no history and their locality is unknown. It differs from the other species of the genus by the slenderer proportions of the tibio-tarsus, which is 22 inches long by 2·9 inches distal width, as opposed to 24 inches by 4·2 in *elephantopus* and 20 inches by 3·5 in *ponderosus*, the two nearest in size. Femur: length 10·6 as opposed to 12·5 inches in *elephantopus*.

PACHYORNIS PONDEROSUS (HUTT.)

Euryapteryx ponderosus Hutton, Trans. N.Z. Inst., p. 137 (1892).

THIS species is slightly smaller than *P. elephantopus*, the tarso-metatarsus varying from 8·25 to 8·0 inches, as opposed to from 9·4 to 9·25 in *elephantopus*; the tibio-tarsus varies from 18·5 to 18·6, as opposed to 24 to 21·1; femur, 10, as opposed to 13 to 11·8.

The skull can be distinguished by the processes at the hinder angles of the basi-sphenoid, which are higher and rounder in *ponderosus*, flatter and more elongated in *elephantopus*. Type: Hamilton.

Habitat: Middle Island, New Zealand.

Cast of egg in Tring Museum, taken from specimen in Otago Museum, dredged up in 1901 in the Molyneux River, also incomplete skeleton from Kapua Swamps.

PACHYORNIS INHABILIS HUTT.

Pachyornis inhabilis Hutton, Trans. N.Z. Inst. XXV, p. 11 (1893).

DIFFERS from *ponderosus* by having the great inward expansion at the distal end of the tibio-tarsus. This expansion has induced some ornithologists to separate the species of *Pachyornis* into two genera—*Euryapteryx* and *Pachyornis*—but I do not think this expansion of sufficient importance to warrant generic separation.

Habitat: Middle Island, New Zealand.

PACHYORNIS VALGUS (HUTT.)

Euryapteryx valgus Hutton, Trans. N.Z. Inst. XXV, p. 12 (1893).

THIS species is at once distinguishable from all others by the extraordinary internal expansion of the distal end of the tibio-tarsus. The tarso-metatarsus is 8·5 inches = 216 mm. in length and the proximal width 3·5 inches = 89 mm., and does not differ much from *crassus* except in the great proximal width, necessary to articulate with the distal internal expansion described above.

The type came from Enfield in New Zealand.

Habitat: Middle Island, New Zealand.

PACHYORNIS PYGMAEUS (HUTT.)

Euryapterxy pygmaeus Hutton, Trans. N.Z. Inst. XXIV, p. 739 (1892).

As implied by its name, this is the smallest species of *Pachyornis*, the tarso-metatarsus only measuring 6 inches in length. The type came from Takaka.

Habitat : Middle Island, New Zealand.

PACHYORNIS COMPACTA (HUTT.)

Euryapteryx compacta Hutton, Trans. N.Z. Inst. XXV, p. 11 (1893).

APPROACHES nearest to *pygmaeus* in size, but can be at once distinguished by the distal extremity of the tibio-tarsus not being expanded inwards. The tarso-metatarsus has the trochleae considerably more expanded than in *pygmaeus*.

Type from Enfield in New Zealand.

Habitat : Middle Island, New Zealand.

PALAEOCASUARIUS FORBES.

DR. FORBES founded this genus of *Dinornithidae* on remains of Moas of three distinct sizes as regards femora collected by him at Manitoto. Dr. Forbes has kindly placed these bones at my disposal, and the following summarises the results of my examination. I find that Dr. Forbes' original idea as to the distinctness of *Palaeocasuarius* is perfectly justified, as not only are his characters of the tibio-tarsus, as opposed to those in the other genera, correct, but the proportions between femur, tibio-tarsus and tarso-metatarsus are quite different to those of other genera. I give the proportions of the three bones in *Palaeocasuarius elegans*, *Megalapteryx tenuipes*, and *Pachyornis elephantopus*, which are the three most nearly allied genera:

	Pal. elegans.	*M. tenuipes.*	*Pach. elephantopus.*
Femur, length	10⅝ inches	11 inches	12 inches
Width over condyles	3½ ,,	3½ ,,	5 ,,
Tibio-tarsus, length	16 ,,	15½ ,,	33 ,,
Width at distal end	2 ,,	2¼ ,,	3½ ,,
Tarso-metatarsus, length	7 ,,	6 ,,	9 ,,
Width at centre	1½ ,,	1¼ ,,	2¼ ,,

The original diagnosis was as follows, being founded on the tibio-tarsus: "The tibio-tarsus differs from that of all other genera in being straighter and less twisted on itself, so that the position of the ridge forming the inner wall of the groove for the tendons of the extensor muscles run along the inner side of the bone as in *Casuarius*. As in the latter genus it takes a marked turn inwards and backwards before joining the epicnemial crest, while a line joining the centre point between the distal condyles and the epicnemial ridge leaves a considerable space between it and the wall of the groove. There is no intercondylar eminence in the intercondylar channel, and the orifice of the extensor foramen opens more longitudinally than in the other genera, and points downwards."

Type of the genus: *Palaeocasuarius haasti* Forbes.

Number of species: 3.

In the following descriptions of the three species I only rely on the measurements of the femora, as not all the other leg bones of the three species are available.

PALAEOCASUARIUS HAASTI FORBES.

Palaeocasuarius haasti Forbes, Trans. N.Z. Inst. XXIV, p. 189 (1892).

FEMUR: length approximately 8·5 inches; width across head and great trochanter 2·25 inches. Tarso-metatarsus: length 7 inches; width in centre 1·15 inches, at distal end 2·75 inches.

Type from Manitoto in Liverpool Museum.

"This bird exceeded considerably the cassowary in size," is all the author tells us of this bird. It is a pity that Dr. Forbes did not insist on the publication in full of his paper, as proper descriptions of all the twelve new species are wanting.

Habitat: New Zealand.

PALAEOCASUARIUS VELOX FORBES.

Palaeocasuarius velox Forbes, Trans. N.Z. Inst. XXIV, p. 189 (1892).

FEMUR: length 9·5 inches; width across head and trochanter 2·75 inches, across distal end 2·5 inches. Tarso-metatarsus: length 7 inches; width in centre 1·5 inches, across distal end 3 inches.

Type specimen from Manitoto in Liverpool Museum.

Habitat: New Zealand.

PALAEOCASUARIUS ELEGANS FORBES.

Palaeocasuarius elegans Forbes, Trans. N.Z. Inst. XXIV, p. 189 (1892).

FEMUR: length 10·75 inches; width across head and trochanter 3·25 inches, across distal end 3·4 inches. Tarso-metatarsus: length 7·8 inches, width over centre 1·75, over distal end about 3·3 inches.

Type specimen from Manitoto in the Liverpool Museum.

Habitat: New Zealand.

AEPYORNITHIDAE.

THE first notice we have from a scientific man of the existence on Madagascar of large Struthious birds is the description by Isidore Geoffroy-Saint-Hilaire of two eggs and a few osseous remains, in the Annales des Sciences naturelles III, Zoologie, vol. XIV (1850). These important objects were sent to the describer by a colonist of Réunion, Monsieur de Malavois, but were obtained from the natives in Madagascar by Captain M. Abadie. A third egg arrived smashed. The name given on this evidence was *Aepyornis maximus*.

Since then some 40 eggs at least and a large number of odd bones have been collected by Monsieur Grandidier, Messrs. Last and others, and Dr. Forsyth Major, but only one practically complete, and one less complete skeleton of a smaller species, named *Aepyornis hildebrandti* by Dr. Burckhardt.

A large number of species has been diagnosed on the evidence of these bones and eggs by Professor Milne-Edwards, Mr. Dawson Rowley and Mr. Andrews, and a second genus, *Mullerornis*, established.

The following is the diagnosis of the family

AEPYORNITHIDAE.

Head less flattened than in the *Dinornithidae*, much longer and narrower. Brain case much greater in volume. Occipital condyle strongly pedunculate. Temporal fossae deep and narrow. The basisphenoid has on each side a well marked pterygoidal apophysis. The lower mandible is straight and stout, recalling somewhat that of *Rhea*, but the maxillary branches are higher and stouter. The symphysis is long, contracted, and hollowed out in the shape of a ladle. The sternum presents many affinities to that of *Apteryx*. It is a thin plastron, flattened, and much widened. The coracoidal articular surfaces similar to those of *Apteryx*. The Coraco-scapulars are feeble, and have so faint an articular surface that the humerus must have been rudimentary. Hallux absent, outer digit has five, the middle digit four, and the inner digit three phalanges.

There are three genera and twelve species.

A striking character is that in the genus *Aepyornis* the proximal extremity of the tarso-metatarsus is larger than the distal extremity, a feature not found in the majority of other birds.

Monsieur Grandidier has expressly pointed out that *Aepyornis* had only three toes, I cannot, therefore, understand why Messrs. Lydekker and Evans both state that the hallux is present.

In spite of the researches of Messrs. Grandidier, Last, and Forsyth Major and the large collections sent home by them, the number of *Aepyornis* bones is infinitesimal compared with the vast masses of bones of the *Dinornithidae* contained in the museums. This paucity of material quite prohibits us from making a critical study of the described species, so that we are at present unable to say if too many or too few species have been diagnosed. I am inclined, however, to think that if we ever get complete skeletons of the larger forms, *Ae. grandidieri* and *Ae. cursor* will prove to be sexes of one species, and also *Ae. titan* and *Ae. maximus*. For the present, however, the measurements are too different to allow of their being united without further investigation.

The three genera are as follows:—

AEPYORNIS T. GEOFF.

Aepyornis Geoffroy Saint Hilaire.
Epiornis Geoffroy Saint Hilaire.
Epyornis Auct.

MULLERORNIS MILNE-EDWARDS & GRANDIDIER.

Mullerornis Milne-Edwards and Grandidier.

FLACOURTIA ANDREWS.

Flacourtia Andrews.
Mullerornis Milne-Edwards and Grandidier (part).

AEPYORNIS GEOFF.

CHARACTERS same as those of the family; but in opposition to *Mullerornis* the species are very heavy, ponderous, and clumsy, the bones being both actually and comparatively much stouter. Differs from *Flacourtia* in not having an ossified boney bridge over lower end of groove for adductor of outer digit.

Type: *Aepyornis maximus* Geoff.

Number of species: 9.

AEPYORNIS TITAN ANDR.

Aepyornis titan Andrews, Geol. Mag. 1895, p. 303.

THIS appears to be the largest species of the genus, though *Ae. maximus* is considerably stouter. In the original description of *Ae. ingens*, however, the tibio-tarsi referred to that species are really those of *Ae. titan*:—

Smallest Femur.	
Length about	430 mm.
Circumference, narrowest point	280 ,,
Width, distal end	190 ,,
Width of shaft at narrowest part	97 ,,
Largest Femur.	
Length	470 mm.
Circumference at narrowest point	280 ,,
Width, distal end	210 ,,
Distal part of tibio-tarsus.	
Width at distal end	180 mm.
Width of shaft at narrowest point	77 ,,
Circumference of shaft at narrowest point....	210 ,,
Tarso-metatarsus.	
Length	480 mm.
Width at proximal end	190 ,,
Width at distal end	165 ,,
Width at narrowest point of shaft	80 ,,
Circumference at narrowest point of shaft....	200 ,,

The skull, pelvis, and most vertebrae, as well as the sternum of this form are unknown.

Habitat : S. W. Madagascar.

Three Femora, two tarsi-metatarsi, and two incomplete tibia-tarsi are in the Tring Museum, collected by Last in the Antinosy country.

There are two eggs of this species at Tring, the measurements of which are as follows :—

No. 1, Antinosy Country, Last.

Large circumference	....	....	....	862·5 mm.
Small circumference	....	....	....	631·5 ,,

No. 2 (traded).

Large circumference	....	....	....	883 mm.
Small circumference	....	....	....	763 ,,

The egg mentioned by Mr. Lydekker in Cat. Foss. Birds B.M., page 214, No. 41847 is, judging from its size, undoubtedly an egg of this species, and I quote the measurements, as they are very large :—

Largest circumference	....	....	....	921 mm.
Smallest circumference	....	....	....	768 ,,

The egg purchased in 1854 in the Paris Museum measures :—

Large circumference....	....	....	....	925 mm.
Small circumference	....	....	....	753 ,,

In addition to these four eggs which are undoubtedly of *Ae. titan*, there are the following which I consider to belong to that species :—

1 Paris Museum, Mr. Armange.

1 Hamburg.

1 Messrs. Gilford, Orange, New Jersey.

1 Rowley collection.

These four eggs range from 900 mm. to 863·5 mm. in large circumference, and 770 mm. to 736 mm. in small circumference.

AEPYORNIS MAXIMUS GEOFF.

Aepyornis maximus I. Geoffrey St. Hilaire, Ann. Sci. Nat. sér 3, vol. XIV, p. 209 (1851).
Aepyornis ingens Milne-Edwards & Grandidier, C.R. CXVIII, pp. 122-127 (1894).

THIS is the stoutest and bulkiest species, though not so tall as *Ae. titan*. All the largest eggs next to those of *Ae. titan* must belong to this species. It will be argued that I have no right to use the name *maximus* for this form, but the name of *maximus* is based on one of the eggs in the Paris Museum, and as these evidently belong to this form and not to the form subsequently called *maximus*, I must apply to that the name of *grandidieri*, given by Mr. Dawson Rowley in 1867 to a portion of eggshell of the lesser form.

The measurements of the limbs are as follows :—

Femur.

Total length	440 mm.
Width at proximal end	190 ,,
Width at distal end	200 ,,
Circumference at narrowest part of shaft	265 ,,

Tibio-tarsus.

Total length	780 mm.
Width at proximal end	180 ,,
Width at distal end	160 ,,
Circumference at narrowest part of shaft	210 ,,

Tarso-metatarsus.

Total length	420 mm.
Width at proximal end	170 ,,
Width at distal end	160 ,,
Circumference at narrowest part of shaft	200 ,,

The description of the foot in the diagnosis of the family is based on the pes of this species. It is true that the two mounted skeletons in the British and Tring Museums of *Aepyornis hildebrandti* show a larger number of phalanges ; but as neither is composed of the bones of a single individual it is more than likely that the articulator made a mistake.

The dimensions of the type egg are as follows :—

Large diameter	340 mm.
Small diameter	225 ,,
Large circumference	850 ,,
Small circumference	710 ,,

Habitat: S. W. Madagascar.

There are about 16 eggs known of this form, varying from 854 mm. to 816 mm. in large circumference, and from 743 mm. to 715 mm. in small circumference.

AEPYORNIS GRANDIDIERI ROWLEY.

Aepyornis Maximus Auct.

Aepyornis grandidieri Rowley, P.Z.S. 1867, p. 892.

THIS is the form which nearly all the bones, referred erroneously to Geoffroy's *Ae. maximus*, belong. The original description of Dawson Rowley was founded on a piece of eggshell, and is as follows:— "The granulation is in a marked degree different from that of the other pieces. The air pores which in the other specimens appear like a comet with a tail are here only small indentations without any tail; the shell also is only half the thickness, is much finer, and presents an aspect so diverse that the difference is detected by the most careless observer, even when the pieces are all mixed. These fragments belonged to the egg of much smaller birds, the embryo of which required less strength in the shell. Yet the colour, quality and locality of that shell clearly point to a bird of the same family as *Aepyornis maximus*—in short, a smaller and more delicate *Aepyornis*. For this species I propose the name of *Aepyornis grandidieri*."

The measurements of bones of the hind limb are as follows:—

Femur.

Length	320 mm.
Width at distal end....	190 „

Tibio tarsus.

Length	640 mm.

There are at Tring two eggs of this species.

No. 1, traded.

Length	283·0 mm.
Width	215·0 „
Large circumference	777·5 „
Small circumference	670·0 „

No. 2 Ambondo, Ambovombé in the district of Fort Dauphin.

Large circumference	775 mm.
Small circumference	662·5 „

There are recorded of these eggs, besides the two mentioned above, eight further specimens, varying from 810 mm. to 771·5 mm. in large circumference, and 686 mm. to 654 mm. in small circumference.

In addition to these there are in various collections about eight or nine eggs whose species is doubtful.

AEPYORNIS CURSOR M.-E. & GRAND.

Aepyornis cursor Milne-Edwards & Grandidier, C.R. CXVIII, p. 124 (1894).

ORIGINAL description as follows: *Ae. cursor* is almost as large as *Ae. grandidieri* = *maximus* auct., nec. Geoffroy, but is more slender.

Length of tarso-metatarsus	380 mm.
Width at proximal end	140 ,,
Width at distal end	120 ,,
Circumference of shaft	155 ,,
Width of shaft	65 ,,

Habitat: Madagascar.

AEPYORNIS MEDIUS M.-E. & GRAND.

Aepyornis medius Milne-Edwards & Grandidier, Ann. Sci. Nat. ser. V, vol. XII, p. 179 (1869).

Aepyornis medius Milne-Edwards & Grandidier, Rech. Faune. Orn. Et. Masc. & Mad. (1866-73), p. 97, note 2.

THIS form was founded on a femur found at Amboulitsate in W. Madagascar, and is described as follows: "It presents the same general characters, and evidently belongs to an *Aepyornis*, but to a different species, which we will call *Aepyornis medius*. The femur in question is not only distinguished by its lesser proportions but by the narrower external face of the bone; which variation results in causing the whole area between the trochanter and the base of the femoral neck to be much less depressed. The intermuscular line, which marks the insertion surface of the deep portion of the femoral triceps muscle, is hardly indicated, whereas it is very pronounced in the larger femur. The posterior side is also more rounded, and the distance which separates the popliteal depression from the proximal extremity is larger; the shape of this large depression is, however, the same as in the larger femur, and although the articular surfaces above it do show some differences, we know that these characters are not very reliable as they are subject to individual variations.

Circumference of shaft 215 mm."

Habitat: West Madagascar.

AEPYORNIS HILDEBRANDTI BURCKH.

Aepyornis hildebrandti Burckhardt, Pal. Abh. (VI) II, p. 127 (1893).

I MUST refer my readers to Dr. Burckhardt's description, as it is too long and too technical to be reproduced here, especially as it is not comparative. I, however, give here some of his measurements :—

Tibio-tarsus.

	A. grandidieri.	*A. hildebrandti.*
Length	640 mm.	480 mm.
Breadth at proximal end	190 ,, ...	130 ,,
Breadth at distal end	135 ,, ...	82 ,,

Tarso-metatarsus.

Length circa	375 mm.	275 mm.
Breadth at proximal end	145 ,, ...	103 ,,
Breadth at distal end	145 ,, ...	95 ,,

The locality of the type is Sirabé.

Habitat : Madagascar.

AEPYORNIS LENTUS M.-E. & GRAND.

Aepyornis lentus Milne-Edwards & Grandidier, C.R. CXVIII, p. 124 (1894).

ORIGINAL description as follows: "*Ae. lentus* is remarkable from its short and massive feet.

Length of tarso-metatarsus	360 mm.
Width of proximal end	150 ,,
Circumference of shaft	170 ,,
Width of shaft	68 ,, "

Habitat : Madagascar.

AEPYORNIS MULLERI M.-E. & GRAND.

Aepyornis mulleri Milne-Edwards & Grandidier, C.R. CXVII, pp. 124-125 (1894).

THE original description commences: "The new species which we owe to the researches of M. G. Muller, and which we shall name *Ae. mulleri*, is smaller. Nevertheless, it is superior in size to *Ae. hildebrandti*, described by M. Burckhardt, which also came from Antsirabé. We possess the almost complete skeleton of this bird, the skull, mandible, vertebrae, ribs, sternum, a part of the pelvis, the leg bones, and a few phalanges of the pes; so that we can now exactly define the position and affinities of the genus *Aepyornis*." Then follows the diagnosis of the family, which I have given before.

Habitat: Central Madagascar.

AEPYORNIS MODESTUS M.-E. & GRAND.

Aepyornis modestus Milne-Edwards & Grandidier, Ann. Sci. Nat. (5) XII, p. 189 (1869).

MESSRS. MILNE-EDWARDS & GRANDIDIER state at pages 180-181 that the bone (a portion of a femur) which is the type of the above name, had a shaft-circumference of 120 mm., while in *Ae. medius* this circumference was 215 mm., and in *Ae. grandidieri* (= *maximus* auct. nec. Geoffroy), it was 270 mm.

Type locality: Amboulitsate, in West Madagascar.

MULLERORNIS MILNE-EDWARDS & GRANDIDIER.

BIRDS of medium size, not having the heavy and massive build of *Aepyornis*. They appear to resemble more closely the *Casuaridae*. Known only from leg bones.

Number of species: 2.

MULLERORNIS BETSILEI MILNE-EDW. & GRAND.

Mullerornis betsilei Milne-Edwards and Grandidier, Compt. Rend., CXVIII, p. 125 (1894).

ORIGINAL description as follows:—" The leg bones are slender, the tarso-metatarsus is not enlarged as in the preceding genus, and the section through the shaft shows almost an isosceles triangle. The bone itself having more the proportion of *Dromaius*.

" Length of tibio-tarsus	390 mm.
Circumference of tibio-tarsus	90 ,,
Width of tibio-tarsus	30 ,,
Width of proximal end	75 ,,
Width of distal end	60 ,,
Length of tarso-metatarsus	310 ,,
Circumference of tarso-metatarsus....	80 ,,
Width of shaft of tarso-metatarsus	27 ,,
Width of proximal end	70 ,,

" *Mullerornis betsilei* inhabited the same area as *Ae. mulleri* but was much rarer." (Translated.)

Habitat : Central Madagascar.

MULLERORNIS AGILIS MILNE-EDW. & GRAND.

Mullerornis agilis **Milne-Edwards and Grandidier, Compt. Rend., CXVIII, pp. 125-126 (1894).**

ORIGINAL description as follows:—" *M. agilis* inhabited the South-west Coast; we only possess, of this species, one tibia, which is remarkable for the manner in which the intermuscular bony ridges and the tendon-grooves are marked. The exterior border of the bone above the lower articular surface has developed into a very pronounced crista." (Translated.)

" Length of tibio-tarsus	....	....	....	....	440 mm.
Circumference of tibio-tarsus		....	....	....	97 ,,
Width of tibio-tarsus	....	....	...	....	34 ,,
Width at proximal end	....	....	....	....	65 ,,
Width at distal end	....	....	....	....	75 ,, "

Habitat : South-west Madagascar.

FLACOURTIA ANDREWS.

DIFFERS from *Mullerornis* in having a completely ossified bony bridge over the lower end of the groove for the adductor of the outer digit, in the tarso-metatarsus.

Number of species : 1.

FLACOURTIA RUDIS (MILNE-EDW. & GRAND.)

Mullerornis rudis Milne-Edwards & Grandidier, Compt. Rend. CXVIII, p. 126 (1894).
Flacourtia rudis Andrews, Nov. Zool. II, p. 25 (1895).

ORIGINAL description as follows :—"The third species *M. rudis* (= *F. rudis*) was discovered by M. Grevé in the fossiliferous beds of the West Coast. The tibio-tarsus is of about the same length as in *M. betsilei*, but is more massive. The tarso-metatarsus is remarkable on account of the great enlargement of the distal extremity, and of which the digital articular attachments are extremely large. Between the middle and outer ones there is a bony opening for the passage of the adductor muscle of the outer digit, which passage is not present in *Aepyornis* (or *Mullerornis*, W.R.)." (Translation.)

Length of tibio-tarsus	400 mm.
Circumference of tibio-tarsus	100 ,,
Width of tibio-tarsus	35 ,,
Width of distal end	75 ,,

Habitat : West Madagascar.

DROMAIUS PERONI NOM. NOV.

(PLATE 40.)

Casoar de la Nouvelle Hollande Péron, Relat. Voy. Terr. Austr. I p. 467, pl. XXXVI (1807).

Dromoius ater Vieillot, Gal. des Ois, pl. 226 (not text).

Dromaeus ater Blyth, Ibis 1862, p. 93.

IT is most unfortunate that the larger number of authors have neglected to go carefully into the synonymy of this bird; if they had done so it would not have been necessary, after 81 years, to reject the very appropriate name of *ater*, and to rename the Emu of Kangaroo Island. Vieillot, in the Nouveau Dictionnaire D'Histoire Naturelle X, page 212, distinctly states that his *Dromaius ater* was a name given to Latham's *Casuarius novaehollandiae*, and makes no mention of Péron or of the Isle Decrès.

The figures in Péron's work of the adult male and female are not good, but those of the young and nestlings appear to me to be very accurate, and the plate in the Galérie des Oiseaux is quite excellent. The latter and my own are taken from the type specimen in the Paris Museum, while the plate in Péron was done by Lessieur from a series of sketches from life made by himself on Decrès Island and in the menagerie of the Jardin des Plantes. The only known specimens of this extinct species are the mounted skin and skeleton in Paris and the skeleton in the Florence Museum. All these are what remain of the three living birds brought to Paris by Péron, and no other authentic specimens exist anywhere. There is in the Museum at Liverpool a full-grown, though immature Emu of the same size as *Dromaius peronii*, but owing to its proportionally longer legs and very scanty plumage it is not absolutely safe to identify it as a second mounted specimen of *D. peronii*. I will recur to this lower down.

Description of adult male (ex Cat. Birds Brit. Mus.): Similar to *D. novaehollandiae*, but much smaller, and with feathers of the neck entirely black; feathers of the body brown fulvous, with the apical half very dark blackish brown; bill and feet blackish, naked skin of the sides of the neck blue. Total length about 55 inches, tarsus 11·40, culmen 2·36.

Immature in first plumage entirely sooty black. Nestling whitish with longitudinal bands of rufous brown. In addition to Decrès or Kangaroo Island, also Flinders, King Islands, and Tasmania had Emus living on them at the time of Péron's visit, and I believe, if authentic specimens from these localities were in existence we should find that each of these islands had had a distinct species or race of Emus. Taking this for granted, and also taking into account that it is slightly different from the type of *D. peronii*, I have come to the conclusion that the Liverpool specimen is an immature, though full-grown individual from one of these other islands; but it is not possible from this one rather poor specimen to separate it from the Kangaroo Island species, especially as there is absolutely no indication of the origin of this specimen.

Habitat: Island of Decrès or Kangaroo Island.

One stuffed specimen (Type) and one skeleton in Paris, one skeleton in Florence, and one stuffed specimen in Liverpool (an species diversa?). Also some leg-bones in Adelaide, Australia.

Dr. H. O. Forbes, who kindly lent me the last-named specimen, was the first to point out the differences of this bird from *D. novaehollandiae*. It is certainly totally distinct from birds of similar age of either *D. novaehollandiae* or *D. n. irroratus*.

DROMAIUS MINOR (SPENCER).

Dromaeus minor Baldwin Spencer, Vict. Nat. XXIII, p. 140 (1906).

As Mr. Bernard H. Woodward, of Perth, West Australia, was organising an expedition to Kangaroo, Flinders, and King Islands (December, 1906), to hunt for Emu remains on these islands, I had hoped to be the first to describe what I felt sure would be two new species of *Dromaius*. I have, however, been forestalled by Professor Baldwin Spencer in the case of King Island, whence a collection of 17 femurs, 19 tibio-tarsi, 28 tarso-metatarsi, and portions of 8 pelves, made by Messrs. Alex. Morton and R. M. Johnston, T.S.O., formed the material for the description of a new species.

The diagnosis is as follows: "Smaller than *D. ater* (= *D. peronii* mihi). Tibia not or only slightly exceeding 330 mm. in greatest length. Tarso-metatarsus not exceeding 280 mm. in greatest length. Pelvis, length not or only slightly exceeding 280 mm."

D. minor was a smaller but stouter bird than *D. peronii*. Comparative dimensions -—

	D. peronii.	*D. minor.*
Tibio-tarsus	342 mm.	320—332 mm.
Tarso-metatarsus	290 „	277—277 „
Femur	180 „	170—180 „
Pelvis	340 „	274—280 „
Pelvis, front width	75 „	64 „
Pelvis, width behind acetabular cavity	92 „	78— 86 „

Habitat: King Island, Bass Strait. Now extinct.

INDEX.

PLATES.

FREGILUPUS VARIUS
(NATURAL SIZE)

1. FOUDIA BRUANTE
(NATURAL SIZE)

2. NECROPSAR RODERICANUS
(TWO-THIRDS NATURAL SIZE—*from description*)

3. NECROPSAR LEGUATI
(TWO-THIRDS NATURAL SIZE)

1. GEOSPIZA MAGNIROSTRIS
2. GEOSPIZA STRENUA
3. NESOENAS MEYERI
4. CHAUNOPROCTUS FERREIROSTRIS

(ALL THREE-FOURTHS NATURAL SIZE—*from skins*)

1. HEMIGNATHUS ELLISIANUS
2. HETERORHYNCHUS LUCIDUS
3. PSITTIROSTRA PSITTACEA DEPPEI
4. CIRIDOPS ANNA

(ALL FIVE-SIXTHS NATURAL SIZE—*from skins*: NO. 3 *from type*)

1. MIRO TRAVERSI (FOUR-FIFTHS NATURAL SIZE) 2 & 2A. TRAVERSIA LYALLI ♂ ♀ (FOUR-FIFTHS NATURAL SIZE) 3. BOWDLERIA RUFESCENS

SIPHONORHIS AMERICANA
(NATURAL SIZE)

FIG. 1. NESTOR NORFOLCENSIS
From the plate in the Bulletin of the Liverpool Museum

FIG. 2. HEAD OF NESTOR PRODUCTUS
From the specimen in the Tring Museum
(FIVE-SIXTHS NATURAL SIZE)

LOPHOPSITTACUS MAURITIANUS
(ELEVEN TWENTY-NINETHS NATURAL SIZE—*from drawing and description*)

NECROPSITTACUS BORBONICUS
(TWO-FIFTHS NATURAL SIZE—*from a description*)

MASCARINUS MASCARINUS
(THREE-QUARTERS NATURAL SIZE)

ARA TRICOLOR
(ELEVEN-THIRTEENTHS NATURAL SIZE—*from specimen in Liverpool Museum*)

ARA GOSSEI

(FOUR-FIFTHS NATURAL SIZE—*from Gosse's description*)

ARA ERYTHROCEPHALA
(SIX-TENTHS NATURAL SIZE—*from Gosse's description*)

ANADORHYNCHUS PURPURASCENS
(TWO-FIFTHS NATURAL SIZE—*from a description*)

ARA MARTINICUS
(TWO-FIFTHS NATURAL SIZE—*from description*)

ARA ERYTHRURA
(ONE-HALF NATURAL SIZE—*from description*)

CONURUS LABATI
(NATURAL SIZE—*from Labat's description*)

AMAZONA VIOLACEUS
(TWO-THIRDS NATURAL SIZE—*from description*)

AMAZONA MARTINICANA
(TWO-THIRDS NATURAL SIZE —*from Labat's description*)

PALAEORNIS EXSUL
(THREE-QUARTERS NATURAL SIZE)

PALAEORNIS WARDI
(THREE-QUARTERS NATURAL SIZE)

HEMIPHAGA SPADICEA
(TWO-THIRDS NATURAL SIZE)

ALECTROENAS NITIDISSIMA
(NATURAL SIZE)

PEZOPHAPS SOLITARIA
(About One-Third Natural Size—*from descriptions and drawings*)

DIDUS CUCULLATUS

(ONE-THIRD NATURAL SIZE—*from drawings*)

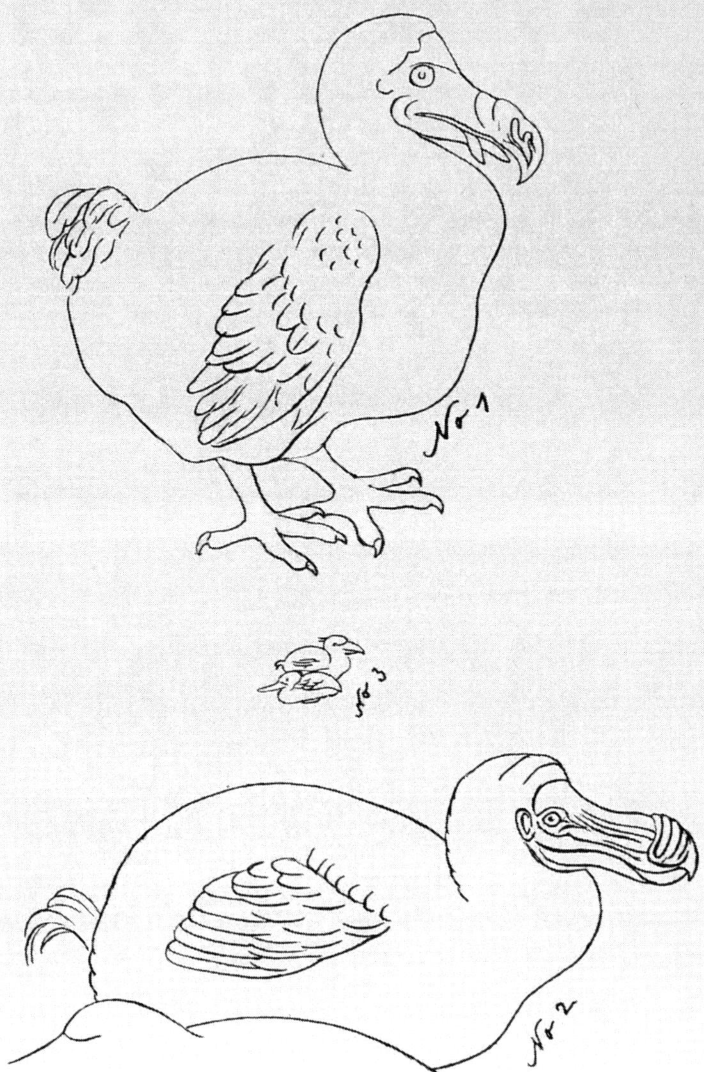

1, 2, 3. DIDUS CUCULLATUS *(see explanation)*

1—9. DIDUS CUCULLATUS

10—13. DIDUS CUCULLATUS

DIDUS SOLITARIUS

(ONE-THIRD NATURAL SIZE—*from a Dutch picture taken from living bird in Amsterdam, beak and wing restored*)

DIDUS SOLITARIUS
(ONE-THIRD NATURAL SIZE—*from Dubois' description*)

FIG. 1, 2, 3. PEZOPHAPS SOLITARIA
FIG. 4, 5, 7, 8. DIDUS SOLITARIUS

1. HYPOTAENIDIA PACIFICA
(TWO-THIRDS NATURAL SIZE—*from Forster's drawing in British Museum*)

2. PENNULA SANDWICHENSIS
(THREE-FIFTHS NATURAL SIZE—*from skin*)

3. PENNULA MILLSI
(THREE-FIFTHS NATURAL SIZE—*from skin*)

NESOLIMNAS DIEFFENBACHI
(SEVEN-EIGHTHS NATURAL SIZE)

1. CABALUS MODESTUS
(NATURAL SIZE)

2. COTURNIX NOVAEZEALANDIAE
(SEVEN-EIGHTHS NATURAL SIZE)

APHANAPTERYX BONASIA
(ONE-HALF NATURAL SIZE—*from a drawing*)

ERYTHROMACHUS LEGUATI

(ONE-HALF NATURAL SIZE—*from a description and a tracing*)

LEGUATIA GIGANTEA
(ONE-SIXTH NATURAL SIZE—*from description and drawings*)

APTERORNIS COERULESCENS

(ONE-HALF NATURAL SIZE—*from descriptions*)

NOTORNIS ALBA
(FIVE-NINETHS NATURAL SIZE)

NOTORNIS HOCHSTETTERI
(ONE-HALF NATURAL SIZE)

1

2

1. AECHMORHYNCHUS CANCELLATUS
(NATURAL SIZE)

2. PROSOBONIA LEUCOPTERA
(NATURAL SIZE)

CAMPTOLAEMUS LABRADORIUS
(ONE-HALF NATURAL SIZE—*from Nature*)

AESTRELATA CARIBBAEA

(FIVE-SIXTHS NATURAL SIZE—*from stuffed specimen in Dublin Museum*)

ALCA IMPENNIS
(FIVE-EIGHTHS NATURAL SIZE—*from stuffed specimen*)

CARBO PERSPICILLATUS

(SEVEN-SIXTEENTHS NATURAL SIZE)

DROMAIUS PERONI

(ONE-THIRD NATURAL SIZE—*from type specimen*)

MEGALAPTERYX HUTTONI

(ONE-QUARTER NATURAL SIZE—*restored drawing from feathers and mummified remains*)

DINORNIS INGENS

(ONE-ELEVENTH NATURAL SIZE—*restoration from skeleton and feathers*)